International Order of Twelve of Knights ...

Manual of the International Order of Twelve of Knights and Daughters of Tabor

Containing general laws, regulations and ceremonies

International Order of Twelve of Knights ...

Manual of the International Order of Twelve of Knights and Daughters of Tabor
Containing general laws, regulations and ceremonies

ISBN/EAN: 9783337221546

Printed in Europe, USA, Canada, Australia, Japan

Cover: Foto ©Andreas Hilbeck / pixelio.de

More available books at **www.hansebooks.com**

Rev. MOSES DICKSON,
Founder of the International Order of Twelve.

MANUAL

OF THE

International Order of Twelve

OF

Knights and Daughters of Tabor,

CONTAINING

GENERAL LAWS, REGULATIONS, CEREMONIES, DRILL,

AND A

TABORIAN LEXICON,

BY

Rev. MOSES DICKSON.

ST. LOUIS, MO.:

A. R. FLEMING & CO., PRINTERS, 522 N. Third Street.

1891.

INTRODUCTION.

Orders, societies and governments were instituted for the purpose of making a united effort in a given direction. What one man cannot accomplish, many men united can. Hence great enterprises for the well-being of mankind are carried foward by companies. Governments are formed by uniting a number of people under one form or code of laws. Societies are organizations of a number of persons to accomplish a certain object, or to obtain a desired end. Man was made a social being; he must have society, or the company of a fellow-being, or he will drift into barbarism and brutality. Man is an intelligent being. Civilization, art, science, and architecture, and government, must come only from an united effort. Therefore, the members of the International Order of Twelve have formed one band, united by the strongest ties of friendship, and bound together by solemn obligations, and established on a firm basis, for the purpose of making a united and effective effort in aiding each member in sickness or distress, to protect and defend each other, to aid and help the widows and orphans of members that died in good standing, to inculcate true morality, that the members of the International Order of Twelve may be an example to the masses of mankind.

It is the highest and bounden duty of every
member of the Knights' and Daughters of Tabor
to individually and collectively help to spread and
build up the Christian religion. The Order of
Twelve is non-sectarian—all members of the Order
are free to make their choice of any Evangelical
Church. The members of this Order are reminded
that education and a cultivated mind will open the
way to a useful and respected life. We are ad-
monished to use every honorable method to advance the cause of education. The members of the
International Order of Twelve are advised to
acquire real estate—this makes a man or woman
a substantial and reliable citizen. Avoid intem-
perance; cultivate true manhood; eschew immoral
and degraded people. Let your bearing and deportment be such that will show you to be a lady
or a gentleman. Live an exemplary life, and you
will die respected. Knights and Daughters of
Tabor, it is in your power to make the International Order of Twelve a real and lasting benefit
to mankind.

THE FOUNDER AND FATHER.

"Rev. Moses Dickson was born in the City of Cincinnati, Ohio, April 5th, 1824. His parents, Robert and Hannah Dickson, were natives of Virginia. They moved to Ohio just three months before the subject of this sketch was born. Mr. Dickson's father died A. D. 1832; his mother departed this life A. D. 1838. She was truly a Christian mother, and became a member of the first A. M. E. Church that was organized in Cincinnati. Her children were all christened by Elder Wm. Paul Quinn, a number of years before he was made a bishop.

"Mr. Dickson had five sisters and three brothers— all have passed away—and he has not a relative living at this date, A. D. 1891. He learned the barber's profession with the well-known William Darnes. While learning the tonsorial art, he attended school, and mastered all the branches of study that were taught in that early day. At the age of sixteen he felt a desire to see the South. He embarked on a steamboat, and traveled for three years, on various boats, upon the different southern rivers and bayous.

"In these travels he saw slavery in all its horrors; he witnessed such scenes of monstrous cruelty as caused his African blood to boil with suppressed indignation at the sight of the outrageous suffering

7

of his people. What he saw in these three years
made a lasting impression on his heart, and he became a life-foe to the slave-owner, the slave-driver
and the slave-trader. In his travels he made the
acquaintance of a few true and trusty young men,
who were ready to enter into any plan that would
assure freedom to the African race. These men
knew that the magnitude of the work would require time, courage and patience to make a success
of any plan they might adopt. They resolved to
take two years to study out a plan, and meet in the
City of St. Louis, Mo., the second Tuesday in the
month of August, 1846, to prepare for business.

"Mr. Dickson embarked on board of the steamer
'Oronoco,' at New Orleans, in the month of May,
1844; and made the trip to St. Louis, remaining in
that city during the summer. For two years he
traveled through Iowa, Illinois and Wisconsin.
August, 1846, he was in the City of St. Louis, preparing to meet his young friends. He had in the
meantime prepared a plan to be submitted to them.
On the second Tuesday in August, as per agreement, twelve men assembled in the second story of
an old brick house, on the southeast corner of
Green and Seventh streets. (The name of Green
St. has since been changed to Lucas Ave.) They
were just the kind of men to carry to success the
secret and great work of obtaining liberty for the
bondsmen. Mr. Dickson read his plan for operat-
ing, and, after a very careful discussion of all its
parts, it was adopted. Organizations were secretly
to be made in the Southern States. None but reliable, fearless men were to be enrolled. The

organizers were to carefully pick the men that were courageous, patient, temperate, and possessed of sound common sense. This was what was required in every man that was enrolled. The oath that bound them together was so binding that it could not be broken. One feature of it was: 'I can die, but I cannot reveal the name of any member until the slaves are free.' This oath never was broken. · All the matter pertaining to the business was finished, and each man understood his part. Mr. Dickson was elected Chief; he was to remain North and watch events, and keep the members posted. Ten years was the time fixed on to open battle for freedom.

"It will not be amiss now to give the names of the men who, like the Twelve Apostles, commenced the great work for Liberty: John Patton and Henry Wright, in South Carolina; James Bedford and Silus W. Green, in Mississippi; Irvin Hodges, in Alabama; Peter Coleman and Willis Owens, in Virginia; James Orr, in Louisiana; Miles Graves, in North Carolina; Henry Simpson, in Georgia; Lewis Williams, in Tennessee, and Moses Dickson, their Chief. These men, with their aides, formed organizations in all the Slave States, except Missouri and Texas. Silently, like the falling of Autumn leaves, the organizations multiplied, until, in 1856, the army of true and trusty men numbered forty-seven thousand, two hundred and forty Knights of Liberty.

"Mr. Dickson will give, in another place, details of this wonderful organization, its secrecy, its mode of operation, its drill, the many incidents in its

history, and why the battle was not opened in
1856.

"One incident I must name: The first organization that was created, under the distinct name of
the Order of Twelve, was organized in the City of
Galena, Ills., by Mr. Dickson, at the residence of
Alfred H. Richardson, in August, 1855. The secret work of the Knights of Liberty was not im-
parted to this Society.

"Mr. Dickson was married to Mrs. Mary Elisabeth
Peters, in Galena, Ills., on the 5th day of October,
1848. She has been his companion in joys and
sorrows for forty-two years (up to 1891, when she
departed this life). She was an exemplary Christian, a true and loving wife, a sound and able coun-
selor. She was loved by all that were acquainted
with her throughout the South and West. She
was known by the dear name of Mother Dickson.

"Mr. Dickson has one child, Mrs. Mamie Augusta
Hayden, the widow of Harry Halyard Hayden. They have one child, Zennie Arvesta.
This child was adopted by the Order of Twelve at
their National Grand Session, held in Louisville,
Ky., in 1885. Her title is Princess of the Knights
and Daughters of Tabor. Mr. Dickson fixed his
headquarters in St. Louis, Mo., in 1859, that he
might be near the Knights of Liberty to guide their
affairs. After the war was over, the work begun
by the *twelve*—seemingly his work for his people
—was finished, but he could not rest; schools for
Colored children must be opened. He, with a number of other stalwart men, worked with energy in
the lobby at Jefferson City, Mo. At length, under

the administration of Governor McClurg, the present school laws for Missouri were adopted. Mr. Dickson's next move was to procure Colored teachers for Colored Schools. It was a hard fight, but the move was a success. Now, throughout the State of Missouri, Colored schools have Colored teachers.

"Mr. Dickson took an active part in the founding of 'Lincoln Institute,' at Jefferson City, Mo. He was Trustee and Vice-President of the Board for several years, and remained in the Board until the success of the Institute was a fixed fact. Mr. Dickson is a member of the Republican Party, and he remains true to it. He was a Delegate to every State Convention of Missouri, from 1864 to 1878, and stumped the State several times in the interests of the party; he was Elector-at-Large on the Grant ticket in 1872, and did good work. Mr. Dickson was President of the Refugee Relief Board, in St. Louis, Mo., in 1878. This Board received and cared for about sixteen thousand men, women and children, who were fleeing from Southern oppression. The whole North and East was stirred up, and thousands of dollars were received by the Board from the East and North to aid the fugitives. This money, with hundreds of large boxes of clothing and provisions that were received, enabled the President and the Board to send the refugees to their destinations comfortably clothed and with ample provisions to last them for several months. Kansas, Nebraska, Colorado, and other Northern States received these fugitives from oppression. Mr. Dickson has not lost sight of them in the several States wherein they have settled. He finds them good citizens and doing well. Kansas received over ten thousand of them.

"Mr. Dickson was converted and joined the A. M. E. Church in 1866, and was licensed to preach in 1867. He has held large and small charges for a number of years, and has had invariably good success in the management of churches. He is known as a church-builder, a debt-payer and a revivalist. Thirteen hundred and ninety persons have been converted in the different charges during his pastorship. Mother Dickson has been a great help to him in his pastoral work.

"The International Order of Twelve, of Knights and Daughters of Tabor, is an evidence of Mr. Dickson's skill as an organizer. The Society that was organized by him in Galena, in 1855, disbanded in 1859. The Knights of Liberty had become extinct after the War of the Rebellion. At the close of that war, not a man, so far as known, of that great number, returned from the battle-field, except Mr. Dickson; he, as an independent fighter, was in thirteen hard-fought battles, and returned home in 1864, not having received a scratch from the enemy's bullets.

"In 1865, all that was found of the Galena Society were seven; their names are in the Manual. In 1868 Mr. Dickson decided to create a Beneficial Order to perpetuate the memory of the *twelve* that organized the Knights of Liberty. After three years of preparation, in 1871, he was ready to commence the work. He organized a Temple and Tabernacle in Independence, Mo.; a Tabernacle in

Kansas City, Mo.; a Temple and Tabernacle in Lexington, Mo. With these five organizations a Convention was called to meet in Independence, Mo., the second Tuesday in August, 1872. This Convention organized the National Grand Temple and Tabernacle of the Order of Twelve, of Knights and Daughters of Tabor. The Child of Destiny was born and named. Mr. Dickson, with his usual energy and perseverance, pushed the work of organizing, aided by a number of Knights and Daughters.

"The Order grew rapidly, spreading from State to State, gathering strength in its onward march. Mr. Dickson did not spare time nor money; he used all the means that were at his command to build a lasting Beneficial Order. Within eighteen years this Order has taken its place and rank with the greatest Colored organizations of the world. It has had strong opposition at every step put forward; but, 'forward' was the motto. The father and founder has lived to see his work firmly fixed on a solid basis, going onward, gaining strength daily, and a benefit to thousands. This Order meets the necessities and wants of the Colored people. It encourages Christianity, education, morality and temperance; it teaches the art of governing, self-reliance and true manhood and womanhood. It recommends to its members the getting of homes and the acquiring of wealth. It teaches the greatness, goodness and mercy of God, and man's responsibility to the Supreme Being.   TABOR.

Dec. 1st, 1890."

Extract of the I. C. G. M.'s Message to the Triennial Grand Session, held in St. Louis, Mo., August, A. D. 1890:

A CHANGE OF TIME.

"We have been much perplexed and bothered in explaining the two dates of the original organization. Our public speakers are hampered when they come to this part of our history. The organization of the Order of Twelve that was made in Galena, Ills., in 1855, was made to perpetuate the names of the Twelve Knights of Tabor, who were so successful in enrolling the 47,000 Knights of Liberty, for the purpose of aiding in breaking the bonds of our slavery. This secret organization of the Knights of Liberty was one of the strongest and most secret of any organization ever formed by men. The question of giving the history of this organization to the world is one that has had my most earnest thoughts for several years. There are so many families of the old men of renown, both in this country and England, that are now living and hold high positions, that they might be injured by revealing the secrets of the Knights of Liberty and giving the names of their fathers. I had almost decided to let this part of our history rest in the grave, more especially since God found other means to give us our manhood and freedom; but the names of the *twelve* men who were instruments in God's hands in preparing and organizing 47,000 men of undoubted courage to do battle for our freedom shall be perpetuated. God fixed the time, and every man was at his post. In their death struggles they gave to us the boon of liberty. Precious be their memory.

"The organization that was made in Galena, Ills., was no part of the Knights of Liberty. They were simply organized to perpetuate the name, "Order of Twelve, of Knights of Tabor." I made the organization in the residence of Alfred H. Richardson. The names of the Knights that were known to be alive in 1872 were given in the old Manual, and are: A. H. Richardson, R. H. Cain, Wm. P. Emery, James T. Smith, J. Garrett Johnson and G. Christopher. This organization closed its doors at the beginning of the great Rebellion and never opened again. I have given this statement, that we may be enabled to change the date of our Order's birth. This Order, in its present form, was changed from the original warlike order, Order of Twelve, into a Beneficial Secret Order, and the real date of the birth of our Order is the 12th of August, A. D. 1872. On that day the Representatives of three Tabernacles and two Temples assembled in the City of Independence, State of Missouri, and organized the Order of Twelve, of Knights and Daughters of Tabor, and elected Grand Officers. The birthday of this great Order of ours is the 12th day of August, 1872. The first Grand Session was held in the same city the second Tuesday in August, A. D. 1873.

"I refer to these matters as a part of the history of the Order, and that all official papers may give the correct date, the 12th of August, 1890, A. O. T., age of Taborians—18 years. I recommend that the 12th of August be made the day to celebrate the birthday of the International Order of Twelve. I recommend that the Triennial Grand Session be changed from the second Tuesday in August. The

fourth Tuesday in the month of August was fixed
by this Triennial Grand Session as the day to
assemble. The 12th day of August was made the
day for our annual celebration, in commemoration
of the birthday of the Order.

KNIGHTS OF LIBERTY.

"This organization was known among its members by the name of Knights of Tabor—a name
that gave the members courage. That God was
with Barak and Deborah, in Israel's great battle
with the immense army of Sisera; they, with only
ten thousand men, assembled on Tabor, to fight
Jabin's army, and, if possible, win the victory and
break the bondage of the Israelites. God was with
Israel, and gave the victory to the bondsmen,
though they were opposed by twenty times their
number. Our cause was just, and we believed in
the justice of the God of Israel and the rights of man.
Under the old name of Tabor, we resolved to make
full preparation to strike the blow for liberty. We
felt sure that the Lord God was on the side of
right and justice, our faith and trust was in him,
and that he would help us in our needy time.

SECRECY.

"From the very origin of the organization of the
Knights of Liberty, the necessity of secrecy was
impressed on each member. Let not your right
hand know what your left hand does; trust no one,
and test every man before he is admitted to membership. A part of the oath was: 'We can die,
but we can't reveal the name of a member, or make
known the organization and its objects.' It was

absolutely a secret organized body. We know of
the failure of Nat. Turner and others, the Abolition-
ist in the North and East. The under-ground
railroad was in good running order, and the Knights
of Liberty sent many passengers over the road to
freedom.

"We feel that we have said enough on this subject.
If the War of the Rebellion had not occurred just
at the time it did, the Knights of Liberty would
have made public history. Let the past sleep;
enough has been said.

Faithfully Yours,

MOSES DICKSON.

Mrs. MARY ELIZABETH DICKSON.

Born August 18th, 1818. Died February 1st, 1891, aged 72
years, 5 months and 13 days.

18

Extract from an eulogy delivered by Rev. Sir R. L. Beal, at the memorial services of Mother Dickson, held at Independence, Mo., February 23d, 1891:

"Mrs. Mary Elizabeth Dickson was born in the town of Ste. Genevieve, County of Ste. Genevieve, State of Missouri, August 18th, 1818. Her parents were members of the Roman Catholic Church. She was the youngest of ten children. When she was twelve years old her parents sent her to St. Louis to reside with her sister Louisa and attend school. She received her education at the old Sacred Heart Convent. Her father, John Sebastian Butcher, was a German, born near the boundary line between France and Germany. He was a stone-cutter and builder, and one among the first settlers of Ste. Genevieve. Her mother's name was Mary Butcher. The family was highly respected by all who knew them, and were owners of considerable property in the town of Ste. Genevieve. Miss Mary E. Butcher was married at the age of 17 years to Mr. Caleb Peters, and in 1838 they moved to Galena, Ills. Mr. Peters opened a provision store, and continued in that business until his death, in 1846. Mrs. Peters was converted and joined the A. M. E. Church, in 1845. She remained a widow until she married Moses Dickson. The ceremony was performed by the then famous A. M. E. Elder, George W. Johnson, Oct. 5th, 1848, in the City of Galena, Ills. For over forty-two years Rev. and Mrs. Dickson have traveled together, living in peace and harmony, bearing each other's troubles and trials. Their home-life was pleasant, loving and trusting.

Mother Dickson is the honorable title that she was known by. She has been a consistent and earnest Christian, and a member of the A. M. E. Church for more than 45 years. She was a faithful and zealous worker in the church for many years, until she became too old for active work; she was full of fire, and one of God's greatest women. The International Order of Twelve, of which the Rev. Moses Dickson is the Founder and Father, recognizing the influence and part that Daughter Dickson had in building up the Order, did, at the Grand Session, August, 1882, by a unanimous vote, elect and install her into the honorable office and title of Mother of all Knights and Daughters of Tabor, for life. She is held in great esteem and honored by all the members of the great Order. Rev. Moses Dickson is the founder of the Court of Heroines. At the organization of St. Mary's Court, A. D. 1865, in St. Louis, Mo., Sister Dickson was made a charter member. St. Mary's Court is the first and oldest regularly organized Court in the United States. Sister Dickson has presided as Most Ancient Matron and Most Ancient Grand Matron. Mother Dickson was a member of R. H. Gleaves Tabernacle of Brothers and Sisters of Love and Charity in this city. When the Grand Lodge of Good Samaritans and Daughters of Samaria, for Kansas and Missouri, was organized at St. Joseph, Mo., Mother Dickson was made an honorary member. She has been in ill health for four years. Sunday, January 18th, she was confined to her bed; she gradually grew weaker from day to day; day and night her doctor, family and friends did everything to retain her on earth; but the Lord said to his faithful follower—*come home!* Sunday night, at 10:35 P. M., her spirit obeyed the summons; she bid farewell to the church on earth; in the church triumphant she has taken her place among the redeemed from earth. She leaves a husband, a daughter and a grand-child, and a large number of relations in various parts of the United States, to mourn her departure. Her age was 72 years, 5 months and 13 days when she entered into rest.

"We are brought together by order of the Chief Grand Mentor, to pay tribute to a noble woman, whose influence has done more to cement the bonds by which we are bound together in common brotherhood, than to any other individual. effort put forth for the promotion of our mystic Order. To-day hundreds—yea, thousands—rise up to call her blessed. All over this land, wherever our Order has gained a foothold, the name of Mother Dickson is a household word, for she was the hidden force behind the executive chair which urged her husband to the first place in the scale of human endeavor, that we must look elsewhere for proof. After careful investigation, we reach the conclusion that the Creator has planted in the breast of every human certain innate principles. Some of which are will to do and power to act in human affairs, which, if cultivated, make us useful in whatever sphere we are placed. With hearts willing, minds to plan and hands to execute, our possibilities are unlimited. Our venerable mother was possessed of these qualifications, and cultivated them, and looked forward to the time when opportunity would favor her

to put into practice schemes that would lead to
deeds of lofty heroism.

"But wherein lay the secret of her success, that
wraps itself, as if by magic spell, around our
hearts?

"Let us enter the laboratory of human character, and analyze the elements which make up the
good and the great. It is claimed by some high in
authority that lineal descent, through the law of
heredity, transmits greatness from the parental
stock to the children; but history has so often re-
futed this, by the splendid achievements she has
recorded of some lowly born, who, in the humble
walks of life surmounted every difficulty, took the
front ranks in the annals of Fame, thereby prov-
ing their right to which, she conceived, would promote the best interests of the race. The geomet-
rical truism, which says: 'If equals be added to
equals, the remainder will be equals,' is a fitting
analogy of the conjugal ties between Father and
Mother Dickson; each was suited and equal to the
other. If certain qualities appeared more prominent in him, such as the marshaling and organizing the crude material of which the Taborian
Order is composed, she was the refiner of these
forces; his nature was the more rugged, hers was
the more gentle. He, the impetuous commander,
at times became discouraged at the gigantic undertaking of building up a society that should have
a national reputation. She was the patient, steady
plodder, who encouraged and kept up his spirit.

"When truth shall give a hearing to our cause,
and the work done by our great men shall be prop-

erly accredited, the Africo-Americans will be allowed to build upon some public thoroughfare a monument to Father Dickson, the master-organizer of the race. As its shaft will rise heavenward, our youth, with uncovered head, will point with pride to the illustrious name engraved thereon. Love, fairest daughter of the virtues, will continue to write on the hearts of the coming children, who are to perpetuate this Order, the name of Mary E. Dickson. She was a mother to us in the fullest sense of the word. She knew no creed, no denomination, simply for its name.

"While a member of the Methodistic family, she practiced that broad religion which comes from a pure heart. Her doors were always opened to the distressed. She fed the hungry, clothed the naked, comforted the lowly in spirit. There are some here to-night that received counsel from her, when you needed the advice of a friend. Some in this city, and many in other places where she has been, when she would give up her bed to see you comfortable.

"Her sainted face presents itself before me to-night; that sweet voice, which has soothed so many sad hearts, whispers from across the mystic river. But why do we mourn for her as one lost. She is not dead, no; for those sainted souls can never die. Her influence lives on. She will never be seen by us with the natural eye, but we can hold communion with her in spirit. Her seraph wing will stretch over us, and her works will live, although she is removed from us. We shall all see her again when the despised Galileean shall step from the throne of His sovereign mercy to that of His sovereign justice; when the revivified, at the shrill blast of the trumpets, shall wake to life, and throw off their winding sheets at the world's glad re-union.

"We close with this climax, borrowed from Dr. Munsay's last sermon on the resurrection of the human body. (Mother Dickson will be with all the sanctified.) When the battlefields of the world: Troy and Thermopylæ, Palavera and Marengo, Austerlitz and Waterloo, Marathon and Missolough, the battlefields of Europe, Asia, Africa and America, will produce their armies, and crowd the world with their revivified legions, Indian maidens will leap from the dust of our streets, and our houses overturning, will lead their chiefs to Judgment. Abraham will shake off the dust of Machpelah, and arise with Sarah by his side. David will come with harp in hand. The Reformer of Geneva and the Apostles of Christianity will come side by side.

"Our village church-yards and family burial-grounds will be deserted. All will come: patriarchs, prophets, Jews and Gentiles, and Heathens, bond and free, rich and poor, fathers and mothers, children, sisters, brothers, husbands, wives. All from Adam down will come forth. And all the good from around the world, all together, will hail this redemption's grand consummation with one proud anthem, whose choral thunders rolling along all the paths of space will shake the universe with its bursting chorus: 'O, death, where is thy sting? O, grave, where is thy victory?'"

Power Defined.

When a Temple, Tabernacle, Palatium or Tent fails to meet for business every month in the year, they forfeit their charter, and the C. G. M. must declare them closed, unless a dispensation has been obtained, permitting them to omit one session.

Closed Up.

When a Temple, Tabernacle, Palatium or Tent is closed up or becomes defunct, all the money and property belonging to the Temple, Tabernacle, Palatium or Tent that has been closed up or has become defunct must be taken by the C. G. M., and record of it made in the C. G. S.'s office, and put in care of the C. G. T. If the said closed or defunct organization is not re-opened within one year, all property that belonged to said closed or defunct organization must be sold, and the proceeds turned over to the Grand Treasurer.

Withdrawals.

When a Temple, Tabernacle, Palatium or Tent withdraws from the International Order of Twelve, and from the authority of the Grand Temple and Tabernacle, the charter, rituals, and property of all kinds must be surrendered to the C. G. M., or his Deputy. Members who withdraw are not permitted to use the ritualistic works, or the name, "Knights and Daughters of Tabor," in any other organization.

Grand Temples and Tabernacles.

If a Grand Temple and Tabernacle withdraws from the International Grand Temple and Tabernacle; that is, from the general government of the International Order of Twelve, without the consent of all other Grand Temples and Tabernacles, it is hereby ordained that the withdrawing Grand Temple and Tabernacle shall forfeit every right and privilege of the Knights and Daughters of Tabor; that is, the right to use the name, the rituals and laws of the International Order of Twelve. Their copy-rights shall be annulled by the act of withdrawing. The International Grand Temple and Tabernacle shall have authority to enforce this law. ✦

CONSTITUTION

OF THE

International Order of Twelve

OF

Knights and Daughters of Tabor,

AND

GENERAL LAWS

OF THE

International Grand Temple and Tabernacle.

By order of the International Grand Temple and Tabernacle every Temple, Tabernacle, Palatium and Tent must have and own a Manual, and keep the same for the use of their members.

New Temples, Tabernacles, Palatiums and Tents are hereby ordered to obtain a Manual within sixty days after their organization. Learn and know the laws, and obey them. All parts of the Manual are general laws, except the biographies, history and lexicon.

CONSTITUTION.

ARTICLE I.

SECTION 1.—This organization shall be known as the "International Order of Twelve, of Knights and Daughters of Tabor."

SEC. 2.—This organization is vested with full power and authority to organize and charter Temples or Plateaus of the Knights of Tabor, Tabernacles or Saba Meroe of the Daughters of Tabor, Palatiums of the Royal House of Media, and Tents of the Maids and Pages of Honor, in any part of the civilized world.

SEC. 3.—The International Grand Temple and Tabernacle is hereby authorized to charter Grand Temples and Tabernacles in any State, Territory or country, when they have a lawful number of Temples, Tabernacles, Palatiums and Tents within their boundaries.

SEC. 4.—The International Grand Temple and Tabernacle shall have the authority to enact general laws for the government of the Order.

SEC. 5.—The International Grand Temple and Tabernacle shall assemble in Grand Session triennially, the fourth Tuesday in the month of August, at 10 o'clock A. M , and assemble from day to day, until its business is finished.

SEC. 6.—Special sessions can be called by the International Chief Grand Mentor, whenever he may find it is necessary; or it shall be his duty to call a special session, when officially requested by a two-third vote of the Chief Grand Mentors.

ARTICLE II.

SECTION 1.—Membership of the International Grand Temple and Tabernacle shall be as follows: Present and Past International Chief Grand Mentors. Present and Past International Chief Grand Preceptresses.
Present and Past International Grand Queen Mothers.
Present and Past Chief Grand Mentors.
Present and Past Chief Grand Preceptresses.
Present and Past Grand Queen Mothers.
Present and Past Chief Mentors.
Present and Past Chief Preceptresses.
Present and Past Queen Mothers.
Present and Past Presiding Princes.
Present and Past Vice-Princesses.
Present and Past International Grand Deputies.
Present and Past International Deputy Grand Mentors.

Sec. 2.—A Grand Temple and Tabernacle shall
have twelve votes in the International Grand
Session, these votes to be cast by the Chief Grand
Mentor or the Chief Grand Preceptress. If both of
these officers are present in the Grand Session, they
shall divide the vote, each casting six votes. A
Past Grand Mentor, three votes; a Past Grand Preceptress, three votes; a Grand and Past Grand
Queen Mother, three votes; International Grand
Officers, one vote each; Chief Mentors, one vote;
Past Chief Mentors, one vote; Chief Preceptress,
one vote; Past Chief Preceptress, one vote; Presiding Prince, one vote; Past Presiding Prince one
vote; Vice-Princess, one vote; Past Vice-Princess,
one vote; Queen Mother, one vote; Past Queen
Mother, one vote; International Grand Deputies,
one vote; Past International Grand Deputies, one
vote; Present or Past International D. G. M., one
vote.

Sec. 3.—A member of the International Grand
Temple and Tabernacle cannot be represented in
the Triennial Grand Session by proxy. A proxy
vote for any purpose will not be permitted in the
International Grand Sessions.

Sec. 4—The Chief Grand Mentors and the Chief
Grand Preceptresses are the Representatives of
their Grand Temples and Tabernacles in the International Grand Sessions.

ARTICLE III.

POWERS AND AUTHORITY.

Section 1.—The International Grand Temple
and Tabernacle shall have the authority to organize

and charter Temples of the Knights of Tabor, Tabernacles of the Daughters of Tabor, Palatiums of the Royal House of Media, and Tents of Maids and Pages, in any part of the civilized world.

SEC. 2.—When an organization is formed inside of the boundaries of any Grand Temple and Tabernacle by an International Grand Deputy, or I. D. G. M., the Deputy must report to the Chief Grand Mentor for a charter or warrant.

SEC. 3.—The International Grand Temple and Tabernacle shall receive, hear and decide all appeals that come from Grand Temples and Tabernacles, and shall adjust all grievances and complaints arising between Grand Temples and Tabernacles.

SEC. 4.—The International Grand Temple and Tabernacle shall have the authority to provide for its own support.

ARTICLE IV.
OFFICIAL TITLES.

SECTION 1.—The titles of the officers of the International Grand Temple and Tabernacle shall be as follows:

1.—International Chief Grand Mentor.—I. C. G. M.
2.—International Chief Grand Preceptress.—I. C. G. P.
3.—International Vice-Grand Mentor.—I. V.-G. M.
4.—International Vice-Grand Preceptress.—I. V.-G. P.
5.—International Chief Grand Scribe.—I. C. G. S.
6.—International Chief Grand Recorder.—I. C. G. R.
7.—International Chief Grand Treasurer.—I. C. G. T.
8.—International Grand Queen Mother.—I. G. Q. M.
9.—International Chief Grand Orator.—I. C. G. O.
10.—International Chief Grand Priestess.—I. C. G. Ps.
11.—International Grand Drill-Master.—I. G. D.-M.
12.—International Grand Inner Sentinel.—I. G. I. St.

The above officers are elected and installed at each Triennial Grand Session.

SEC. 2.—The following officers are appointed by the International Chief Grand Mentor, and installed with the other officers:

1.—International Grand Color Bearer.—I. G. C. B.
2.—International Chief Grand Sentinel.—I. C. G. St.
3.—International Chief Grand Guard.—I. C. G. G.
4.—International Chief Grand Guard.—I. C. G. G.
5.—International Chief Grand Guard.—I. C. G. G.
6.—International Chief Grand Guard.—I. C. G. G.
7.—International Chief Grand Guard.—I. C. G. G.

———

1.—International Chief Grand Judge.—I. C. G. J.
2.—International Chief Grand Judge.—I. C. G. J.
3.—International Chief Grand Judge.—I. C. G. J.
4.—International Chief Grand Judge.—I. C. G. J.
5.—International Chief Grand Judge.—I. C. G. J.
6.—International Chief Grand Judge.—I. C. G. J.
7.—International Chief Grand Judge.—I. C. G. J.

Three Knights are appointed by the International Chief Grand Mentor, and four Daughters are appointed by the International Chief Grand Preceptress.

The International Chief Grand Preceptress appoints the following Daughters:

1.—International Chief Grand Tribune.—I. C. G. Te.
2.—International Chief Grand Tribune.—I. C. G. Te.
3.—International Chief Grand Tribune.—I. C. G. Te.
4.—International Chief Grand Tribune.—I. C. G. Te.
5.—International Chief Grand Tribune.—I. C. G. Te.
6.—International Chief Grand Tribune.—I. C. G. Te.
7.—International Chief Grand Tribune.—I. C. G. Te.

33

ARTICLE V.

SECTION 1.—The officers of the International Grand Temple and Tabernacle are elected during the Triennial Session, and installed before the Session closes.

SEC. 2.—The ballots shall be written or printed. A majority of all the votes shall be necessary to elect. Nominations shall be made in open Session. In case there is no election on the ballot, the candidate receiving the lowest number of votes is to be dropped, until some one else is elected.

SEC. 3.—The I. C. G. M. shall appoint five Tellers, whose duty it is to count the ballots and announce the result.

SEC. 4.—A Knight cannot be elected and installed as International Chief Grand Mentor, who has not served one year as Chief Grand Mentor of a Grand Temple and Tabernacle.

SEC. 5.—A Daughter cannot be elected and installed as International Chief Grand Preceptress, until she has served one year as Chief Grand Preceptress of a Grand Temple and Tabernacle.

ARTICLE VI.

PERPETUATION.

SECTION 1.—In the event of the death, resignation or the disqualification of the I. C. G. M. and I. V.-G. M., the I. C. G. S. is authorized to issue a summons to the Chief Grand Mentors, requesting them to meet within ten days from date of summons, and elect and install an I. C. G. M., to serve the balance of the term.

(2—Dickson's New Manual.)

ARTICLE VII.

DUTIES OF INTERNATIONAL GRAND OFFICERS.

Section 1.—The International Chief Grand Mentor shall preside at all Sessions of the International Grand Temple and Tabernacle, and call Special Sessions when he deems it necessary, or when requested by two-thirds of the Chief Grand Mentors. He shall decide all points and questions of order in the Triennial Grand Session—appoint officers *pro-tem.* in the absence or disqualification of the officer elected or appointed. He can open and close the Triennial Session without a motion. He shall make to the Triennial Session a report of the business that has been transacted during the interval since the last Session. He shall appoint all committees not otherwise ordered by the Triennial Session. He can order the I. C. G. S. and I. C. G. T. to report to him the condition of the treasury at any time. His signature to a warrant on the Treasurer makes it legal. No money can be paid out of the treasury without his signature. He shall organize Grand Temples and Tabernacles under the International Charter, in any State, Territory or country, when he is satisfied that they have the constitutional number of organizations within their boundary. He must supply the Grand Temples and Tabernacles that he organizes with all the requisites to commence business as a Grand body. He can organize Temples, Tabernacles, Palatiums and Tents in person or by Deputy, in any part of the civilized world, and assign such organizations to the nearest Grand Temple and Tabernacle, or organize them into International Districts. He must issue the quarterly Pass in the months of March, June, September and December, and furnish a sufficient supply to the C. G. Ms., for all Temples and Tabernacles. He must decide on all matters that are requested of him by the C. G. Ms. or C. G. Ps.

INTERNATIONAL CHIEF GRAND PRECEPTRESS.

SEC. 2.—It shall be the duty of the I. C. G. P. to assist the I. C. G. M. during the business of the Triennial Session, when he is absent from the Chair at any time during the Session. She must give such instructions and assistance to Chief Grand Preceptresses as they may request of her. She is authorized to organize Tabernacles, Palatiums and Tents in any part of the civilized world, and, if in a State where there is a Grand Temple and Tabernacle, report her organizations to the C. G. M. for a charter. She must make a full report to the Triennial Session of her work and official business during the interval since the last Triennial Session.

INTERNATIONAL VICE-GRAND MENTOR.

SEC. 3.—It shall be the duty of the I. V.-G. M. to assist the I. C. G. M. in keeping order during the Triennial Session. In the event of the death or mental inability of the I. C. G. M., the I. V.-G. M. shall attend to and perform all the duties of the I. C. G. M. until another is elected at the Triennial Session and installed.

INTERNATIONAL VICE-GRAND PRECEPTRESS.

SEC. 4.—It is the duty of the I. V.-G. P. to assist the I. V.-G. M. in his duties during the Triennial Session. Should the I. C. G. P. be re-

moved by death, or resign her office, the I. V.-G.
P. must fill her station and attend to its duties
until the regular election.

INTERNATIONAL CHIEF GRAND SCRIBE.

Sec. 5.—The I C. G. S. shall have charge of
all the records, and keep a journal of the proceedings of the Triennial Session. He must keep and
preserve all official papers. He shall keep a register
of all Grand Temples and Tabernacles, and a copy
of their seals. He shall attest all official papers
that are issued from his office with the seal of his
office. He shall collect the International Grand
dues and other moneys due the International Grand
Temple and Tabernacle, and pay them to the I. C.
G. T. He shall draw all warrants for money on
the Grand Treasurer, and have them signed by the
I. C. G. M., and sign his name and impress his
seal thereon. He must make a full report of all
business that has been transacted in his office to
each Triennial Session. At the expiration of his
term of office he must deliver to his successor all
books, papers and property that are in his possession
belonging to the International Grand Temple and
Tabernacle.

INTERNATIONAL CHIEF GRAND RECORDER.

Sec. 6.—It shall be the duty of the I. C. G. R.
to assist the I. C. G. S. in the business of the
Triennial Session, and aid him in getting the proceedings ready for the printer, and perform such
other duties pertaining to her office as may be
assigned to her.

INTERNATIONAL CHIEF GRAND TREASURER.

SEC. 7.—It shall be the duty of the I. C. G. T. to receive all moneys and valuables belonging to the International Grand Temple and Tabernacle, and keep a correct account of what he receives. He must pay all warrants drawn on the Treasurer that are signed by the I. C. G. M. and I. C. G. S. He shall make a full report to the Triennial Session of the amount of money received and disbursed. His books shall always be ready for the inspection of the I. C. G. M., or any committee appointed by him. At the expiration of his term of office he must deliver to his successor all books, papers, moneys and valuables, belonging to the International Grand Temple and Tabernacle.

INTERNATIONAL GRAND QUEEN MOTHER.

SEC. 8.—It is the duty of the I. G. Q. M. to communicate with the Grand Queen Mothers of the Grand Temples and Tabernacles, and receive from them the annual reports of the Tents and their condition, the number of Tents, and the number of children in the Tents. She must make a triennial report of all Tents to the Triennial Session.

INTERNATIONAL CHIEF GRAND ORATOR.

SEC. 9.—The I. C. G. O. shall conduct the devotional exercises of the Triennial Session, and perform the functions of Chaplain on public occasions, and preach the triennial sermon, and conduct the funeral services of all International Grand Officers.

INTERNATIONAL CHIEF GRAND PRIESTESS.

Sec. 10.—It is the duty of the I. C. G. Ps. to assist the I. C. G. O. in the exercises of the Triennial Session; and when he is absent from the Session, she shall attend to the opening and closing of the Session in the usual form.

INTERNATIONAL GRAND DRILL-MASTER.

Sec. 11.—The I. G. D.-M. shall assist the I. G. I. St. in her duties at the inner door of the hall. He shall perform the functions of Chief Marshal at all public processions of the International Grand Temple and Tabernacle, and has authority to appoint Aides. He must give instructions to the Grand Drill-Masters, when they so request. He must arrange the hall for the Triennial Session, assisted by the I. C. G. Gs.

INTERNATIONAL GRAND INNER SENTINEL.

Sec. 12.—It is the duty of the I. G. I. St. to guard the inside door during the Triennial Session, and to admit none, unless they give the proper Pass and are properly clothed. She must report all applicants for admission to the I. V.-G. M., and admit or reject them on his order.

INTERNATIONAL GRAND COLOR BEARER.

Sec. 13.—It is the duty of the I. G. C. B. to take care of the International Banner, and carry it in public processions.

INTERNATIONAL CHIEF GRAND SENTINEL.

Sec. 14.—The I. C. G. St. shall have charge of the outer door of the hall during the International Grand Session. He must notify the I. G. I. St.

when a Knight or Daughter desires admittance. It is his business to see that they are properly clothed before he permits them to enter.

INTERNATIONAL CHIEF GRAND JUDGES.

SEC. 15.—The Board of International Chief Grand Judges shall consist of seven members—three Knights and four Daughters. This Board shall investigate all appeals, grievances and complaints that are referred to it by the International Session; they must report their decisions to the International Session. This Board shall have authority to impeach an International Chief Grand Mentor in accordance with Article XVII of the International Constitution.

INTERNATIONAL CHIEF GRAND TRIBUNES.

SEC. 16.—It shall be the duty of the I. C. G. Tes. to assist the I. C. G. Gs. in their several duties. This Board shall consist of seven Daughters.

INTERNATIONAL CHIEF GRAND GUARDS.

SEC. 17.—This Board shall consist of five Knights, whose duty it is to attend on the members under the orders of the I. C. G. M., and they shall assist the I. G. D.-M. in preparing the hall for the International Sessions.

ARTICLE VIII.

INTERNATIONAL DEPUTIES.

SECTION 1.—Commissions are issued by the I. C. G. M. to none but those distinguished members of the Order who have by their zeal and earnest work aided in building up and enlarging the Order.

Their commissions are evidence of their high standing in the International Order of Twelve. This constitutional provision is not to be departed from, except when a Deputy is needed for organizing.

SEC. 2.—An International Deputy Grand Mentor shall have authority to organize and set up Temples, Tabernacles, Palatiums and Tents in any part of the United States of North America, and in any part of the civilized world.

SEC. 3.—An International Grand Deputy shall have the authority to organize and set up Tabernacles, Palatiums and Tents in any part of the United States of North America, and in any part of the civilized world.

SEC. 4.—The I. C. G. M. can appoint Special International Deputy Grand Mentors, and assign them to special duty, with specific instructions.

SEC. 5.—When an International Deputy organizes within the boundaries of a Grand Temple and Tabernacle, the organization must be reported to the Chief Grand Mentor of the State in which the organization has made application for a charter or warrant.

SEC. 6.—When an International Deputy organizes at any place that is not within the boundaries of a Grand Temple and Tabernacle, the organization must be reported to the International Chief Grand Mentor for charter or warrant.

SEC. 7.—An International commission creates and makes the bearer a life member in the International Grand Temple and Tabernacle, with all of its rights and privileges. If the bearer is a Knight, he must be and remain a member in good standing in a Temple; if a Daughter, she must be and remain a member in good standing in a Tabernacle.

ARTICLE IX.

REVENUE.

SECTION 1.—The revenue of the International Grand Temple and Tabernacle shall be derived from the following sources:

1.—All members of Temples and Tabernacles shall each pay two cents annually.

2.—Tents of Maids and Pages of Honor shall pay one dollar each annually, and Palatiums two dollars each annually. The fee shall be fixed by the Triennial Session.

3.—The C. G. S. of Grand Temples and Tabernacles are required to collect these International Grand dues, and forward them annually to the I. C. G. S., and take his receipt therefor.

The International Grand Temple and Tabernacle must furnish to each Grand Temple and Tabernacle, on their organization, the following requisites: Four dozen Saba Meroe Rituals, four dozen Daughters' Third Degree Rituals, two dozen Knights' Rituals, six dozen Daughters' Constitutions, four dozen Knights' Constitutions, four dozen Daughters' Traveling Certificates, three dozen Knights Traveling Certificates, four dozen Daughters' Transfers, three dozen Knights' Transfers, sixteen dozen Blank Daughters' Petitions, twelve dozen Knights' Petitions, twenty dozen Daughters' Monthly Cards, twelve dozen Knights' Monthly Cards, twenty dozen Tent Constitutions, twenty dozen Children's Monthly Cards, twenty Blank Tabernacle Warrants, sixteen

Blank Temple Charters, twelve Blank Tent Charters, one Grand Temple and Tabernacle Seal Press, one C. G. S. Seal Press, ten Palatium Charters, four dozen Palatium Rituals, and four dozen Past Arcanum Rituals.

The amount required for organizing a Grand Temple and Tabernacle shall be as follows: For the Charter, fifty dollars; to the I. C. G. M., for organizing and expenses, fifty dollars; for Requisites, one hundred and fifty dollars; total, two hundred and fifty dollars. To cover these expenses the I. C. G. M. shall assess each Temple, Tabernacle, Palatium and Tent *pro-rata*.

ARTICLE X.

PAY-ROLL OF INTERNATIONAL OFFICERS.

Section 1.—The I. C. G. M. shall receive five cents per mile for traveling expenses to and from the Triennial Session, and three dollars per day during the Triennial Session.

The I. C. G. P. shall receive the same amount.

The I. C. G. S. shall receive the same amount.

The I. C. G. R. shall receive the same amount.

The I. C. G. T. shall receive the same amount.

That is, these four officers shall receive the same amount that is paid to the I. C. G. M.

Sec. 2.— The salary of the above officers must be fixed, from time to time, by the Triennial Session.

Sec. 3.—The I. C. G. O., I. C. G. Ps., I. G. Q. M., I. G. D.-M., I. C. G. St. and I. G. I. St. shall receive three dollars per day during the Triennial Session.

ARTICLE XI.

INTERNATIONAL BOARD OF GRAND CURATORS.

SECTION 1.—This Board shall consist of five members, namely: The I. C. G. M., I. C. G. P., I. C. G. S., I. C. G. R. and I. C. G. T.

SEC. 2.—This Board shall be the Trustees of the International Grand Temple and Tabernacle. All deeds, donations, gifts or devises, for the benefit of the International Grand Temple and Tabernacle, shall be made to them.

SEC. 3.—They shall invest in stocks, loans or securities, the funds, as the Grand Session may direct. They shall call in, sell and realize on loans, stocks and investments, collect interest, rents and dividends accruing or arising from any investments belonging to the International Grand Temple and Tabernacle, and pay all that is collected to the I. C. G. S., and he shall turn it over to the I. C. G. T

SEC. 4.—The International Grand Temple and Tabernacle shall furnish the Board with such books and requisites as are needed to conduct their business.

SEC. 5.—The Board shall make a Triennial report to the Triennial Session of all the business; when their successors in office are installed and qualified, they shall deliver to them all books, securities, deposits, stocks, deeds, papers and moneys belonging to the International Grand Temple and Tabernacle.

ARTICLE XII.

BONDS.

SECTION 1.—The I. C. G. S. and the I. C. G. T. must give bond, with such security as shall be ap-

proved by the I. C. G. O., I. C. G. Ps. and I. V.-
G. M., for the faithful application of all moneys
and valuables belonging to the International Grand
Temple and Tabernacle, in accordance with the
Constitution and the orders of the Triennial Session.

ARTICLE XIII.

SECTION 1.—The I. C. G. M. must appoint the
following committees immediately after the Trien-
ninal Session is opened, and shall consist of seven
members each—three Knights and four Daughters:

1.—On Credentials.

2.—On Returns of Grand Temples and Tabernacles.

3.—On I. C. G. M.'s Message and I. C. G. P.'s
Report.

4.—On Finance and Accounts.

5.—On Ways and Means.

6.—On Obituaries.

7.—On Collecting the Membership Fee.

8.—On the Condition of the Colored People of
the World.

9.—On I. C. G. S.'s and I. C. G. T.'s Reports.

10.—On Board of Grand Curators' Report.

11.—On the Condition of the Order.

12.—On Edowment Benefits.

ARTICLE XIV.

DUTIES OF COMMITTEES.

SECTION 1.—The Committee on Credentials must
make a full report of all the Members of the International Grand Temple and Tabernacle, divided as
follows:

1.—The Representatives of Grand Temples and Tabernacles.

2.—The Chief Mentors and Past Chief Mentors.

3.—The Chief Preceptresses and Past Chief Preceptresses.

4.—The Presiding Princes and Vice-Princesses.

5.—The Queen Mothers and Past Queen Mothers.

6.—The International Deputies.

This report must include those that are present and absent. When members are absent, *absent* shall be marked opposite their names.

SEC. 2.—The Committee on Returns of Grand Temples and Tabernacles are to examine the returns of the Grand Temples and Tabernacles, and report the number of Temples, Tabernacles, Palatiums and Tents, and the number of members belonging to each Grand Temple and Tabernacle, and the dues that are due to the International Grand Temple and Tabernacle.

SEC. 3.—The Committee on I. C. G. M.'s Message and the I. C. G. P.'s Report must examine the message, and make such disposition of it as in their judgment it requires, and they must also recommend what shall be done with the I. C. G. P.'s report.

SEC. 4.—The Committee on Finance and Accounts must report the amount of money in the treasury after all dues have been collected in Triennial Session. Members who have accounts against the International Grand Temple and Tabernacle must put their accounts into the hands of this committee. This committee shall read their report just before the election of the Grand Officers. The report must itemize and give the amount of money received from each Grand Temple and Tabernacle and other sources, and the total amount that is in the International Grand treasury, and the amount of the accounts against the treasury, and the balance remaining in the treasury after all bills are paid.

SEC. 5.—The Committee on Ways and Means shall examine all business that is referred to them by the Triennial Session, and recommend what it considers the best action the Session shall take.

SEC. 6.—It shall be the duty of the Committee on Obituaries to report the names of the members of the International Grand Temple and Tabernacle who have died since the last Triennial Session, and prepare a programme for the Session, and recommend that an hour be set apart during the Session for the obituary exercises.

SEC. 7.—The Committee on Collecting the Membership Fee must collect the fee that is ordered by the Triennial Session, and report the names of the members that have paid.

SEC. 8.—The Committee on the Condition of the Colored People of the World shall be a standing committee, and shall hold their office for three years. It is the duty of this committee to prepare a detailed report of what the Colored People are doing. Their report should be complete, and cover all the avenues of life.

SEC. 9.—It is the duty of the Committee on the I. C. G. S.'s and I. C. G. T.'s Reports to examine and compare these reports carefully, and submit their decision to the Session.

SEC. 10.—The duty of the Committee on the Board of Grand Curators must examine the business of this Board, and report upon its correctness.

SEC. 11.—The Committee on the Condition of the Order must prepare a carefully written report of the condition of the Order, and make any recommendation that will in their judgment be of benefit in administering the affairs of the Order.

SEC. 12.—It shall be the duty of the Committee on Endowment Benefits to carefully examine the workings of the Taborian endowment, and widows' and orphans' benefits in the Grand Temples and Tabernacles, and report to the Session, and recommend such measures as they may think necessary.

The reports of the I. G. Q. M., I. D. G. M.s and I. G. D.s must be referred to a Special Committee.

ARTICLE XV.

BUSINESS RULES.

1.—The International Grand Temple and Tabernacle shall assemble in Triennial Session on the constitutional day and hour, and open with the usual ceremonies in the Saba Meroe Degree.

2.—The International Grand Chief appoints the committees.

3.—The Committee on Credentials makes a partial report.

4.—The International Grand Chief reads his message, and the International Grand Preceptress makes her report; the I. G. Q. M., I. D. G. M.s and I. G. D.s make their reports.

5.—Reports of Regular Committees.

6.—Reports of Special Committees.

7.—Reports of the Board of Grand Curators.

8.—Reports of the I. C. G. S. and I. C. G. T. are not made until all returns are made from Grand Temples and Tabernacles and other sources from which money is received.

9.—Motions, resolutions and new business.

10.—A special meeting of the C. G. M.s, to ex-emplify the Knights' ritualistic work.

11.—A special meeting of C. G. P.s, to exemplify the Daughters' and Priestesses' ritualistic work.

12.—A special meeting of the G. Q. M.s, on the best manner of conducting the Tent work and bus-iness.

13.—A special meeting of the P. P.s and V.-P.s on the Palatium ritualistic work.

14.—Nomination and election of International Grand Officers.

15.—Installation of Grand Officers.

16.—The I. C. G. M. declares the International Grand Temple and Tabernacle at rest until the next Triennial Grand Session, unless a Special Session is called.

FORM OF TRIENNIAL SESSION.

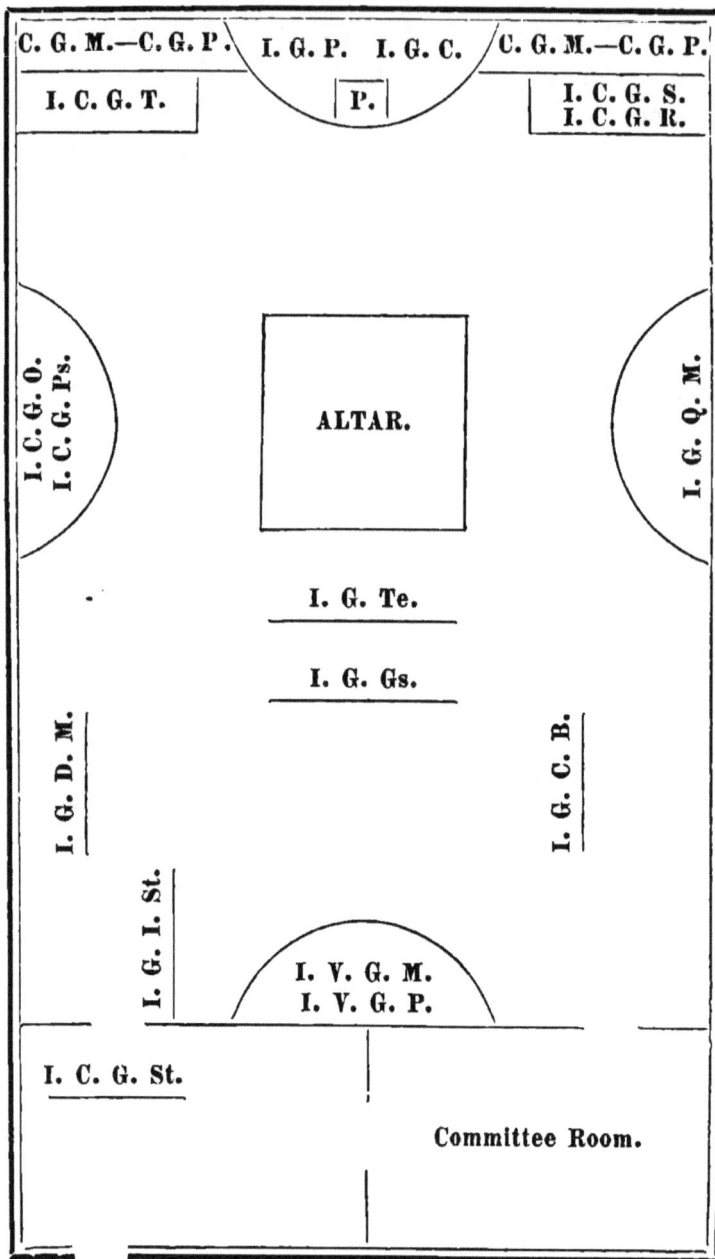

```
C. G. M.—C. G. P.    I. G. P.    I. G. C.    C. G. M.—C. G. P.

I. C. G. T.               P.                    I. C. G. S.
                                                I. C. G. R.




I. C. G. O.                                              I. G. Q. M.
I. C. G. Ps.          ┌──────────────┐
                      │              │
                      │    ALTAR.    │
                      │              │
                      └──────────────┘

                         I. G. Te.


                         I. G. Gs.

I. G. D. M.                                              I. G. C. B.




I. G. I. St.
                         I. V. G. M.
                         I. V. G. P.


I. C. G. St.

                                            Committee Room.
```

49

ARTICLE XVI.

SECTION 1.—He can organize and set Grand Temples and Tabernacles to work, and constitute them by International Charter.

SEC. 2. His decisions are final on all questions that are submitted to him from the C. G. M.s of Grand Temples and Tabernacles.

SEC. 3.—His decisions on International and General Laws and Rules remain in force until reversed by his successor.

SEC. 4.—He can visit any Grand Temple and Tabernacle when in Session, and have his traveling expenses paid by the Grand Session that he visits.

SEC. 5.—He can arrest the charter and suspend a Grand Temple and Tabernacle, when it is clear that they are in rebellion against the International and General Laws of the Order of Twelve.

SEC. 6.—He can preside at all meetings of the International Grand Temple and Tabernacle.

SEC. 7. — He can assemble the International Grand Temple and Tabernacle in Special Session at any time, if he decides that it is necessary for the interests of the Order.

SEC. 8.—He can call all the C. G. M.s and C. G. P.s into a council whenever grave and important business concerning the Order demands an united consultation and action.

SEC. 9.—When complaint or charges are made against a C. G. M. for violation of the criminal laws of the State, county or city, or for immorality or imbecility, by a majority of the elected Grand

Officers, the I. C. G. M., when he receives the charges and specifications, properly signed, shall suspend the said C. G. M. from his official duties, and notify the V.-G. M. to take charge of the C. G. M.'s official business. The I. C. G. M. shall order a committee of three C. G. M.s to meet and investigate the case. If this committee reports him guilty, as charged, the I. C. G. M. shall suspend him from the Order, and notify him to meet the Triennial Session for trial. If the committee decides that he is innocent in their report, the I. C. G. M. shall restore him to his office and official duties. The Grand Temple and Tabernacle that has a case of this kind, must pay the traveling expenses and *per diem* of the committee. The I. C. G. M. must fix the place, and notify the accused and the committee where to assemble. The committee shall have the authority to summons witnesses for and against the accused.

SEC. 10.—The I. C. G. M. can confer the Temple and Tabernacle degrees on all persons of distinction, and assign them to any Temple or Tabernacle for membership. Such persons are to be enrolled without ballot, but they must obey the laws and rules governing the Temple or Tabernacle.

SEC. 11.—The I. C. G. M. can give a dispensation to open a Grand Temple and Tabernacle, and allow them to proceed with their business. When their charter is lost or misplaced, the dispensation will hold good until it is found or another one is granted.

SEC. 12.—He can appoint as many International Deputies as he desires.

Sec. 13.—He cannot be disciplined for his official acts after he has passed out of office.

ARTICLE XVII.

IMPEACHMENT.

Section 1.—An International Chief Grand Mentor can be impeached for the following offenses: First, for violating the criminal laws, if he is arrested and found guilty, and sentenced to prison; second, for immoral conduct; and third, for imbecility.

Sec. 2.—When an I. C. G. M. is found guilty in a criminal court and sentenced to prison, the Chairman of the Board of International Grand Judges must assemble the Board, and investigate the case, and if they find that the evidence is clear and that he was justly sentenced, they are authorized to declare his seat vacant, and notify the I. V.-G. M. to take charge of the I. C. G. M.'s office and attend to all its duties.

Sec. 3.—If the I. C. G. M. is accused of immoral conduct, and it is notoriously the common talk of his neighbors, a charge can be made by three or more members of the Order, who must be eye-witnesses of his immorality. The charge and specifications, with the names of the witnesses signed to it, must be given to the International Board of Judges. It shall be the duty of the Chairman to call his Board together, and examine the witnesses in the presence of the I. C. G. M., or, if he refuses to attend, the Judges shall proceed with the examination. If they decide that it is a case requiring a trial, the Judges must notify the I. C. G. S. to summons five C. G. M.s or Past C.

G. M.s to try the case. The I. C. G. S. shall fix the day and date and the place of meeting, also to notify the I. C. G. M. to be present. If the I. C. G. M. is found guilty, he must be suspended and ordered to meet the Triennial Session for trial. The I. V.-G. M. takes charge of the office.

SEC. 4.—If the I. C. G. M. becomes weak-minded or insane, so that he cannot attend to the duties of his office, the I. C. G. S. must notify the I. G. C. J.s, and they must meet and investigate. If they find that the I. C. G. M. is incapable of attending to the duties of the office, they shall declare the office vacant and put the I. V.-G. M. in charge.

ARTICLE XVIII.

AMENDMENTS.

SECTION 1.—The International Constitution can be amended by submitting the amendment or amendments to the International Grand Session. If said amendment or amendments are recommended by a three-fourths vote, they must be printed in the Proceedings, and submitted to every Grand Temple and Tabernacle at their First Annual Session after the said amendment or amendments have been recommended by the Triennial Session.

SEC. 2.—The Grand Temples and Tabernacles shall read the amendment or amendments in open Session, and order them printed in the Annual Grand Session Proceedings, with instructions that each Temple and Tabernacle call a special meeting to act on the amendment or amendments.

SEC. 3.—When a Temple is opened to act on the amendments, the amendment or amendments should first be carefully read, and then put to a vote. The

C. S. shall thereupon record the names of the members who voted for or against the amendment or amendments, and shall forward the result to the C. G. S.

SEC. 4.—Tabernacles shall proceed in the same manner as Temples in regard to the reading of and voting for the amendment or amendments, only that the C. R. shall record each member who voted yes or no, and shall forward the result to the C. G. S.

SEC. 5.—The C. G. S. shall report to the Grand Temple and Tabernacle Session the vote of each Temple and Tabernacle. If three-fourths of the Temples and Tabernacles approve of the amendment or amendments, and the Grand Session recommends the adoption by a two-thirds vote, the C. G. S. shall forward the entire vote cast to the I. C. G. S. If there is not the required number of Temples and Tabernacles voting for the adoption of the same, the C. G. S. shall inform the I. C. G. S. that the amendment or amendments are rejected by the Grand Temple and Tabernacle for the State of ———.

SEC. 6.—The I. C. G. S. shall report the vote from all the Grand Temples and Tabernacles to the Triennial Session. If seven-eighths of the Grand Temples and Tabernacles approve the amendment or amendments, the I. C. G. M. shall announce that the amendment or amendments have been regularly adopted, and are a part of the International Constitution. If they have not been approved by the required number, the I. C. G. M. shall declare that the amendment or amendments have been rejected.

KNIGHTS OF TABOR

INTERNATIONAL
ORDER OF
TWELVE

INTERNATIONAL GRAND OFFICERS' JEWEL
OF OFFICE.   (Insert Initials of Each Officer.)

CONTINUATION

OF

GENERAL LAWS.

GENERAL LAWS.—CONTINUATION.

ARTICLE I.

SECTION 1.—The International Grand Temple and Tabernacle shall have the authority to enforce the General Laws of the International Order of Twelve, of Knights and Daughter Priestesses of Tabor. The General Laws cover and comprise the Constitution and all Installing Ceremonies, all Funeral Ceremonies, Corner-stone Laying, Dedicating Ceremonies, Taborian Drill, Color of Regalia, Form of Jewels and Badges, Duties of Grand Officers, and General Taborian Rules and Instructions. The International Grand Temple and Tabernacle shall be an advisory and appellate body, whose decisions shall be final. During the interim between the Triennial Grand Sessions, the International Chief Grand Mentor shall hear all appeals, and adjust all differences occurring between Grand Temples and Tabernacles. He shall also have authority to enforce all of the General Laws.

(See Code, constituting part of the General Laws, with the Law of Impeachment and Trials of I. C. G. M.s and I. C. G. P.s, and Chief Grand Mentors and Chief Grand Preceptresses.)

ARTICLE II.

GRAND TEMPLES AND TABERNACLES.

SECTION 1.—A Grand Temple and Tabernacle of the Knights and Daughters of Tabor can be organized within the boundaries of any State or Territory of the United States, also in any State, Province or country in the civilized world.

SEC. 2.—Grand Temples and Tabernacles cannot be organized with less than forty organizations, composed of chartered and warranted Temples, Tabernacles, Tents and Palatiums.

SEC. 3.—The Temples, Tabernacles, Palatiums and Tents are required to pay the expenses for organizing a Grand Temple and Tabernacle within the boundaries of their State or Province.

SEC. 4.—When a State, Territory or Province has forty organizations, composed of Temples, Tabernacles, Palatiums and Tents, within its boundaries, a Grand Temple and Tabernacle must be organized. Two or more States adjoining each other may, for the convenience of their organizations, unite in forming a Grand Temple and Tabernacle.

SEC. 5.—It is the duty of an International Deputy, living within the boundaries of a State, Territory or Province that has not organized, to inform the I. C. G. M. when there is a lawful number of Temples, Tabernacles, Palatiums and Tents within those boundaries willing to organize a Grand Temple and Tabernacle. The International Grand Chief Mentor, when he receives this information, shall notify the Temples, Tabernacles, Palatiums and Tents to prepare to organize. He is required to give them at least three months to prepare for organizing a Grand Temple and Tabernacle.

SEC. 6.—The International Chief Grand Mentor may give a dispensation to organize a Grand Temple or Tabernacle with less than forty organizations, if he is satisfied that it will be for the best interests of the International Order of Twelve.

ARTICLE III.

POWER AND AUTHORITY.

SECTION 1.—A Grand Temple and Tabernacle shall have power and authority over all Temples, Tabernacles, Palatiums and Tents within the boundaries of the State, Territory or Province in which it is organized.

SEC. 2.—A Grand Temple and Tabernacle shall have authority to organize Temples, Tabernacles, Palatiums and Tents in any State, Territory, Province or country in the civilized world, where there is no Grand Temple and Tabernacle, and have jurisdiction over all of its organizations until a Grand Temple and Tabernacle is organized.

SEC. 3.—A Grand Temple and Tabernacle shall have authority to enact laws and rules for its government (but not to conflict with the International General Laws), grant charters and warrants, suspend or revoke charters and warrants for cause, receive and hear appeals, redress grievances and complaints arising in Temples, Tabernacles, Palatiums or Tents, and to provide for its support and government.

SEC. 4.—A Grand Temple and Tabernacle shall have an Annual Grand Session. A Special Grand

Session can be called by the Chief Grand Mentor at any time, if he finds it is necessary or when he is requested to call a special Grand Session by two-thirds of the Temples and Tabernacles, Palatiums and Tents.

SEC. 5.—Grand Temples and Tabernacles shall have exclusive jurisdiction within the boundaries of the State, Territory or Province in which they are organized, provided they do not conflict with the International General Laws.

SEC. 6.—When a Grand Temple and Tabernacle organizes in any State, Territory or Province where there is no Grand Temple and Tabernacle, their organization does not give them exclusive jurisdiction over the State, Territory or Province; their jurisdiction extends only to their organization, other Grand Temples and Tabernacles have the same right to organize Temples, Tabernacles, Palatiums and Tents in the same State, Territory or Province, and have jurisdiction over their own organizations.

ARTICLE IV.

APPEALS.

SECTION 1.—Members who have been suspended or expelled, and think that they have not received justice, have the right to appeal to the Grand Temple and Tabernacle Session.

SEC. 2.—The method of making out an appeal is as follows: First, give the day and date of the trial, and the name and number of the Temple or the Tabernacle; second, give the character of the offense upon which the charge and specifications are based; third, state the reason why you appeal; fourth, tell in what manner you were unjustly sentenced; and, fifth, give the names of witnesses. If it is a Temple, a copy of the appeal must be filed with the Chief Scribe; if a Tabernacle, with the Chief Recorder. The appellant must retain a copy. The appeal must be filed with the C. G. S. within ten days after the trial.

SEC. 3.—The C. S. or C. R. who receives an appeal must retain a copy, and forward the original appeal to the C. G. S.

SEC. 4.—When the Grand Session assembles, the C. G. S. must read the appeal in open Session, and the C. G. M. shall refer the same to the Board of Grand Judges.

SEC. 5.—The Grand Judges shall examine the complaint in the appeal and the witnesses, and deliver their decision to the Grand Session. If adopted by a majority vote, their decision is sustained.

SEC. 6.—If the appellant is not satisfied, an appeal can be taken to the Triennial Grand Session, by giving notice to the C. G. S. within ten days after the Grand Session closes. The C. G. S. must forward a copy of the appeal, with the other papers pertaining to the same, to the I. C. G. S.

SEC. 7.—When the Triennial Grand Session assembles, the I. C. G. S. shall read the appeal, and the other papers that accompany it, in open Session. The I. C. G. M. shall refer the appeal and papers to the International Board of Grand Judges, who shall investigate and examine witnesses, and render their decision to the Session. If adopted, it settles the matter. If a majority refuse to adopt the decision, the Triennial Session shall dispose of the appeal by a majority vote.

ARTICLE V.

ANNUAL SERMONS.

SECTION 1.—The International Order of Twelve, by the teachings of its Constitutions and Degrees, shows the belief of its members in the Lord God, the Supreme Ruler of Heaven and Earth. It is but right and just that the Knights and Daughters of Tabor should set apart one Sunday in each year to unite their voices in prayer and thanks that He has preserved our Order.

SEC. 2.—The third Sunday in the month of June of each year is hereby fixed as the day for the Knights and Daughters of Tabor to assemble and have an Annual Sermon preached. The members of Temples, Tabernacles, Palatiums and Tents are required to meet together that day, and make a united service to God.

SEC. 3.—The members can turn out in full regalia, or in undress regalia, as may be decided by their various Temples, Tabernacles, Palatiums and Tents.

SEC. 4.—In large cities, where the members are too numerous to all meet in one church, they can divide and hold the services in two churches of different denominations at the same hour.

ARTICLE VI.

SEC. 1.—Every Grand Temple and Tabernacle must formulate a plan for building halls, and insist that the Temples and Tabernacles working under its jurisdiction build or buy a suitable hall to hold their meetings in.

SEC. 2.—Every Grand Temple and Tabernacle must know that all Temples and Tabernacles take care of their sick, distressed or disabled members, and that the weekly benefits are paid regularly.

SEC. 3.—Every Grand Temple and Tabernacle must impress on the members that, when they start on a journey, they must take traveling certificates and monthly cards from Temples or Tabernacles, to show that they are in good standing, and warn all Temples and Tabernacles that they must not receive strangers without their certificates, cards and Quarterly Pass.

HALLS.

The halls used by the Knights and Daughters of Tabor must be dedicated within three months after they are occupied. Secret meetings in private houses are positively prohibited.

INTERNATIONAL DEPUTIES.

1. The business of the International Deputies is to organize Temples, Tabernacles, Palatiums and Tents in any part of the civilized world.

2. When they make an organization, they shall report that organization, if it is within the borders of a Grand Temple and Tabernacle, to the Chief Grand Mentor for a charter.

3. When they make an organization in any State, Territory or Province, where there is no Grand Temple and Tabernacle organized, the Deputy shall

report to the International Grand Chief for a charter.

4. An International Deputy Grand Mentor must be a member in good standing in a Temple of the Knights of Tabor, and is amenable to the laws the same as any other member. When his membership ceases, his commission is revoked.

5. An International Grand Deputy must be a member in good standing in a Tabernacle of Saba Meroe Priestesses, and is amenable to the laws the same as any other member. When her membership ceases, her commission is revoked.

6.—International Deputies, or Past International Deputy Knights or Daughters, shall be members of the International Grand Temple and Tabernacle as long as they remain in good standing in a Temple or Tabernacle.

INTERNATIONAL DISTRICTS.

The International Grand Chief may, for the convenience of the members, organize and arrange International Districts. These Districts shall not conflict with the Grand Temples and Tabernacles, or prevent them from making organizations in such Districts. The Districts shall be represented in the Triennial Grand Session by their District Grand Mentor and District Grand Preceptress. These Districts shall be required to conform to the Laws and Rules of the International Order of Twelve.

SUSPENSIONS AND EXPULSIONS.

When a member is suspended or expelled from a Temple or Tabernacle by due process of law, the member shall remain suspended or expelled, as the case may be, until restored to membership by the same Temple or Tabernacle, or by the Grand Temple and Tabernacle; *provided*, however, that if the Temple or Tabernacle becomes defunct before the suspended or expelled member is restored, the member can apply by petition to the Grand Session, which is authorized to restore the member (if after an investigation they are found worthy), and give a transfer.

Members of the International Grand Temple and Tabernacle.

The membership of the International Grand Temple and Tabernacle shall be as follows:
1.—Chief Mentors and Past Chief Mentors.
2.—Chief Preceptresses and Past Chief Preceptresses.
3.—Presiding Princes and Past Presiding Princes.
4.—Vice-Princesses and Past Vice-Princesses.
5.—Queen Mothers and Past Queen Mothers.
6.—International Deputy Grand Mentors.
7.—Past International Deputy Grand Mentors.
8.—International Grand Deputies.
9.—Past International Grand Deputies.

To continue their membership in the International Grand Temple and Tabernacle, they must be and remain members in good standing in their Temples or Tabernacles.

Members of Grand Temples and Tabernacles.

The members of Grand Temples and Tabernacles shall be as follows:
1.—Chief Mentors and Past Chief Mentors.
2.—Chief Preceptresses and Past Chief Preceptresses.
(3—Dickson's New Manual.)

3.—Presiding Princes and Past Presiding Princes.

4.—Vice-Princesses and Past Vice-Princesses.

5.—Queen Mothers and Past Queen Mothers.

6.—Deputy Grand Mentors and Past Deputy Grand Mentors.

7.—Deputy Grand Preceptresses and Past Deputy Grand Preceptresses.

To continue their membership in the Grand Temples and Tabernacles, they must be and remain members in good standing in their Temples or Tabernacles.

HONORARY MEMBERS.

The only department in the International Order of Twelve that has the authority to make honorary members is the Temples and Tabernacles, and they are permitted under the following instructions to honor a member of their Temple or Tabernacle: First, the member to receive this honor must be an old member, for years in good standing, and one who has been active in building up the Order. If a Temple desires to invest one of their members with this honor, it will require a unanimous vote of all the members who are present at a regular meeting. If a Tabernacle desires to honor a Daughter who is a member of their Tabernacle, it can be done by a unanimous vote of all the members present at a regular meeting. An honorary member is entitled to all the benefits and privileges of a contributing member.

THE UNITY OF THE INTERNATIONAL ORDER OF TWELVE.

The Ritualistic work of the Order is unchangeable and uniform, the same everywhere; new degrees cannot be added or new signs and tokens be given, except it is so ordered by amending the General Laws. To add to the Ritualistic work, or to make a new degree or degrees for any of the departments, will require the unanimous vote of every Temple and Tabernacle in the affirmative, and the unanimous vote of every Grand Temple and Tabernacle, when in Grand Session. The Triennial Grand Session may, when satisfactory evidence is given that it is the unanimous desire of every member of the International Order of Twelve to add new degrees, signs, words and tokens to the Ritualistic work, the Triennial Grand Session is authorized to prepare such degrees, by appointing a committee to draft the degrees, signs, words or tokens, and submit their work to the next Triennial Grand Session; then, if approved by the unanimous vote of the Triennial Grand Session, said degree or degrees, signs, words and tokens shall be lawful.

FULL UNIFORM.

Within three months after the Uniform Rank of Tabor or the Fourth Degree in the Temple is conferred, the member must have his full uniform, as follows: Helmet, sword and belt, gloves and gauntlets, cap, cup and badges. A Knight failing to comply with this law, shall be and stand suspended until he has his full uniform. If a C. M. fails to enforce this law, the C. G. M. is authorized to remove him from office and appoint another C. M. This law is to be enforced when the Temple is one year old. The members of every Temple that is one year old must have their full uniform.

777—THE ORGANIZATION—333.

The International Order of Twelve, of Knights and Daughters of Tabor, was organized in the City of Independence, State of Missouri, August the 12th, A. D. 1872. This is the birthday of the Order, and is hereby set apart as the proper day to celebrate. It is the Taborian day—a day to be remembered.

INSTALLATION

OF

International Grand Officers.

FULL CEREMONIES.

INSTALLING CEREMONY

OF

INTERNATIONAL GRAND OFFICERS.

————: o :————

The installing ceremony is performed by a Past International Chief Grand Mentor, or a Present or Past Chief Grand Mentor.

When the time arrives to install, the I. G. Drill-Master (or Marshal, who is appointed for that occasion) receives the Jewels, or badges of office from each officer, and places them on the altar. The Marshal forms the officers elected and appointed in a semi-circle around the altar, the International Chief and International Preceptress elect in the center of the circle, and the other officers on each side of them, according to the roll of office. The band plays until the installing ceremony is ready to commence.)

The Marshal salutes the installing Grand Officer, and says: Sir Grand, I have the high honor of presenting to you these Sir Knights and Daughters of Tabor, who have been regularly elected to fill the several offices in the International Grand Temple and Tabernacle of the International Order of Twelve for the ensuing term. I also present to you the appointed officers; they all have signified their readiness to enter upon their official duties.

The Installing Grand to Marshal:—Sir Marshal, please form the Sir Knights and Daughters in a circle around these elected and appointed officers. (A double circle is formed, the Daughters forming the inner and the Knights the outer circle.)

Sir Grand to the officers elect:—Sir Knights and Daughters of Tabor, you have been honored by receiving the suffrage of the members of the International Grand Temple and Tabernacle; you have been elected to the highest offices that are in the gift of the International Order of Twelve. We are here to invest and entrust to your care the responsibility of conducting the business and work of the Knights and Daughters of Tabor. The honor, stability and perpetuity of the Order are to be placed in your charge. I admonish you to vigilantly guard every avenue, and be ready to meet and repel any danger that would deter or obstruct our Order in fulfilling its mission for the benefit of mankind. It becomes my duty to administer to you an obligation that all International Grand Officers have taken before they were installed. If you are willing and ready, place your right hands on your hearts and repeat your full names, and say after me:

OBLIGATION.

I, —— —— ——, do solemnly promise that I will defend and support the International Constitution and General Laws of the International Order of Twelve. I will faithfully attend to the duties of the office that I am about to be installed in.—*In Solo Deo Salus!*

The Grand:—Sir Knights, uncover; let us Knights and Daughters unite in prayer with the Grand Orator.

PRAYER.

Almighty and Everlasting God, in the name of Jesus, Thine Only Begotten Son, our Savior, we come unto Thee. We confess our many sins and omissions of duty unto Thee, Thou who art full of mercy and love to mankind, and have given to us the inestimable privilege of coming unto Thee at all times to plead for pardon and forgiveness. Hear us at this hour and let the light of Thy Godly Presence illumine our hearts, and in the name of Jesus fit us and prepare us that we may worship Thee in the beauty of holiness. We come to Thee, our Heavenly Father to ask Thy blessings for the members of the International Order of Twelve, wherever they are dispersed around the world. In an especial manner bless these Knights and Daughters of Tabor that are about to be invested with the governing power of the International Grand Temple and Tabernacle. Oh Lord, endow them with wisdom, that they may be enabled to carry forward the business of the Order to Thy honor and glory, and for the best interests of its members and for the benefit of humanity. Direct us in all our ways, and prosper the work of the Order in the hands of these Grand Officers. May Thy Godly and Fatherly care and protection accompany us all through life. This we humbly beg, in the name of Thy Exalted Son, Jesus Christ, our Lord, Redeemer and Savior.—*In Solo Deo Salus!*

Response by the members: Amen! Honor and Glory to God! One rap, and all are seated—Music.

Sir Grand:—Sir Knights, cover.

The Marshal then places the elected Grand Chief in proper position, and says:

Sir Grand, I present to you Sir —— —— ——, who has been elected International Chief Grand Mentor, and is now ready for installation.

Sir Grand:—Sir Knight, you have been chosen by the members of this Triennial Session to the most exalted position in the gift of the International Grand Temple and Tabernacle. You have my congratulations upon your elevation to that eminent station; you will find your official duties in the Constitution and General Laws of the International Order of Twelve. I now invest you with the Jewel of your office. Be faithful to the Taborian Knighthood.

The Marshal affixes the badge to the left breast of the Most Faithful Grand Chief, and conducts him to the Grand Seat in the South.

INSTRUCTIONS TO THE INTERNATIONAL CHIEF GRAND PRECEPTRESS.

Marshal:—Sir Grand, I present to you Daughter —— —— ——, who has been elected International Chief Grand Preceptress, and is now ready to be installed.

Sir Grand:—Most Faithful Daughter, you have been elected by the members of this Triennial Session to the most exalted position that is given to a Daughter of the Tabernacle. Your duties in the International Grand Temple and Tabernacle you will find in the Constitution and General Laws of the International Order of Twelve. I now invest you with the Jewel of your office. Be faithful to every duty that is required of you in your eminent station.

The Marshal affixes the badge to her left breast, and seats her at the left side of the I. C. G. M.

Sir Grand gives three raps, and all stand. He then says:—By virtue of the power and authority as Installing Officer, I now and here declare that Sir —— —— —— is regularly installed International Chief Grand Mentor of the International Order of Twelve, of Knights and Daughters of Tabor.

All repeat after the Grand: *We Declare!* and give one clap. (This is repeated three times.)

Sir Grand:—By virtue of the power and authority as Installing Officer, I now and here declare that Daughter —— —— —— is regularly installed International Chief Grand Preceptress of the International Order of Twelve, of Knights and Daughters of Tabor.

All repeat after the Grand: *We Declare!* and give one clap. (This is repeated three times.)

All say after the Grand: *We welcome our International Grand Chief!* and clap three times three.

All repeat after the Grand: *We welcome our International Grand Preceptress!* and clap three times three.

The Grand gives one rap, and all are seated. If the International Grand Chief and International Grand Preceptress desire to make any remarks, this is the proper time.

INTERNATIONAL VICE-GRAND MENTOR, AND INTERNATIONAL VICE-GRAND PRECEPTRESS.

Marshal:—Sir Grand, I have the honor of presenting to you Sir —— —— ——, who has been elected International Vice-Grand Mentor, and Daughter —— —— ——, who has been elected International Vice-Grand Preceptress. They are now ready to be installed.

Sir Grand:—Right Faithful Sir and Right Faithful Daughter, you have been elected by the members of this Triennial Session to fill the important duties of International Vice-Grand Mentor and International Vice-Grand Preceptress. These positions are next in rank to the Presiding Grand Officers'. You will find your duties fully laid down in the International Constitution. I congratulate you on the high position to which you have been called in the order. You are hereby invested with the Jewel of office.

The Marshal attaches the badges of office to their left breasts, and seats them properly in the North.

INTERNATIONAL CHIEF GRAND SCRIBE AND INTERNATIONAL CHIEF GRAND RECORDER.

The Marshal:—Sir Grand, I take pleasure in introducing to you Sir —— —— ——, who has been elected I. C. G. S., and Daughter —— —— ——, who has been elected I. C. G. R. They are now ready to be installed.

Sir Grand:—Sir Knight and Daughter, you have been elected by the members of this Triennial Session, and it shows the confidence they place in your ability to perform the duties of these very impor-

—

tant offices. You will find your instructions in the International Constitution. Read it carefully. I now invest you with the Jewel of office.

The Marshal attaches the badges, and seats them.

INTERNATIONAL CHIEF GRAND TREASURER.

The Marshal:—Sir Grand, I take pleasure in introducing to you Sir —— —— ——, who has been elected I. C. G. T. He is now ready for installation.

Sir Grand:—Sir Knight, you have been elected by the members of this Triennial Session to an office of trust and responsibility; it is an honor conferred on you, and an evidence that the members have confidence in your integrity. You will find your duties in the International Constitution. Read it carefully. I now invest you with the Jewel of office.

The Marshal affixes the badge, and seats him.

INTERNATIONAL GRAND QUEEN MOTHER.

The Marshal:—Sir Grand, I have the pleasure of introducing to you Daughter —— —— ——, who has been elected I. G. Q. M. She is now ready to be installed.

Sir Grand:—Daughter, you have been elected by the members of this Triennial Session to the very distinguished position of International Grand Queen Mother. The office is one of great usefulness, and you will find pleasure in attending to its several duties. The International Constitution will give you the full instructions regarding your position.

The Marshal affixes the badge of office, and seats her in the East.

International Chief Grand Orator and International Chief Grand Priestess.

The Marshal:—Sir Grand, I am pleased to introduce to you Sir —— —— ——, who has been elected I. C. G. O., and Daughter —— —— ——, who has been elected I. C. G. Ps. They are now ready for installation.

Sir Grand:—Sir Knight and Daughter, you have been elected by the members of this Triennial Session to the honorable offices of I. C. G. O. and I. C. G. Ps., these are high and sacred positions to which you have been called; may you be thoroughly furnished and abundantly provided for the good work. Your duties are found in the International Constitution. I now invest you with the Jewel of your office.

The Marshal affixes the badges of office, and seats them in the West.

International Grand Inner Sentinel.

The Marshal:—Sir Grand, I have the pleasure of presenting to you Daughter —— —— ——, who has been elected I. G. I. St., and is now ready to be installed.

Sir Grand:—Daughter —— —— ——, you have been elected to the very important position of I. G. I. St. I admonish you to be zealous in your duties. You will find your instructions in the International Constitution. I now invest you with the Jewel of your office. Please be seated.

International Grand Drill-Master.

The Marshal:—Sir Grand, it gives me pleasure to present to you Sir —— —— ——, who has been elected I. G. D.-M., and is now ready for installation.

Sir Grand:—Sir Knight, your election to the responsible office of I. G. D.-M. is proof of the confidence that is reposed in your ability to discharge the duties of the office. You will find your instructions in the International Constitution. I now invest you with the Implements of your office and the Jewel. Please be seated.

INTERNATIONAL GRAND COLOR BEARER.

The Marshal:—Sir Grand, I have the honor of presenting to you Sir —— —— ——, who has been appointed I. G. C. B., and now ready to be installed.

Sir Grand:—Sir Knight, you have been appointed International Grand Color-Bearer. The office is one of honor, and requires courage. Your duties are fully laid down in the International Constitution. I now invest you with the Jewel of office.

The Marshal affixes the badge, and seats him.

INTERNATIONAL CHIEF GRAND SENTINEL.

The Marshal:—Sir Grand, I have the pleasure of presenting to you Sir —— —— ——, who has been appointed International Chief Grand Sentinel. He is now ready to be installed.

Sir Grand:—Sir Knight, you have been honored with the appointment of International Chief Grand Sentinel. It is an office of great responsibility. I admonish you to be vigilant in your several duties. You will find your instructions in the International

Constitution. Be faithful. I now invest you with the Jewel of office and Sword of defense.

The Marshal affixes the badge, and seats him.

INTERNATIONAL CHIEF GRAND GUARDS.

The Marshal:—Sir Grand, I have the honor of presenting to you Sir Knights (gives each of their names). They are now ready for installation.

Sir Grand:—Sir Knights, you have been appointed to the honorable position of International Chief Grand Guards. Be punctual to the trust that is given to you, that you may merit the approval of the members of the International Grand Temple and Tabernacle. You will find your instructions in the International Constitution. I now invest you with the Jewel of office.

The Marshal affixes the badges, and seats them.

INTERNATIONAL CHIEF GRAND JUDGES.

The Marshal:—Sir Grand, I have the honor of introducing to you Sir Knights (gives their names), and Daughters (gives their names), who have been appointed International Chief Grand Judges, and are now ready to be installed.

Sir Grand:—Sir Knights and Daughters, you have been appointed to the exalted office of International Chief Grand Judges. This distinguished position is one that requires a thorough knowledge of the Laws governing the Order. You will find your instructions in the International Constitution and General Laws. I now invest you with the Jewels of office.

The Marshal affixes the badges, and seats them.

INTERNATIONAL CHIEF GRAND TRIBUNES.

The Marshal:—Sir Grand, I have the honor of presenting to you Daughters (gives their names). They have been appointed International Chief Grand Tribunes, and are now ready to be installed.

Sir Grand:—I am pleased to hear that you are appointed to the honorable offices of International Chief Grand Tribunes. This high position is one of dignity and usefulness. May you fill its duties with honor. You will find your instructions in the International Constitution. I now invest you with the Jewels of office.

The Marshal affixes the badges, and seats them.

Singing, or music by the band.

After the music has finished, the Sir Grand gives three raps; all Knights and Daughters stand, except those that have just been installed.

CLOSING CEREMONY.

The Sir Grand gives three claps, and says: By virtue of the authority in me vested as Installing Grand Officer, I now and here declare that the Officers of the International Grand Temple and Tabernacle have been regularly installed and inducted into their several official positions for the ensuing International Grand Temple and Tabernacle term.

All the members repeat after the Sir Grand: *We Declare! We Declare!! We Declare!!!*

All give claps, three times four.

The Sir Grand gives one rap, and all are seated.

Singing or music by the band.

ORATION.

The I. C. G. M. gives three raps, and all stand. He says: By virtue of the authority in me vested, I now declare the International Triennial Grand Session from work to rest, until the next Triennial Session, unless special business makes it necessary to call an Extra Session. If so, all the members will be officially notified.

"Home, Sweet Home," is sung or played by the band.

The I. C. G. M. then gives one rap.

KNIGHTS OF TABOR

INTERNATIONAL
ORDER OF
TWELVE

333

777

BADGE OF KNIGHTS OF TABOR.

82

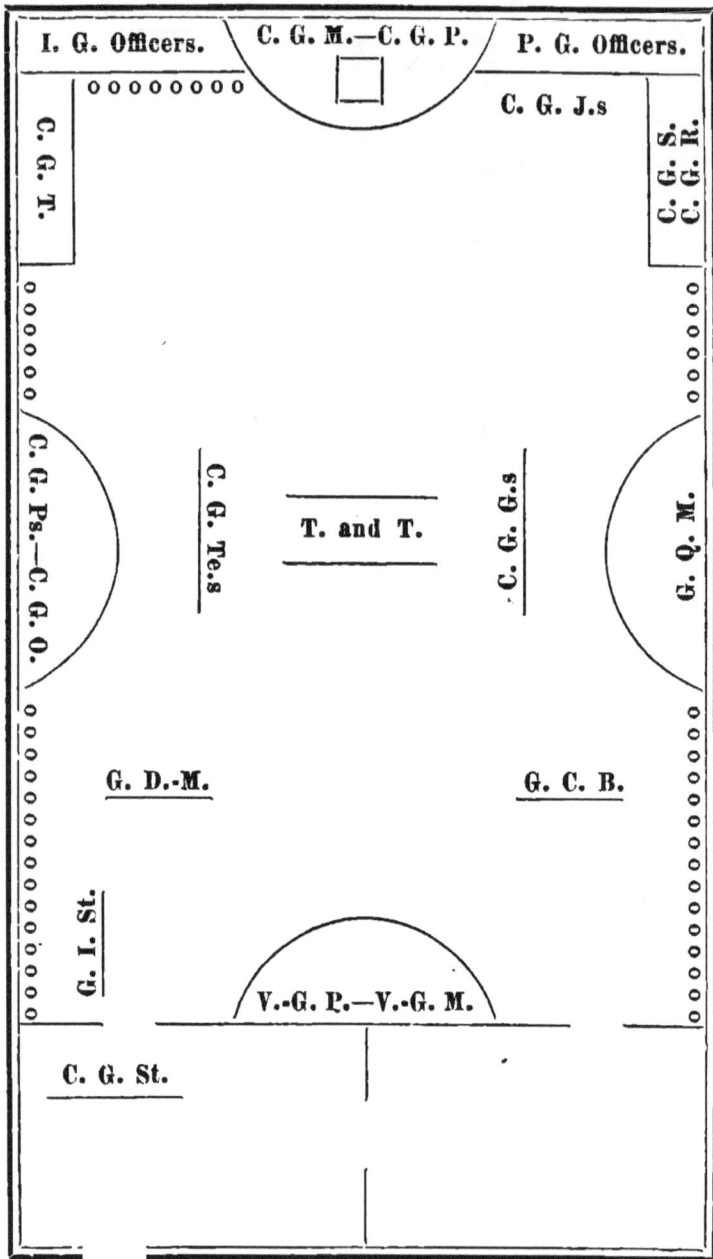

I. G. Officers.   C. G. M.—C. G. P.   P. G. Officers.

o o o o o o o o

C. G. J.s

C. G. T.

C. G. S.
C. G. R.

o o o o o o

o o o o o o

C. G. Ps.—C. G. O.

C. G. Te.s

T. and T.

C. G. G.s

G. Q. M.

o o o o o o o o o o o o o o o o o

G. D.-M.

G. C. B.

o o o o o o o o o o o

G. I. St.

V.-G. P.—V.-G. M.

C. G. St.

GRAND TEMPLE AND TABERNACLE OFFICER'S JEWEL.

Twenty-seven Grand Officers—Each Jewel with Initials of Office.

84

ARTICLE VII.

GRAND TEMPLE AND TABERNACLE OFFICERS.

SECTION. 1.—The official titles of the officers of
the Grand Temple and Tabernacle shall be as follows:

1.—Chief Grand Mentor.—C. G. M.
2.—Chief Grand Preceptress.—C. G. P.
3.—Vice-Grand Mentor.—V.-G. M.
4.—Vice-Grand Preceptress.—V.-G. P.
5.—Chief Grand Scribe.—C. G. S.
6.—Chief Grand Recorder.—C. G. R.
7.—Chief Grand Treasurer.—C. G. T.
8.—Grand Queen Mother.—G. Q. M.
9.—Chief Grand Orator.—C. G. O.
10.—Chief Grand Priestess.—C. G. Ps.
11.—Grand Drill-Master.—G. D.-M.
12.—Grand Inner Sentinel.—G. I. St.

The above officers are elected and installed at
each Grand Session.

SEC. 2.—The following officers are appointed by
the C. G. M., and installed with the other officers:

1.—Grand Color Bearer.—G. C. B.
2.—Chief Grand Sentinel.—C. G. St.
3.—Chief Grand Guard.—C. G. G.
4.—Chief Grand Guard.—C. G. G.
5.—Chief Grand Guard.—C. G. G.

1.—Chief Grand Judge.—C. G. J.
2.—Chief Grand Judge.—C. G. J.
3.—Chief Grand Judge.—C. G. J.

SEC. 3.—The C. G. P. appoints the following
officers—all Daughters—who are installed with the
other officers:

1.—Chief Grand Judge.—C. G. J.
2.—Chief Grand Judge.—C. G. J.
3.—Chief Grand Judge.—C. G. J.
4.—Chief Grand Judge.—C. G. J.

1.—Chief Grand Tribune.—C. G. Te.
2.—Chief Grand Tribune.—C. G. Te.
3.—Chief Grand Tribune.—C. G. Te.

SEC. 4.—A Sir Knight must serve as Chief Mentor of a Temple one year, before he can be elected and installed as Chief Grand Mentor. A Daughter must serve as Chief Preceptress of a Tabernacle one year, before she can be elected and installed as Chief Grand Preceptress. A Daughter must serve one year as Queen Mother of a Tent, before she can be elected and installed as Grand Queen Mother.

SEC. 5.—The Grand Temple and Tabernacle must make a constitutional provision defining the number of votes to be cast in each department, and who shall have the right to vote.

SEC. 6.—A Sir Knight cannot be elected and installed as C. G. M., unless he is a member in good standing in a Temple. A Daughter cannot be elected as C. G. P., unless she is a member in good standing in a Tabernacle.

SEC. 7.—All the officers in the Grand Temple and Tabernacle must be and remain members in good standing during their terms of office, in a Temple or Tabernacle. If they lose their membership in either of these departments, they forfeit their offices.

ARTICLE VIII.

DUTIES OF GRAND OFFICERS.

SECTION 1.—The Chief Grand Mentor shall preside at all Sessions of the Grand Temple and Tabernacle. He shall have authority to call Special Sessions when he decides it is needed, or when requested to call a Session by a two-thirds of the Temples and Tabernacles. He must enforce the laws, decide all questions of law or points of order, and appoint officers *pro-tem.* in case of the absence or disqualification of the officer elected or regularly appointed. He can give permission, by dispensation, to Temples, Tabernacles and Palatiums, to reduce the constitutional fee for receiving members for thirty, sixty or ninety days. He can give dispensations for public turn-outs and entertainments, and for Temples, Tabernacles, Palatiums and Tents to continue work when their charters or warrants are lost. He can grant a charter or warrant upon proof that they are destroyed or lost. He can organize Temples, Tabernacles, Palatiums and Tents in person, or by commissioned Deputies. He can constitute new Temples, Tabernacles, Palatiums and Tents by charter or warrants. He can install the officers, dedicate halls and lay cornerstones, either in person or by deputy. He can visit Temples, Tabernacles, Palatiums and Tents at any time when he deems it necessary. He must appoint all committees not otherwise ordered. He must open and close the Grand Session without a motion. He must issue the Quarterly Pass to all Temples and Tabernacles. He must make an annual report to the Grand Session of the condition of all the Temples, Tabernacles, Palatiums and Tents. He must sign all warrants and other papers that require his signature to make them legal.

Sec. 2.—He must furnish new Temples, Tabernacles, Palatiums and Tents with charters or warrants, and books and blanks. He must report monthly, to the C. G. S., the names and numbers of all new Temples, Tabernacles, Palatiums and Tents, with the names and addresses of the C. M., C. P., P. P. and Q. M., and with the monthly report he must pay to the C. G. S. all moneys that he has received for charters, warrants, books and blanks.

Sec. 3.—He can suspend a Temple, Tabernacle, Palatium and Tent, if he decides it is necessary for the good of the order. He can revoke the suspension at any time, or order them to meet the Grand Session for trial.

Sec. 4.—He can suspend a Chief Mentor, Chief Preceptress, Presiding Prince or a Queen Mother when a grave charge is made against either by two-thirds of their members, and order them to trial either before a committee of peers or before the Grand Session. In the event that a presiding officer is suspended, the C. G. M. must fill the vacancy by appointment; *provided*, there is no Vice to fill it.

Sec. 5.—He can give the Degrees of the Temple, Tabernacle and Palatium to any distinguished person or persons at will, and have them enrolled as members in any Temple, Tabernacle or Palatium within the boundaries of his State and jurisdiction.

This, however, will not constitute them honorary members.

SEC. 6.—When he visits any Temple, Tabernacle or Palatium within his State and jurisdiction, his traveling expenses and *per diem* must be paid by the organization which he visits. He can preside in any Temple, Tabernacle, Palatium and Tent which he honors with a visit.

SEC. 7.—He shall decide all questions or points of the State laws or rules. His decisions are final, until reversed by his successor, or by the Triennial Session.

SEC. 8.—He can appoint Special Grand Deputies to represent him in any Grand Temple and Tabernacle, or for the transaction of any business in his own State and jurisdiction.

SEC. 9.—He can appoint as many Deputy Grand Mentors and Deputy Grand Preceptresses as he may need for organizing.

CHIEF GRAND PRECEPTRESS.

SEC. 10.—It shall be the duty of the C. G. P. to assist the C. G. M. when he is presiding, and preside during his temporary absence from the Chair. She has the authority to organize and set up Tabernacles, Palatiums and Tents. She is authorized to install the officers of Tabernacles and Palatiums. She is authorized to make an annual visit to all Tabernacles in her State and jurisdiction that need instruction, and have her traveling expenses and *per diem* paid by the Tabernacles that she visits. She must correspond with all the Chief Preceptresses in her State and jurisdiction, on the condition and prospects of the Order. The commissions of Deputy Grand Preceptresses must have her signature to make them legal. It is her duty to make a full report to the Grand Session, annually, of her official business, and with the report make such recommendations as she believes to be for the best interests of the Order, and the success of Tabernacles.

VICE-GRAND MENTOR.

SEC. 11.—In the absence of the C. G. M. and the C. G. P., the Vice-Grand Mentor shall preside over the business of the Grand Session. In case of the death, mental inability or removal out of the State and jurisdiction, or lawful disqualification of the C. G. M. during the interim between the Grand Sessions, the V.-G. M. shall attend to all the official business of the C. G. M., until another is duly elected and installed.

VICE-GRAND PRECEPTRESS.

SEC. 12.—It shall be the duty of the Vice-Grand Preceptress to perform the duties of the C. G. P. in the absence of that officer from the Grand Session; and in case of the death or lawful disqualification of the C. G. P. during the time between the Grand Sessions, the V.-G. P. must attend to all the business of the C. G. P., until another is duly elected and installed.

CHIEF GRAND SCRIBE.

SEC. 13.—The Chief Grand Scribe shall have the custody and control of the records of the Grand Temple and Tabernacle, and preserve all official papers; he shall also have authority to provide his office with all necessary books and stationery to enable him to perform his duties; he shall keep a journal of the business of the Grand Temple and Tabernacle, and the proceedings of the Grand Session; he shall keep a register of all Temples, Tabernacles, Palatiums and Tents, with date of charter and warrant, name of the town or city, county and State where they are situated; he shall keep a record of all members of the Grand Temple and Tabernacle; he shall keep in his office a copy of the seal of each subordinate Temple, Tabernacle, Palatium and Tent; he shall receive and give notice to all the subordinate Temples and Tabernacles of all rejected candidates, and of members that have been suspended or expelled; he shall attend to and carry on the correspondence of the Grand Temple and Tabernacle, and give notice to the Temples, Tabernacles, Palatiums and Tents when and where to meet the Grand Session; he shall perform such other duties as are assigned to him by the Grand Temple and Tabernacle; he shall receive all moneys coming to the Grand Temple and Tabernacle, and pay them over to the Chief Grand Treasurer without delay, taking his receipt therefor; draw all warrants on the Grand Treasurer, and attest them; keep his accounts ready for examination at any time; he shall, at the expiration of his term of office, deliver to his successor all books, papers, warrants, charters, rituals, blanks and other property belonging to the Grand Temple and Tabernacle.

CHIEF GRAND RECORDER.

SEC. 14.—It is the duty of the C. G. R. to assist the C. G. S. in taking the proceeding of the Grand Session, and to help him in arranging the proceedings for the printer, and to attend to such other business as may be assigned to her by the Grand Session.

CHIEF GRAND TREASURER.

SEC. 15.—It shall be the duty of the Chief Grand Treasurer to receive all moneys and valuables belonging to the Grand Temple and Tabernacle, and keep a correct account of the same; he shall pay all warrants when duly signed by the Chief Grand Mentor, and countersigned by the Chief Grand Scribe; he shall make an annual report to the Grand Temple and Tabernacle of the business of his office; his books shall be open for the inspection of the Chief Grand Mentor, or any committee that he may appoint, at all times; he shall give to the Chief Grand Scribe a receipt for all moneys he receives; his books shall show the amount of moneys received and paid out; he shall give a statement, in writing, at the Grand Session, exhibiting the amounts of his receipts and the amounts of his disbursements, and for what purpose the money was drawn; at the expiration of his term of office he shall deliver all books, papers and moneys belonging to the Temple and Tabernacle to his successor.

GRAND QUEEN MOTHER.

SEC. 16.—It shall be the duty of the Grand Queen Mother to correspond with all the Queen Mothers in the State and jurisdiction, and receive their reports of the condition of their Tents, with the number of children in each Tent. It is her duty to visit a Tent when requested by the Queen Mother, and give needed instructions. It is also her duty to report annually to the International Grand Queen Mother the number of Tents, with the number of children in the Tents. She shall report to the Grand Session, and make any recommendation that will be for the good of the Tents. She is authorized to organize Tents, and install the Officers of Tents of Maids and Pages of Honor.

Chief Grand Orator.

Sec. 17.—It shall be the duty of the Chief Grand Orator to lead the devotional exercises of the Grand Temple and Tabernacle, and perform the functions of a Chaplain on all public and private occasions. It is his duty to preach the sermon at the Annual Grand Session.

Chief Grand Priestess.

Sec. 18.—It shall be the duty of the Chief Grand Priestess to assist the Chief Grand Orator during the opening and closing of the Grand Session.

Grand Drill-Master.

Sec. 19.—It shall be the duty of the Grand Drill-Master to conduct the drill exercises during the Grand Session, and to act as Marshal in the public turn-outs of the Grand Temple and Tabernacle. He must arrange the hall for the Grand Session, and shall give instructions to the Chief Drill-Masters of Temples, when requested.

GRAND INNER SENTINEL.

SEC. 20.—It is the business of the G. I. St. to have charge of the Inner Door of the Grand Session, and to admit none but members who are properly clothed and have the Pass. She must report to the Vice-Grand Mentor the names of all who desire admittance.

GRAND COLOR BEARER.

SEC. 21.—It shall be the duty of the Grand Color Bearer to guard and protect the banner of the Grand Temple and Tabernacle, and to unfurl and carry it on all public turn-outs of the Grand Temple and Tabernacle.

CHIEF GRAND SENTINEL.

SEC. 22.—The Chief Grand Sentinel shall have charge of the outer entrance of the Grand Session. He shall admit none but members of the Order during the Session. He is to inspect all who seek admission, and see that they are properly clothed and have the proper Pass.

CHIEF GRAND GUARDS.

SEC. 23.—It is the duty of the Chief Grand Guards to assist the Presiding Grand Officer in keeping order during the Grand Session. They are the messengers of the Grand Session, and shall attend to any business entrusted to them, under the orders of the Presiding Grand Officer.

CHIEF GRAND JUDGES.

SEC. 24.—The Board of Chief Grand Judges shall consist of seven members—four Daughters and three Sir Knights—whose duty it is to examine all complaints and charges that come before the Grand Session. They shall investigate the charges and complaints when referred to them by the Grand Session. They have authority to call witnesses before them for examination. The C. G. S. must place in the hands of this Board all the papers and documents relating to any case coming before them. This Board shall investigate all appeals and grievances that come before the Grand Session, and report to the Grand Session their findings in all charges, complaints, appeals and grievances. The first named on the Board is the Chairman. The Board organizes by electing a Secretary.

CHIEF GRAND TRIBUNES.

SEC. 25.—It is the business of the Chief Grand Tribunes to assist the Chief Grand Guards in keeping order during the Grand Session, and to attend to the duties of messengers, under the direction of the Presiding Grand Officer.

ARTICLE IX.

BOARD OF GRAND CURATORS.

SECTION 1.—The Board of Grand Curators shall consist of the Chief Grand Mentor, Chief Grand Preceptress, Chief Grand Scribe, Chief Grand Recorder and Chief Grand Treasurer. They shall be the incorporators of the Grand Temple and Tabernacle. The incorporation shall be held in their name. All donations, devises or gifts for the Grand Temple and Tabernacle, or for the benefit of any subordinate Temples, Tabernacles, Palatiums or Tents shall be made to them. They shall invest

in such stocks, loans or securities, the funds of the
Grand Temple and Tabernacle, as the Grand Session may direct. They shall call in, sell and realize
on such loans, stocks and investments, under the
orders of the Grand Session; collect interest, dividends, rents and all money arising or accruing
from any investments belonging to the Grand
Temple and Tabernacle; pay all money that they
collect to the C. G. S., or, if for the benefit of a
subordinate Temple, Tabernacle, Palatium or Tent,
they shall pay to the C. S., C. R., P. P. or Q. M.
The C. G. M. shall be Chairman of the Board.
The Grand Temple and Tabernacle shall furnish the
Board with such books and stationery as they may
need. They shall make an annual report to the
Grand Session of all their business, and, at the expiration of their term of office, shall deliver to their
successors all books, securities, deposits, stocks,
papers, deeds and moneys belonging to the
Grand Temple and Tabernacle, or to Temples, Tabernacles, Palatiums and Tents.

ARTICLE X.

TRUSTEES.

SECTION 1.—The Vice-Grand Mentor, Grand
Queen Mother, Chief Grand Orator, Chief Grand
Priestess and Grand Drill-Master shall be the Trus-
tees of the Grand Temple and Tabernacle.

SEC. 2.—The Trustees shall audit the accounts
of the Board of Grand Curators, also the accounts
of the Chief Grand Scribe and Chief Grand Treasurer, at each Grand Session, and give a full report
to the Grand Session.

Sec. 3.—All officers of the Grand Temple and Tabernacle, who are required to give bond for the faithful discharge of their duties, shall deliver the same to the Trustees and their successors. All bonds must be drawn up in legal form, and when approved by the Trustees of the Grand Temple and Tabernacle, they shall be of binding force during the Temple and Tabernacle year. All bonds must be renewed immediately after the closing of the Grand Session.

ARTICLE XI.

BONDS.

Section 1.—The Chief Grand Scribe and Chief Grand Treasurer shall, before entering upon the duties of their offices, give a bond, with ample security, to the Board of Trustees, for the faithful application of all moneys belonging to the Grand Temple and Tabernacle, in accordance with the laws or orders of the Grand Temple and Tabernacle.

Sec. 2.—The amount of the bond shall be fixed by the Grand Session, with such securities as may be approved by the Board of Trustees. The bond shall be secured by two or more persons, who own unincumbered real estate of double the value of the amount of the bond given.

Sec. 3.—The Grand Temple and Tabernacle shall have power to increase or diminish the bond at every Grand Session.

(4—Dickson's New Manual.)

ARTICLE XII.

WIDOWS AND ORPHANS.

SECTION 1.—A Grand Temple and Tabernacle shall create and sustain a fund for the benefit of Sir Knights' widows and orphans, and the orphans of Daughters of the Tabernacle.

SEC. 2.—The Grand Session shall, within three years after the organization of the Grand Temple and Tabernacle, form and set to work this department, and place it under the control and management of the Board of Grand Curators.

SEC. 3.—The assessment, against the Knights and Daughters shall be liberal and sufficient to meet the requirements of the good name of the Order. The assessments shall be collected from each Temple and Tabernacle quarterly. Temples and Tabernacles are hereby made responsible for the non-payment of assessments of their members.

SEC. 4.—Payment to widows and orphans shall be made quarterly, in accordance with the regulations made by the Grand Session. These regulations must be carefully drawn for the government of this fund so as to insure the regular payment of the quarterly allowances for the widows and orphans, and for the collection of the assessments.

SEC. 5.—When a widow or orphan removes from the jurisdiction of the Grand Temple and Tabernacle, the Board of Grand Curators can, for this reason, refuse to pay the allowance, but if they have good reasons for paying it, and consider it for the best interests of the Order, they may continue the payment.

SEC. 6.—When a widow marries, her allowance ceases. When an orphan arrives at the age of fifteen years, the allowance is discontinued.

SEC. 7.—The above is submitted to the Grand Temples and Tabernacles only as a form to draw a widows' and orphans' plan upon; *provided*, they prefer this to the Taborian Endowment.

SEC. 8.—All Grand Temples and Tabernacles must have some kind of a benefit—either a Widows' and Orphans' Fund, or a Taborian Endowment.

ARTICLE XIII.

GRAND TEMPLES AND TABERNACLES.

SECTION 1.—The Grand Temples and Tabernacles are hereby invested with full authority to make their own Constitutions, By-Laws and Rules for their own Government, but they are not to conflict with the International Constitution or General Laws.

SEC. 2.—Full power is given to the Grand Temples and Tabernacles to conduct their business. The International Grand Temple and Tabernacle cannot interfere with their business in any form, so long as they do not trespass upon or conflict with the International Constitution or General Laws.

ARTICLE XIV.

MEMBERSHIP OF THE GRAND TEMPLES AND TABERNACLES.

The membership of Grand Temples and Tabernacles shall be as follows:

1.—Chief Mentors and Past Chief Mentors.

2.—Chief Preceptresses and Past Chief Preceptresses.

3.—Presiding Princes and Past Presiding Princes.

4.—Vice-Princesses and Past Vice-Princesses.

5.—Queen Mothers and Past Queen Mothers.

6.—Grand Deputies and Past Grand Deputies.

ARTICLE XV.

MEMBERSHIP VOTE.

SECTION 1.—The Grand Temple and Tabernacle Constitution must arrange and state the number of votes each Temple, Tabernacle, Palatium and Tent shall have, and what shall be a Past Officer's vote.

SEC. 2.—A majority of all votes cast shall be necessary to elect a Grand Officer.

ARTICLE XVI.

POWER, STRENGTH AND PERPETUITY.

Just as long as the International Order of Twelve holds together, it will prosper and be a blessing to its members. It is so jointed and arranged that no part can be taken out without weakening the whole fabric. It is just like a wheel. The International Grand Temple and Tabernacle is the hub, the Grand Temples and Tabernacles are the spokes, and the Constitution and General Laws are the tires that bind the Order into one compact body, and make the membership a unit. The International Order of Twelve, of Knights and Daughters of Tabor, is not a monarchy, but it is a Republic, and as it is governed by its members, it has a Central and State Government. The Temples, Tabernacles, Palatiums and Tents form the State Governments, and the Grand Temples and Tabernacles form the Central Government.

ARTICLE XVII.

AMENDMENTS.

This part of the General Laws can be amended or altered in the following manner: First, the amendment or alteration must be read in the Triennial Session. If three-fourths of the members present vote for it, it is recommended; it is then published in the Triennial Proceedings. Second, it is read in each Grand Session of the Grand Temples and Tabernacles, and if all of the members of the Grand Session vote for it, it is then published in the Proceedings, and the Temples, Tabernacles and Palatiums are ordered to vote on the amendments or alterations. If three-fourths of the members of the Temples, Tabernacles and Palatiums vote for it, and it is so reported at the Grand Sessions, then if all of the Grand Temples and Tabernacles adopt said amendments or alterations, and it is so reported to the International Grand Session, and, if adopted by an unanimous vote of the same, the amendments or the alterations become a law.

PENALTY.

There is no effective law without a penalty. In a trial of members and conviction, when the law does not name the penalty, it shall be the duty of the C. M., if it is a Temple, or the C. P., if it is a Tabernacle, to name the penalty and declare the sentence.

For disobeying the laws of the Grand Temple and Tabernacle, when the law does not name the penalty, the C. G. M. shall name the penalty and declare the sentence.

For disobeying or neglecting to obey the General Laws, when there is no penalty named in the law, the International Chief Grand Mentor shall name the penalty and declare the sentence.

Temples, Tabernacles, Palatiums and Tents, disobeying and failing to obey an edict or the laws, shall be notified by the C. G. M. that if they do. not comply with the edict or law within thirty days after notice is given by him, that he will arrest their charters and suspend their members, and fix the duration of their suspension.

The I. C. G. M. is authorized to name the penalty in case Temples, Tabernacles, Palatiums and Tents, working under the International Grand Temple and Tabernacle, fail to obey an edict or the laws.

A KNIGHT'S FANCY BADGE.

INSTALLATION CEREMONY

OF THE

GRAND TEMPLE AND TABERNACLE OFFICERS.

INSTALLING CEREMONY

OF

GRAND OFFICERS.

——: o :——

The Grand Officers may be installed by any C. G. O., C. G. M., Past C. G. M., I. C. G. M. or Past I. C. G. M.

The Installing Officer shall be addressed as Sir Grand. The Presentor or Introducer is addressed as Grand Marshal.

When ready to install, the Grand Marshal shall form all the officers elected and appointed around the altar. The Jewels are laid on the altar. The officers to be installed are so placed that the Knight and Daughter to be installed together will be side by side.

When the Grand Marshal has everything in readiness, he shall salute the Installing Officer and say:—Sir Grand, I have the honor to present to you these officers. They have been duly elected and appointed to serve in the several offices of the Grand Temple and Tabernacle for the ensuing term. They have signified their willingness to enter upon their official duties.

Sir Grand:—Sir Knights and Daughters, you are about to be invested and inducted into the several offices of the Grand Temple and Tabernacle. The responsible positions to which you have been elected and appointed by the members, shows the confidence they repose in your integrity and ability to successfully conduct the business of the Knights and Daughters of Tabor. It becomes my duty to administer to you an oath which all former Grand Officers have taken previous to being installed. Are you willing?

Answer:—We are ready.

Sir Grand:—You will now take the Manual in your right hands, place it upon your breasts, and repeat your names, and say after me:

OATH.

I —— —— ——, do sacredly promise that I will sustain the laws of the International Grand Temple and Tabernacle, of the Knights and Daughters of Tabor, and the Constitution, By-Laws and Rules of the Grand Temple and Tabernacle, I will attend to the duties of my office faithfully, and with all the ability I possess. Amen!

Sir Grand—(Gives three raps, all stand): Sir Knights and Daughters, we are about to commence the business of the International Order of Twelve, for another Taborian year. It is but meet and right that we should implore the blessings of God upon our work. Let us bow our heads, and unite in prayer with the Chief Grand Orator. Sir Knights, uncover.

PRAYER.

Almighty God, who, through Thine Only Begotten Son, Jesus Christ, hast overcome death, and opened unto us the gate of everlasting life, we humbly beseech Thee that, as by Thy special grace helping us, Thou dost put into our minds good desires, so by Thy continual help we may bring the same to good effect. In particular, we implore Thy grace and protection for the ensuing year. Keep us temperate in our meats and drinks, and diligent in our several callings. Grant us patience under any afflictions Thou mayest see fit to lay upon us, and let our minds always be contented with our present condition. Give us grace to be just and upright in all our dealings, quiet and peaceable, full of compassion, and ready to do good to all men, according to our abilities and opportunities. Direct us in all our ways, and prosper the works of our hands in the business of our several stations. Defend us from all dangers and adversities, and be graciously pleased to take us, and all things belonging to us, under Thy fatherly care and protection. These things, and whatever else Thou shalt see necessary and convenient to us, we humbly beg, through the merits and mediation of Thy Son, Jesus Christ, our Lord and Savior. Amen!

Response.—*In Solo Deo Salus!*

Sir Grand:—Sir Knights, cover (he gives one rap, and all are seated.—Music or Singing.)

Grand Marshal then places the C. G. M. and C. G. P. elect in front of the altar, and says:—Sir Grand, I have the honor to present to you Sir ——

—— ——, who has been elected C. G. M., and Daughter —— —— ——, who has been elected C. G. P. of the Grand Temple and Tabernacle for —— and jurisdiction. They are now ready to be installed.

INSTRUCTIONS TO THE CHIEF GRAND MENTOR.

Sir Grand:—Right Faithful Sir, the evident love you have for our beloved Order, and your intimate acquaintance with the duties of every department to work the laws, rules and regulations of the Grand Temple and Tabernacle, makes it unnecessary that I should repeat them at this time. The high honor of this office has its weighty responsibilities. Your authority will be respected by every true Knight and Daughter; your commands and orders will meet with ready obedience. Each Taborian Knight and Daughter will cheerfully sustain you in your care over the interests of your large jurisdiction. You will feel the necessity in your daily life and actions to exemplify the excellent teachings of our beloved Order—an example that all Sir Knights will gladly follow. Be faithful to the end.

INSTRUCTIONS TO THE CHIEF GRAND PRECEPTRESS.

Sir Grand:—Right Faithful Daughter, the Sir Knights and Daughter Priestesses of the Grand Temple and Tabernacle have expressed their confidence in your ability to attend to the duties of C. G. P., and your fidelity to the Order, by electing you to the exalted position of Chief Grand Preceptress. You will find your duties and instructions in the Constitution. Be faithful to the end.

Sir Grand:—Sir Marshal, please invest the C. G. M. and C. G. P. with their Jewels of office, and seat them.

The Sir Grand gives three raps and all stand, except the C. G. M. and C. G. P.

Sir Grand:—Sir Knights, Handle Swords! Draw Swords!! Present Swords!!! Sir Knights and Daughter Priestesses, let us salute our C. G. M. and C. G. P.

The Knights lower and raise their swords, and the Daughters raise and lower their right arms, as they repeat the words after the Grand: *We hail our Chief Grand Mentor!!!* (This is repeated three times.) *We hail our Chief Grand Preceptress!!* (This is repeated three times.) The Knights, at the command of the Sir Grand, return swords. All clap three times three. The Sir Grand gives one rap, and all are seated.

Grand Marshal then places the V.-G. M. and V.-G. P. elect in front of the altar, and says:—Sir Grand, I have the honor to present to you Sir —— —— ——, who has been elected Vice-Grand Mentor, and Daughter —— —— ——, who has been elected Vice-Grand Preceptress. They are ready to be installed.

INSTRUCTIONS TO THE VICE-GRAND MENTOR.

Sir Grand:—Right Faithful Sir, the important station to which the suffrage of your brother Knights and Daughters has called you, demonstrates the confidence that they have in your integrity and ability, and that you will faithfully discharge the duties of the office. You are the nearest successor of the Chief Grand Mentor. Should any unforeseen casualty happen to him, so as to prevent him from fulfilling the duties committed to his care, which the Lord forbid, you are to assume the responsibilities and functions of that office. In his presence, you are to assist him with counsel and advice. I now invest you with the Jewel of your office. Be faithful to duty.

INSTRUCTIONS TO THE VICE-GRAND PRECEPTRESS.

Sir Grand:—Right Faithful Daughter, you have been honored by the suffrage of the Knights and Daughter Priestesses of the Grand Temple and Tabernacle with the honorable office of Vice-Grand Preceptress. You will find your duties and instruction in the Constitution. Be faithful. I now invest you with the . Jewel of your office. Sir Marshal, please seat the V.-G. M. and V.-G. P.

The Grand Marshal then places the C. G. S. and C. G. R. in front of the altar, and says:—Sir Grand, I take pleasure in introducing to you Sir —— —— ——, who has been elected Chief Grand Scribe, and Daughter —— —— ——, who has been elected Chief Grand Recorder. They are now ready to be installed.

INSTRUCTIONS TO THE CHIEF GRAND SCRIBE.

Sir Grand:—Right Faithful Sir, the useful and honorable station that the voice of your brother Knights and Daughters has called you to fill, shows the confidence they repose in your ability to discharge the duties of this most important office. The position is one that requires prompt action and punctuality, and a strict fidelity to matters and

business appertaining to your several duties. I
have no doubt but that you will use due diligence
and correctness in the discharge of the important
duties committed to your care, so that benefit may
accrue to the Grand Temple and Tabernacle, and
honor be awarded to you by the Sir Knights and
Daughters. I now invest you with the Jewel of
your office. Be faithful to your duty.

INSTRUCTIONS TO THE CHIEF GRAND RECORDER.

Sir Grand:—Right Faithful Daughter, you have
been elected to the honorable office of Chief Grand
Recorder by the members of the Grand Temple
and Tabernacle. You will find your duties and instructions in the Constitution. I now invest you
with the Jewel of your office. Be faithful to your
duty. Sir Marshal, you will please seat the C. G.
S. and C. G. R.

Grand Marshal:—Sir Grand, I now present to
you Sir —— —— ——, who has been elected Chief
Grand Treasurer.

INSTRUCTIONS TO THE CHIEF GRAND TREASURER.

Sir Grand:—Right Faithful Sir, the members of
the Grand Temple and Tabernacle, in their choice
of you to the very responsible station of Grand
Treasurer, have proved the confidence they have in
your integrity and honor. The qualities that should
be found in the officer that fills this position are
honesty, accuracy and faithfulness. Be accurate
in keeping a fair account of all receipts and disbursements, and be careful in preserving all the property and moneys that may come into your hands,
with fidelity; render a just account of all your

business with the Order, when called on by the proper authority. I now invest you with the Jewel of your office. Be faithful and prompt in the discharge of the trust we now confide into your hands. Sir Marshal, please seat the C. G. T.

Grand Marshal:—Sir Grand, I have the honor of introducing to you Daughter —— —— ——, who has been elected Grand Queen Mother.

INSTRUCTIONS TO THE GRAND QUEEN MOTHER.

Sir Grand:—Right Faithful Daughter, the members of the Grand Temple and Tabernacle have entrusted to your care the important office of Grand Queen Mother. You will find your duties and instructions in the Constitution. I now invest you with the Jewel of your office. Take care of the children of Mount Tabor. Sir Marshal, you will please seat the Grand Queen Mother.

Grand Marshall:—Sir Grand, I have the pleasure of presenting to you Sir Rev. —— —— ——, who has been elected C. G. O.

INSTRUCTIONS TO THE CHIEF GRAND ORATOR.

Sir Grand: — Right Faithful Sir; Reverend Brother Knight, your high calling as a Christian minister has prepared you for the duties to which you have been elected. Your official duty is of the highest importance to the Sir Knights and Daughters, and so interesting that it requires punctual attendance at all meetings of the Grand Temple and Tabernacle. May you be thoroughly furnished and abundantly provided for the good work. May you be established and perfected in your holy order by Him who presides and rules over the destinies of mankind, and sits as Supreme Grand Chief of the Universe. I now invest you with the Jewel of your office. Be thou faithful until your work is finished on earth, and the Most Faithful Grand Chief of the Heavenly Temple will give you a crown of life. Sir Marshal, please seat the Chief Grand Orator.

Grand Marshal:—Sir Grand, I have the honor of presenting to you Daughter ——— ——— ———, who has been elected Chief Grand Priestess.

Instructions to the Chief Grand Priestess.

Sir Grand:—Right Faithful Daughter, the honorable office to which the Sir Knights and Daughter Priestesses of the Grand Temple and Tabernacle have elected you, is one of highest dignity. You will find your duties and instructions in the Constitution. I now invest you with the Jewel of your office. Be faithful to every duty. Sir Marshal, please seat the Chief Grand Priestess.

Grand Marshal:—Sir Grand, I now present to you Sir ——— ——— ———, who has been elected G. D.-M.

Instructions to the Grand Drill-Master.

Sir Grand:—Right Faithful Sir, having been elected to the important station of Grand Drill-Master, you will find pleasure in the discharge of your several duties. I admonish you to be zealous and active in your teachings and instructions to the Sir Knights, and take command of the Sir Knights when on duty. I would remind you of the necessity of diligence in the duties that devolve upon you. I now invest you with the Jewel of your office. Be thou a faithful soldier, and promptly discharge

every command given to you. You will find your
duties and instructions in the Constitution. Sir
Marshal, please seat the Grand Drill-Master.

Grand Marshal:—Sir Grand, I take pleasure in
presenting to you Daughter —— —— ——, who
has been elected G. I. St.

INSTRUCTIONS TO THE GRAND INNER SENTINEL.

Sir Grand:—Right Faithful Daughter, you have
the high honor of being elected by the members of
the Grand Temple and Tabernacle to the important
station of Grand Inner Sentinel. You will find
you duties and instructions in the Constitution. I
now invenst you with the Jewel of your office and
Staff of Defense. Guard the inner door faithfully.
Sir Marshal, please seat the G. I. St.

Grand Marshal:—Sir Grand, I present to you Sir
—— —— ——, who has been appointed G. C. B.

INSTRUCTIONS TO THE GRAND COLOR BEARER.

Sir Grand:—Faithful Sir, your appointment to
the very important position of Grand Color Bearer
shows the confidence that is placed in your courage
and ability. You will find your duties in the Constitution. I now invest you with the Jewel of your
office, and give into your care the Standard of the
Grand Temple and Tabernacle. Sir Marshal, please
seat the Grand Color Bearer.

Grand Marshal:—Sir Grand, I now present to
you Sir —— —— ——, who has been appointed
C. G. St.

INSTRUCTIONS TO THE CHIEF GRAND SENTINEL.

Sir Grand:—Right Faithful Sir, the responsibility of the station to which you have been appointed

—that of Chief Grand Sentinel—cannot be overestimated. Holding the outpost, and guarding the
entrance of our sacred Grand Temple and Tabernacle, I admonish you to be vigilant and sleepless.
Look well to every avenue of approach. May you
have courage to keep every enemy at bay. Be kind
and courteous to all Sir Knights and Daughters
who hail the outer portals. I now invest you with
the Jewel of your office. Be thou faithful as a
watchman upon the outer lines, and give timely
warning of any approaching danger. Sir Marshal, please seat the C. G. St.

Grand Marshal:—Sir Grand, I now present to
you Sir Knights (gives all their names), who have
been appointed C. G. G.s

Instructions to the Chief Grand Guards.

Sir Grand:—Right Faithful Sirs, you having been
appointed to the station of Chief Grand Guards, I
congratulate you upon the trust that is reposed in
your worthiness to attend to the important duties
pertaining to your office. You will, therefore, be
punctual in the observance of the several official
duties of the station, by which you will merit the
approval of your brother members, and the honorable commendation of all Sir Knights and Daughters. I now invest you with the Jewels of your
office. Be faithful to every duty. Sir Marshal,
please seat the Chief Grand Guards.

Grand Marshal:—Sir Grand, I have the honor of
presenting to you Daughters (gives all their
names), who have been appointed C. G. Te.s

Instructions to the Chief Grand Tribunes.

Sir Grand:—Right Faithful Daughters, the position that you have been appointed to requires the closest attention to your duties. The Constitution will give you full information. I now congratulate you, and invest you with the Jewels of your office. Be faithful to your trust. Sir Marshal, please seat the Chief Grand Tribunes.

Grand Marshal:—Sir Grand, I now present to you Sir Knights and Daughters (gives all their names), who have been appointed C. G. J.s

Instructions to the Chief Grand Judges.

Sir Grand:—Sir Knights and Daughters, the office that you have the honor of being appointed to is one of great importance, and requires a close study of the laws that govern the Grand Temple and Tabernacle. You will find your duties in the Constitution. I now invest you with the Jewels of your office. Be faithful to your official duties. Sir Marshal, please seat the Chief Grand Judges.

Music or Singing.

Sir Grand gives three raps, and all stand, except the officers that have just been installed.

Grand Marshal says:—Sir Knights, Daughter Priestesses, Princes and Princesses, Maids and Pages of Honor, *Hear! Listen!!* and *Receive the Proclamation!!!*

Proclamation.

Sir Grand says:—By virtue of the authority in me vested as Installing Grand Officer, I now and here proclaim that the Grand Officers of the Grand

Temple and Tabernacle, for the State of ——— and its jurisdiction, have been regularly installed into their various official positions for the ensuing Grand Temple and Tabernacle year.

All the members that are standing, shall repeat after the Sir Grand: *We declare! We declare!! We declare!!!* and give claps three times four. The Sir Grand then gives one rap, and all are seated.

Music or singing.

CHARGE TO GRAND OFFICERS.

Sir Grand:—Sir Knights and Daughters, you have been duly elected and installed, with the necessary ceremonies, into the several stations of the Grand Temple and Tabernacle. The duties of your various positions you will find fully laid down in the Constitution of the Order. While your work seems separate and divided, it is really not so. In the erection of our Grand Temple and Tabernacle, a variety of material is used. Workmen of separate callings have their part to perform to make the building complete. Just so we are building a Grand Temple and Tabernacle for the good and interests of humanity. The erection requires sundry talents and various workmen, each in their several departments. Collectively and individually you are to contribute your part in the grand undertaking, so that, by a union of action and a determination to do your whole duty, our Order will continue to move forward to power and usefulness. The past history of the Grand Temple and Tabernacle is a gallant one. Its record is clear and bright. That you will earn-

estly strive to keep it so, I have no doubt. I ask
you to put your trust in the Lord of Hosts. He is
a tower of strength. By the faithful discharge of
your several duties, you will receive the hearty
approval of the Sir Knights and Daughters. May
God, the giver of every good and perfect gift,
guide and direct you in your labor of love. Take
the shield of faith and the sword of the spirit, and
the breast-plate of righteousness, which is the command of God. May peace and harmony, and faith
in the Lord Jesus Christ, be with you all forever.
Amen!

Response:—*In Solo Deo Salus!*

Music or singing. If there is any one who wishes
to deliver an oration, now is time for speaking.

C. G. M. gives three raps, and all stand; he then
says:—By virtue of the authority in me vested, I
now declare the Grand Session of the Grand Temple and Tabernacle from work to rest. "Home,
Sweet Home!"

No. 1.

No. 4.

No. 2.

No. 5.

No. 3.

Palatium Pin.

KNIGHTS OF TABOR PINS AND EMBLEMS.

TEMPLE HOUSE.

OFFICERS

OF

SUBORDINATE TEMPLES

OF

KNIGHTS OF TABOR.

——:o:——

SECTION 1.—The Constitution of the Grand Temple and Tabernacle must be strictly complied with by all subordinate Temples.

SEC. 2.—The officers of the Temple shall be as follows:

1. Chief Mentor,....................C. M.
2. Vice-Mentor, ...V.-M.
3. Chief Scribe,....................C. S.
4. Assistant Scribe,.................A. S.
5. Chief Treasurer,.................C. T.
6. Chief Orator,....................C. O.
7. Chief Drill-Master,..............C. D.-M.
8. Chief Color Bearer,..............C. C. B.
9. Chief Guard,....................C. G.
10. Chief Guard,....................C. G.
11. Chief Guard,....................C. G.
12. Chief Sentinel, ...C. St.

121

KNIGHTS of TABOR·

INTERNATIONAL
ORDER OF
TWELVE

777
P.C.M.
333

TEMPLE OFFICERS' JEWELS—SILVER.

TABORIAN ALTAR.

123

INSTALLATION- CEREMONY

OF

TEMPLE OFFICERS.

————:o:————

The installation of the officers of a Temple can be performed either in public or private. Any C. M. or P. C. M., C. G. M. or P. C. G. M. shall have authority to install the officers.

PUBLIC INSTALLATION.

The Knights assemble in their hall. The Temple is opened in the Fourth Degree. The necessary preparations are made, and instructions given. After which the C. D.-M. forms the procession in marching order, the Knights being in full dress and regalia. If a Grand Officer or a Past Grand Officer is present, proper respect must be paid to him or them.

THE MARCH

Shall be in the usual form, to the place where the ceremony is to be performed.

The procession is marched three times around the hall, the ranks are opened, and the officers are escorted through to the platform.

124

The temple-house and altar are placed in front of the Chief Mentor, in the center of the platform, the officers to the right and left of the C. M.

The Sir Knights, if there is room for them, are in the immediate rear of the officers. If there is not sufficient room on the platform, they are placed in the immediate front of the stage.

LADIES' TABERNACLE.

If the Daughters join in the procession in the hall, they march in the rear of the Sir Knights. The Tribunes' place is in the rear of the Daughters.

The officers of the Tabernacle are seated on the platform to the right and left of the Temple Officers. If there is room, the other Daughters are seated immediately in the rear; if not, they are seated in the rear of the Sir Knights in front of the stage. All are seated.

THE CEREMONY.

Music; or, if there is no band, the following hymn is sung:

OUR KING.

I.

The Lord Jehovah reigns;
  His throne is built on high;
The garments he assumes
  Are light and majesty.
His glories shine with beams so bright,
No mortal eye can bear the sight.

II.

The thunders of His hand
  Keep the wide world in awe;
His wrath and justice stand
  To guard His holy law;
And where His love resolves to bless,
His truth confirms and seals the grace.

The Chief Mentor calls up the Knights and Daughters, and the Sir Chief announces the business that is to be transacted, and states that the duties that devolve upon the officers about to be installed are so important, that it is of the greatest concern that the guidance and blessing of our King, the Mighty Jehovah, remain with them. Our Chief Orator will now address the Almighty Father, our Sovereign Commander, in prayer.

PRAYER.

O Lord, Thy mercy, our sure hope,
The highest orb of heaven transcends;
Thy sacred truth's unmeasured scope
Beyond the spreading sky extends.

Thy justice, like the hills, remains;
Unfathom'd depths Thy judgments are;
Thy providence the world sustains;
The whole creation is Thy care.

Direct us, O Lord, in all our doings, with Thy most gracious favor, and further us with Thy continual help, that in all our works begun, continued, and ended in Thee, we may glorify Thy Holy Name, and finally by Thy mercy obtain everlasting life, through Jesus Christ, our Lord, who hath taught us to pray unto Thee, O Almighty Father, in His prevailing name and words. Amen! Amen!!

All are seated. Music; or the following hymn is sung.

THE THREE MOUNTAINS.

I.

When on Sinai's top I see
God descend in majesty,
To proclaim His holy law,
All my spirits sink with awe,

When in ecstacy sublime
Tabor's glorious mount I climb,
In the too transporting light,
Darkness rushes o'er my sight.

II.

When on Calvary I rest,
God in flesh made manifest
Shines in my Redeemer's face,
Full of beauty, truth and grace;
Here I would forever stay,
Weep and gaze my soul away.
Thou art heaven on earth to me,
Lovely, mournful Calvary.

The Chief Drill-Master, under the instructions of the Sir Chief, forms all the Sir Knights that are to be installed in line in front of the stage, and says:—Faithful Sir, I have the honor to present to you the officers elect of ——— Temple, No. —. They are now ready to be installed.

The Sir Chief will draw his sword, and order the officer elect to draw and lay the sword across their breast, with the point resting on the side of the left shoulder, the left hand on the right breast, and repeat the following

Oath of Office.

I, —— ——, do most solemnly and sincerely promise, upon the word of a Taborian Knight, that I will, to the best of my ability, faithfully discharge and fulfill the duties of the office to which I have been elected. I will support and maintain the Constitution, By-Laws, Rules and Regulations of this Temple, and the Constitution and By-Laws, and Regulations and Edicts of the Grand Temple and Tabernacle, and the Constitution and General Laws of the International Grand Temple and Tabernacle.

INSTRUCTIONS.

The Sir Chief then says:—Sir Knights, you having been elected to the important and responsible duties of the several offices in this Temple, we with pleasure enter upon the duty of installing you, believing that you will attend to the interests of the Temple, and conduct the business of your stations with fidelity. You will study to improve the usefulness of our Order, realizing the importance of the trust that is committed to your care by your confiding brethren. A firm reliance on the teachings, as you find them laid down in our laws, and the practice of those virtues that are inculcated in our rites, and an implicit confidence in the Lord of Lords, will so direct you in the relation in which you are about to be inducted, that you will reflect honor upon your Temple and credit to yourselves.

THE CHARTER.

The charter is presented, and read by the C. O., and its powers explained by the Sir Chief. The Sir Knights are seated, and the C. D.-M. introduces the C M: elect to be installed.

The C. D.-M. says:—Faithful Sir, I take pleasure in presenting to you Sir Knight —— —— ——, who has been elected to the office of Chief Mentor of —— Temple, No. —. He is prepared for installation. (His sword, cap and jewel are laid on the altar.)

INSTRUCTIONS TO THE CHIEF MENTOR.

The Sir Chief says:—Sir Knight —— —— ——, before you are inducted into this important office, you will please answer the following questions relative to the office. If you object to any question, or cannot comply with the request, frankly state your objection, and it will relieve you from the responsibilities of the office, and another must be found to fill the station:

THE TEST.

Ques.—Do you solemnly promise, upon your obligation as a Knight of Tabor, that you will not open the Temple for business unless the charter and a constitutional quorum, not less than seven members, is present?

Ans.—I do.

Ques.—Will you execute the Laws, Rules and Regulations of the Temple with fidelity?

Ans.—I will.

Ques.—Will you support and obey the Constitution, By-Laws, Rules and Regulations, and Edicts of the Grand Temple and Tabernacle, under whose authority you hold your office?

Ans.—I will.

Ques.—Will you endeavor to correct the irregularities, purify the morals, inculcate charity, teach benevolence and true friendship, and promote happiness and harmony in your Temple?

Ans.—I will.

Ques.—Will you preserve the Ritualistic work unalterable,—the solemn ceremonies and instructions,—and continue them, as Chief Mentors have done before you?

Ans.—I will.

Ques.—Will you promise that you will not admit into you Temple a man who has not been knighted

(5—Dickson's New Manual.)

in a regular Temple, nor one who has been expelled or suspended?

Ans.—I will.

Ques.—Do you acknowledge that it is impossible to have intercourse with a Temple that does not work under a charter from the Grand Temple and Tabernacle of the International Order of Twelve?

Ans.—I do.

Ques.—Do you believe that every Sir Knight has a right to his religious opinion, and that you will promise not to permit any denominational discussions in the Temple?

Ans.—I do.

Ques.—Will you support the Constitution, Rules, Regulations and Ritualistic work of the Ladies' Tabernacle?

Ans.—I will.

Ques.—Will you be careful upon whom you confer the degrees, so that our Order may be composed of good and true men only?

Ans.—I will.

Ques.—Will you bind your successor in office to observe the same test that you have taken?

Ans.—I will. So help me God!

The Sir Chief then proceeds as follows:—You will now permit me to cover your head with this helmet, and present to you this sword. Its hilt in your hand reminds you that it is only to be drawn in defense of liberty, equality and innocence. The Jewel of your office I now invest you with. It is composed of three perfect numbers. It is an appropriate emblem of our Order. It will continually remind you of the great principles upon which our

Order is perpetuated. I commit to your care the charter of this Temple. You will carefully guard it as a sacred power and authority that makes your Temple legal. You will also transmit it to your successor in office. I present to you the Constitution, the great instructor of the Knights. Open this book in faith, and follow its teachings without faltering or wavering, and you will exert an influence that will be an honor to yourself and a blessing to the Knighthood. The Constitution of the International Grand Temple and Tabernacle is hereby presented to you, with the Constitution, Rules and Regulations of the Grand Temple and Tabernacle. I admonish you to consult them diligently, and cause them to be read in your Temple frequently, so that all Sir Knights may be informed of their duty. I now seat you in the official chair. May the Lord, our King, protect and keep you in the strict performance of your official duty.

THE SALUTE AND WELCOME.

The Sir Chief then says:—Sir Knights, I present to you your Chief.

(The Knights rise, and present swords; salute, and return swords.)

Let us welcome our Chief.

(The Knights and Daughters give the honors, and repeat the words " *We welcome*," three times, and give the clap seven times, with the words "*Be faithful.*")

The C. D.-M. presents the other officers in regular order, by saying:—Faithful Sir, I present Sir Knight —— —— ——, who has been elected to the office of Vice-Mentor, and is now ready to be installed.

INSTRUCTIONS TO THE VICE-MENTOR.

Sir Chief:—Sir Knight —— —— ——, you have been elected to the office of Vice-Mentor of —— Temple, No. —, and now invest you with the Jewel of your office. Your duty is to fulfill the duties of the Chief Mentor, when that officer is absent; and in his presence, you are to counsel and aid him in the government of the Temple. You will now be seated, and may you faithfully perform your duty.

INSTRUCTIONS TO THE CHIEF SCRIBE.

Sir Chief:—Sir Knight —— —— ——, you have been honored by the suffrage of your brethren to the very responsible office of Chief Scribe. I take pleasure in presenting you with the Jewel of your office. It is your duty to keep the books of the Temple, as also the records and the roll of members. You shall keep a regular account with each member, and collect all dues, fines and other moneys belonging to the Temple, and pay them into the treasury. You shall record the doings of each meeting plainly and neatly, and report to the Temple, when called on, the condition of the treasury. You shall draw all orders for money on the treasury, and see that they are signed by the C. M. and countersigned by yourself. It will be your duty to make an annual report to the Grand Temple and Tabernacle, with a list of all the members. You are also required to make a monthly report to the Grand Chief of the condition of your Temple. You will now be seated. Be thou faithful to duty.

INSTRUCTIONS TO THE ASSISTANT SCRIBE.

Sir Chief:—Sir Knight —— —— ——, you have been elected Assistant Scribe, and I now invest you with the Jewel of your office. It is your duty to assist the Chief Scribe in the several duties of his office, and in the absence of that officer you are to perform his duties. You will be seated. May you honorably fulfill the duties of your station.

INSTRUCTIONS TO THE CHIEF TREASURER.

Sir Chief:—Sir Knight —— —— ——, by the will of your brethren, you have been called to the station of Treasurer of this Temple, and I now invest you with the Jewel of your office. It is your duty to receive all the moneys and valuables belonging to the Temple, and pay all warrants when properly drawn. You shall keep a correct account of all moneys received and paid out. You shall report, when called upon by the C. M., the condition of the treasury. You shall give a bond, to secure the money of the Temple, to the C. M., C. O. and C. S., for the faithful application of the Temple's money, per Constitution—the amount of the bond to be agreed upon at a regular meeting of the Temple. You shall give to your successor a written statement of the condition of the treasury. You shall, when your successor is qualified, turn over to him all books, cash, papers and other property that is in your possession. You will now be seated. Let integrity, probity and faithfulness guide you.

Instructions to the Chief Orator.

Sir Chief:—Sir Knight —— —— ——, you have been elected to the high position of Chief Orator of this Temple, and I now invest you with the Jewel of your office. It is your duty to conduct the devotional exercises of the Temple, to visit the sick or disabled Knights and Daughters, and to attend to the funeral ceremonies. That you may be thoroughly qualified for the work, I present you this Holy Volume. Open and read it; it will give you counsel and instruction. You will now be seated. Be faithful.

Instructions to the Chief Drill-Master.

Sir Chief:—Sir Knight —— —— ——, it is with pleasure that I find that the brethren have honored you by electing you to the station of Chief Drill-Master. I now invest you with the Jewel of your office and your Implement (sword) of duty. It is your business to instruct the members in the march and drill, and the Taborian sword exercise. Your station is at the inner door, which I admonish you to guard well during the time of business. You will now be seated. Look well to your duty.

Instuctions to the Chief Color Bearer.

Sir Chief:—Sir Knight —— —— ——, I am glad to know that the suffrage of your brethren has placed you in the honorable position of Chief Color Bearer of this Temple. I now invest you with the Jewel of your office. I also present you the Standard. It is the Banner of our Order. You will carefully keep it, and defend it in the time of danger. It is your duty to carry it on all public occasions, and in all processions. You will now be seated. Guard well the Banner.

Instructions to the Chief Guards.

Sir Chief:—Sir Knights, you have been elected to the office of Chief Guards, and the responsibility of the position requires your constant attendance at the meetings. I now invest you with the Jewels of your office. It is your duty to assist the Chief Mentor in giving the several degrees, and to preserve order during the session of the Temple. You will now be seated. Be faithful to every duty.

Instructions to the Chief Sentinel.

Sir Chief:—Sir Knight —— —— ——, you have been elected to attend to the responsible duties of Chief Sentinel, and I now invest you with the Jewel of office. I also present to you this sword, and admonish you to use it in defending the post of duty. It is your duty to guard the outside door of the Temple, under orders of the C. M. You shall prepare and keep the Temple in proper order for the meetings. You shall receive such compensation for your services as may be awarded by the Temple. You will now be seated. Look well to your post.

Instructions to the Board of Attendants.

Sir Chief:—Sir Knights, you have been appointed a Board of Attendants. It shall be the duty of the Board to have the oversight of all the members of the Temple, and report to the C. M. when a member is sick or disabled, and what attendance the member needs. Your Board shall draw and pay the sick dues; you shall notify, by order of the C. M., members who are detailed to sit up with sick or disabled members. Your Board shall arrange and prepare the funeral of a deceased Knight. Your Board shall have the oversight of Sir Knights' widows and orphans, and report their condition to the Temple at every regular meeting. Your Board shall keep a book and record its doings, and it shall be your duty to report to the Temple at the regular monthly meeting, what you have done during the month. You will now be seated. Be true to duty.

INSTRUCTIONS TO THE BOARD OF JUDGES.

Sir Chief:—Sir Knights, you have been appointed a Board of Judges. This is truly an important position, and one of great responsibility, and requires that you should be well acquainted with the laws of our Order. This Board shall consist of five members, who shall be appointed by the C. M. on the night he is installed. To this Board shall be referred all matters of difference between members, and all trials of members for any offense whatsoever. This Board shall hold regular meetings, and shall have the power to summons witnesses for the plaintiff and defendant, and carefully hear all sides, make up their decision, and report to the Temple through their Secretary. The Temple shall enforce their recommendation, and their action shall be final when approved by the Temple. You will now be seated. Let justice be your rule and guide.

The Sir Chief then makes the following proclamation (all the Knights and Daughters standing, except the installed officers):

PROCLAMATION.

By virtue of the power and authority in me vested, I proclaim that the officers of ——— Temple, No.—, have been regularly installed, and are now ready for duty for the ensuing term of office. (The seven claps are given, with the words *"Be faithful."* All are seated.)

Music; or the following him is sung:

GOLDEN HILL.

I.

Blest be the tie that binds
Our hearts in Christian love;
The fellowship of kindred minds
Is like to that above.

II.

Before our Father's Throne
We pour our ardent prayers;
Our fears, our hopes, our aims are one,—
Our comforts and our cares.

III.

We share our mutual woes,
Our mutual burdens bear;
And often for each other flows
The sympathizing tear.

IV.

When we assunder part,
It gives us inward pain;
But we shall still be joined in heart,
And hope to meet again.

V.

This glorious hope revives
    Our courage by the way;
While each in expectation lives,
    And longs to see the day.

VI.

From sorrow, toil and pain,
    And sin, we shall be free;
And perfect love and friendship reign
    Through all eternity.

If there is an oration to be delivered, this is the proper time. After which the Knights and Daughters may partake of refreshments, and then the Knights assemble, and march and drill. They then march to their hall, close the Temple, and disperse.

BURIAL SERVICE

OF THE

KNIGHTS OF TABOR.

BURIAL SERVICE

OF THE

KNIGHTS OF TABOR.

———:o:———

FORM OF PROCESSION.

Chief Sentinel.
Musicians.
Sir Knights.
Chief Color Bearer.
Two Chief Guards.
Vice-Mentor and Chief Orator.
Chief Treasurer.
Past Chief Mentors.
Chief Guard.
Chief Mentor.
Grand and Past Grand Officers.
Officiating Clergy.

Mourners.
Tabernacles.

140

GENERAL INSTRUCTIONS.

1.—A Sir Knight, to be buried with the full honors, must be a Uniform Rank Knight, with the T. D. P., and in good standing in his Temple.

2.—When notice of the death of a Sir Knight is received, the Chief Mentor shall summons the Temple to convene, to prepare for the funeral.

3.—The Sir Knights must attend in full uniform, with their sword-hilts and banner dressed in mourning, and Jewels of the officers in appropriate dress.

4.—On the casket of the deceased Sir Knight will be placed his sword and helmet; if an officer, his Jewel, clothed in black crape.

5.—The day on which the body is to be buried, the Knights will assemble in their Temple and march to the residence of the deceased, in the regular order, with swords reversed. The sword and helmet of the deceased Knight is borne in the rear of the Chief Mentor. On arriving at the house, the lines open to the right and left. The bearer passes to the casket, and places the sword and helmet on it. The pall-bearers (Sir Knights) take the casket, and, led by the Chief Drill-Master, pass down through the lines to the hearse.

6.—The procession is then formed, and marched to the church or place of public worship. The Knights will then enter in reversed order, preceding the body, and the mourners following the body.

7.—The Chief Mentor presides during the services, assisted by the Chief Orator. If Grand Officers or Past Grand Officers are present, they must be placed in the procession according to their rank.

8.—If the deceased be a Grand or a Past Grand Officer, the Chief Mentor having jurisdiction will invite the Grand Officers who are present to conduct the burial services.

9.—The pall-bearers should be. Sir Knights, selected by the Chief Mentor. If the deceased was a member of other secret orders, a portion of the pall-bearers can be taken from them, per agreement, they bearing a part of the funeral expenses.

10.—While the body is lying in state, there should be two or more Sir Knights on duty near the body, in full dress.

11.—The Temple of which the deceased was a member must march nearest the body. If a sojourner, then the Temple having charge of the burial shall march nearest. Where more than one Temple joins the procession, the youngest takes the lead.

12.—When other civil and military societies unite with the Knights in the burial, they shall march in front of the Knights.

13.—When the head of the procession shall arrive at the place of interment, the lines should be opened, and the Chief Mentor, or the highest officer in rank, preceded by the Chief Drill-Master, pass through, followed by the others in order, into the cemetery. On arriving at the grave or vault they open ranks, and the casket is carried through to the tomb or grave. The coffin is placed over the grave. The Knights form a circle around it, with the family at the foot, and the Chief Mentor, Chief Orator, and clergy at the head.

14.—At the church or place of worship, after the church services over the body, the Temple's services should begin, the Knights standing during the service of prayer.

15.—The procession will return to the Temple in the same order that it marched to the grave. A Temple of Knights in procession is positively under the rules of an open Temple; therefore, no Sir Knight can enter or leave the ranks without permission from the Chief Mentor, conveyed through the Chief Drill-Master.

16.—Should the Tabernacle join the procession, their carriages or vehicles will follow immediately in the rear of the family. The Daughters shall wear the same dress that they do at a Daughter's burial. In the church, their seats are to the left of the Knights. At the grave, they form around the Knights, or at the foot of the grave.

17.—When the place of worship or church is not convenient for a part of the services before going to the grave, it may be performed at a more convenient place, or at the grave.

18.—The face of the deceased should be uncovered, if possible, during the first part of the ceremony, the Chief Mentor at the head of the casket and the Chief Orator at the foot. The Sir Knights must observe and attend to every command given by the Chief Drill-Master or the Chief Mentor.

THE FUNERAL SERVICE OF SIR KNIGHTS AT THE CHURCH.

After the religious services are concluded, the Sir Knights will commence theirs. Present swords!

Chief Mentor:—Sir Knights, we are daily reminded of the great lessons of time and eternity. We are mortal. Mortality is written upon all living beings on earth. Man's days are short and fleeting. One by one we pass the gates of death. We are reminded to-day that we are born to die. The great and unfailing truth that death is sure, is demonstrated to our view at this sad and mournful hour. The door of our Temple opened to receive a messenger, and there was none to say: "By what right do you enter here?" A Brother Knight has been summoned to appear before the Grand Chief of the Universe. His light has been extinguished in the earthly Temple. He lies mute before us. No more will he meet us around the center square. His voice, so ready in giving knightly greeting, is silent. His hand cannot grasp his sword in defense of innocence, justice and country. All that remains of our beloved Brother Knight is his cold, cold body, stilled in death. (*The Sir Knights return swords.*) Sir Knights, let us attend, while the Chief Orator reads to us from the lessons of the Holy Scriptures. May the impressions fill us with meekness and consolation, that we may be prepared when the last of earth comes to us.

Chief Orator:—O Lord, remember the faithful among the people, for the children of men fail on earth.

Response:—Remember us, O Lord!

C. O.:—There is not a just man on the earth who doeth good and sinneth not.

Res.:—Give ear, O Lord!

C. O.:—Whatsoever God doeth, it shall be forever; nothing can be put to it, nor anything taken from it.

Res.:—Redeem us, O Lord!

C. O.:—Great are Thy tender mercies, O Lord; quicken us according to Thy judgments.

Res.:—Redeem us, O Lord!

C. O.:—We will lift our eyes unto the hills, from whence cometh our help. Our help cometh from the Lord, who made heaven and earth. He that keepeth us will not slumber.

Res.:—The Lord is my keeper!

C. O.:—Give thanks unto the Lord, for He is good; because His mercy endureth forever.

Res.:—Give thanks unto the Lord!

C. O.:—Lord, make us to know our end, and the measure of our days, that we may know how frail we are. There is but a step between us and death.

Res.:—Teach us, O Lord!

C. O.:—God hath made of one blood all nations of men, to dwell on the face of the earth, and hath determined the times before appointed, and the bounds of their habitation.

Res.:—Be nigh unto us, O Lord!

C. O.:—The righteous hath hope in his death. Let me die the death of the righteous. Let my last end be like his.

Res.:—Be merciful unto us, O Lord!

C. O.:—I know that my Redeemer liveth, and that He shall stand at the latter day upon the earth.

Res.:—May we rest in hope!

C. O. :—Christ died for us, whether we wake or sleep.

Res. :—Lord, save us!

C. M. :—Will the memory of our brother be forgotten among his brothers?

Res. :—We will never forget his manly form and virtues.

C. M. :—Shall his name be recorded in our Temple?

Res. :—It is recorded here (*hand on heart*). May he have a clear record in the heavenly Temple.

C. M. :—He was a true and trusted Knight, and has passed from life's turmoils and struggles. May his soul rest in peace!

Res. :—May he rest in peace and be happy! (*The Sir Knights cover.*)

C. M. :—Sir Knights, we are assembled to look upon the last of our Brother Knight. No more will our voices cheer him in this world of sorrow. No more will he meet us in our pleasant retreat— the Temple of our love on earth. Our swords cannot now shield him from danger. The Chief Sentinel's challenge will greet his ear no more. He has hailed the entrance for the last time in our Temple. To the Silent City of the Dead we all must come at last. The manliest form, the bravest heart, that surrounds this spot will be laid captive to death, and bound in the chain of mortality. But he who has been faithful to the teachings of the Chief Mentor of Salvation—the Son of Righteousness— can, by the will of the Sovereign Ruler of the Universe, claim a place in the Eternal Temple of Bliss, then mortality will only be laid aside to put

on the glittering robe of eternal day, and dwell
with the royal, happy company in the Temple of
Eternal Light. Surely the sadness and solemnity
of this occasion are most forcibly felt by all present.
He who now sleeps in death was our brother Knight.
With him we have met often around the hollow
square; with him we have formed the sacred chain
together; we have met life's trials and pleasures.
He is now gone beyond our protecting care. Him
whom we loved and honored, our presence here in
the dress of our Order proves that we revere his
memory. We are here to demonstrate our respect
for his many good qualities; over his errors and
faults, whatever they may have been, we cast the
mantle of forgetfulness. Sir Knights, each suc-
cessive death-call breaks the chain that binds us to
this lower world; make us pause and reflect what
will be our future. If we would meet the Grand
Chief of Heaven and earth in peace and happiness,
we must have a clear passport from His hand. Then,
when the earthen vessel breaks, our souls will soar
away to blissful rest.

Response by the Knights:—*In Solo Deo Salus!*

This closes the ceremony in the church. After
taking a last look at the face of the deceased, the
benediction is pronounced.

The Drill-Master forms the Knights; they then
march out of the church to the place of interment
in the same order as before.

On arriving at the place, and having formed
around the grave (the casket resting over the
grave), the following hymn is sung:

"My flesh also shall rest in hope."

I.

Rest for the toiling hand,
  Rest for the anxious brow,
Rest for the weary, way-worn feet,
  Rest from all labor now.

II.

Rest for the fevered brain,
  Rest for the throbbing eye;
Through these parched lips of thine no more
  Shall pass the moan or sigh.

III.

Soon shall the trump of God
  Give out the welcome sound,
That shakes thy silent chamber-walls,
  And breaks the turf-sealed ground.

IV.

Ye dwellers in the dust,
  Awake! come forth and sing;
Sharp has your frost of winter been,
  But bright shall be your spring.

V.

'Twas sown in weakness here;
  'Twill then be raised in power;
That which was sown an earthly seed,
  Shall rise a heavenly flower!

The following prayer will then be made by the C. O., or an extemporaneous prayer, if preferred by him; or a clergyman may be invited to pray.

PRAYER.

Holy Lord God! Thou that presidest over the destinies of man, in this hour of sorrow we humbly lift our hearts to Thee. Thou hast mercifully proclaimed in Thy Holy Word that Thou wouldst comfort the mourner, and give consolation to the troubled heart. We worship and adore Thee, Maker of Heaven and Earth, for all things that Thou hast given to us. Cleanse Thou the thoughts of our hearts with the inspiration of Thy Holy Spirit, that we may perfectly love Thee, and worthily magnify Thy adorable name. Be Thou a father to the fatherless, and a husband to the widow, and as God administer consolation to those who are sorrowing this day. We have the evidence before us how frail men are, and how uncertain our continuance on earth is held. We are reminded that our lives are but vapor. Oh, let the light of Thy divine countenance shine upon us, and lead us by Thy grace and spirit to turn our thoughts to things that make our everlasting peace and happiness. 'May the burning lamp of Thy pure love light our pathway through the dark valley and shadow of death, that we, by the commendation of Thy Beloved Son, our Lord and Savior, may be enabled to gain admittance to the Heavenly Temple above, and, in the glorious presence of our Lord and Master, enjoy a blissful immortality with the angelic host and the redeemed of earth forever, through Jesus Christ, our Lord. Amen!

Response:—In God alone is safety!

The C. D.-M. removes the sword and cap from the casket. The Knights present swords. It is then lowered into the grave.

The C. O. then says:—I am the resurrection and the life. He that believeth in Me, though he were dead, yet shall he live. Whosoever liveth and believeth in Me, shall never die. To the earth we commit the mortal remains of our deceased Brother. May his soul rest in peace. Earth to earth. (*Cast earth on the casket.*) Dust to dust. (*Cast again.*) Ashes to ashes. (*Cast again.*) Until the morn of the resurrection, when, like our risen Lord and Savior, may he break every chain and bond of death, and ascend to dwell forever in the sunshine of heavenly beams.

Res.:—So may it be. Amen! Amen!!

C. D.-M.:—Sir Knights, return swords.

The V.-M. then presents the sword of the deceased to the C. M.

The C. M. then says:—Sir Knights, you will remember that our deceased Brother Knight was taught while in life that this sword, in the hands of a true and trusty Knight, was an emblem of manly worth; in his grasp, he was to defend the innocent, protect the weak, have mercy on the fallen, and aid the distressed. Be true as steel to a Brother Knight. Obey every order given from justice, and silently admonish an erring Brother Knight. May the sword of Divine Justice open the way, and permit him to enter the blessed abode of saints and angels, and, in their company and companionship, live forever in the realms of eternal joy.

Res.:—Amen! So be it!! Amen!!!

The C. T. then presents the key to the C. O., who says:

C. O.:—This symbol of truth reminds us of Him who said: "I am the way. I am the door. No man can come unto the Father but through Me. I have the keys of death and the kingdom of heaven." We place this upon the breast of our brother, there

to remain as an evidence that he believed in the
Divine Being that has power to save to the utter-
most. May this hope of our brother in life safely
convey his immortal soul, and admit it to the
heavenly mansions, to rest forevermore.

Res.:—Bless the Father! Honor the Son!!

The C. O. casts the key into the grave. The
Knights uncover, and the C. O. repeats the following prayer:—Our Father which art in heaven.
Hallowed be Thy name. Thy kingdom come. Thy
will be done on earth as it is in heaven. Give us
this day our daily bread; and forgive us our trespasses, as we forgive those who trespass against us.
And lead us not into temptation, but deliver us
from evil. For Thine is the kingdom, and the
power, and the glory, forever. Amen!

Res.:—*In Solo Deo Salus!*

The Knights cover, and give the farewell salute
three times. Then they form the wall of steel, and
sing the following, or some other hymn, or the
band may play a solemn dirge:

I.

Friend after friend departs.
Who hath not lost a friend?
There is no union here of hearts
That finds not here an end;
Were this frail world our final rest,
Living or dying, none were blest.

II.

Beyond the flight of time,
Beyond this vale of death,
There surely is some blessed clime
Where life is not a breath,—
Nor life's affections transient fire,
Whose sparks fly upward to expire.

III.

There is a world above,
  Where parting is unknown,—
A whole eternity of love,
  Formed for the good alone;
And fai:h beholds the dying here,
Translated to that happier sphere.

The C. O. pronounces the benediction, the lines are formed, and they march back to their hall; and, after the business is finished, the Temple is closed.

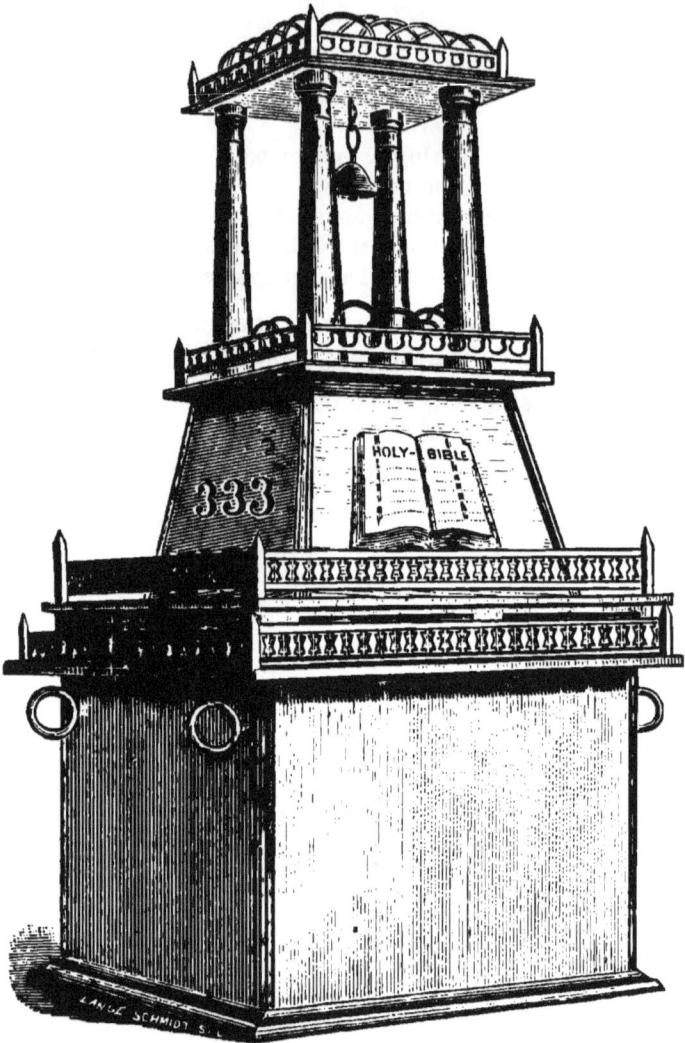

TABERNACLE HOUSE.

153

DAUGHTERS OF
TABERNACLE

INTERNATIONAL
ORDER OF
TWELVE

C. P.
333

TABERNACLE OFFICERS' JEWELS.

154

No. 1.

No. 4—½ Size.

No. 2.

No. 5.

No. 3.

No. 6.

DAUGHTERS' PINS AND EMBLEMS.

INSTALLING CEREMONY

Officers of the Tabernacle.

156

OFFICERS

OF THE

LADIES' TABERNACLE.

——:o:——

SECTION 1.—The Constitution of the Grand Temple and Tabernacle must be strictly complied with by all subordinate Tabernacles.

SEC. 2.—The officers of the Tabernacle shall be as follows:

1. Chief Preceptress, ... C. P.
2. Vice-Preceptress, ... V.-P.
3. Chief Recorder, ... C. R.
4. Vice-Recorder, ... V.-R.
5. Chief Treasurer, ... C. T.
6. Chief Priestess, ... C. Ps.
7. Inner Sentinel, ... I. S.
8. Outer Sentinel, ... O. S.
9. Chief Tribune, ... C. Te.
10. Chief Tribune, ... C. Te.
11. Chief Tribune, ... C. Te.

——

1. Board of Visitors, ... B. V.
2. Board of Visitors, ... B. V.
3. Board of Visitors, ... B. V.

1. Board of Examiners, ... B. E.
2. Board of Examiners, ... B. E.
3. Board of Examiners, ... B. E.

INSTALLATION CEREMONY
OF
TABERNACLE ·OFFICERS.
———: o :———

The officers of the tabernacle may be installed either in public or private. The ceremony can be performed by any C. P., Past C. P., C. G. P., Past C. G. P., C. M., Past C. M., C. G. M., or Past C. G. M.

PUBLIC OR PRIVATE INSTALLATION.

The Daughter Priestesses assemble in a room or place near the hall or room where the installation ceremonies are to be performed, dressed in full regalia, and march in the following order to the place of installation, under the marshalship of one of the Meroes.

THE PROCESSION.

C. P.

C. T.   P. C. T.

V.-P.

C. R.   V.-R.

C. Ps.

O. S.   I. S.

C. Te.s

B. V.   B. V.

B. V.

[HOUSE.]

B. E.   B. E.

B. E., with Banner.

P. C. P.   P. C. P.

P. V.-P.   P. V.-P.

Members by Twos.

Sir Knights,

Meroe.

The Tabernacle House is borne by four Daughters. The procession marches three times around the hall. The officers and past officers are seated on the platform, and the members and Sir Knights in front of the platform. The Tabernacle House is placed in front of the Chief Preceptress, in the center of the platform, the officers to the right and left of her.

THE CEREMONY.

Music; or, if there is no band, the following hymn is sung:

PRAISE TO GOD.

I.

Praise to God, the Great Creator;
  Praise to God from every tongue;
Join my soul with every creature,—
  Join the universal song.

II.

Joyfully on earth adore Him,
  Till in heaven our song we raise;
Then, enraptured, fall before him,
  Lost in wonder, love and praise.

III.

Praise to God, the Great Creator,—
  Father, Son and Holy Ghost;
Praise Him, every living creature,
  Earth and heaven's united host.

The Chief Preceptress gives three sounds, and all the Daughters and Knights stand while the following prayer is said by the C. O., or some one appointed for that purpose:

Eternal God! Eternal King!
  Ruler of heaven and earth beneath!
From Thee our hopes, our comforts spring;
  In Thee we live, and move, and breathe.
Thy word brought forth the flaming sun,
  The changeful moon, the starry host;

In Thine appointed course they run,
  Till in the final ruin lost.
We lift our hearts to Thee,
  Thou Day-Star from on high!
The sun itself is but Thy shade,
  Yet cheers both earth and sky.
Oh, let Thy rising beams
  Dispel the shades of night;
And let the glories of Thy love
  Come like the morning light!

Bless Thou the officers and members of the Tabernacle wherever they may be located, and we give Thee all honor and praise. Amen!

Res.:—In God alone is safety!

The C. P. gives one sound, and all are seated.

Music; or the following (or any other) hymn is sung:

I.

Let all the earth their voices raise,
To sing the choicest psalm of praise;
  To sing and bless Jehovah's name;
His glory let the heathen know,
His wonders to the nations show,
  And all His saving works proclaim.

II.

He framed the globe, He built the sky,
He made the shining worlds on high,
  And reigns complete in glory there;
His beams are majesty and light;
His beauties, how divinely bright!
  His Tabernacle, how divinely fair!

The Meroe lights the candles and places them on the Tabernacle House, and places all the officers' jewels on a stand. The officers elect stand in a semi-circle.

She then says:—Faithful (Here the title of the Installing Officer is to be given), I have the pleasure of presenting to you the officers elect of ———— Tabernacle, No. ——. They are now ready for installation.

Inst. Off. :—You will please open your Manuals, and answer the following questions:

Inst. Off. :—Are you willing to serve in the capacity to which you have been elected?

Ans.:—I am willing to do the duties pertaining to the office.

Inst. Off. :—Will you punctually attend to the business of you office?

Ans. :—I am resolved to attend to all that is required of me under the laws of our Order.

The Installing Officer then requests them to link their right and left hands together, whereupon they repeat the following words after the Installing Officer:

As we are joined together, hand in hand, so we will sustain and support each other in our official duties. We promise to be present at every meeting of the Tabernacle, unless detained at home by sickness, or by absence from the city.

The Inst. Off. gives one sound, and all stand.

The Meroe then places the Chief Preceptress elect in front of the Tabernacle House, and says:— Faithful (give title of Installing Officer), I have the honor of presenting to you Daughter ——— —— ——, who has been elected to preside in this Tabernacle.

6—Dickson's New Manual.)

INSTRUCTIONS TO THE CHIEF PRIESTESS.

Inst. Off. :—Tharbis, you will please receive into your hand the Constitution of the Order, and the By-Laws of this Tabernacle.

Inst. Off. to the Chief Preceptress:—These are the Laws of the Order. It is your duty to have them executed promptly; have them read in your Tabernacle at stated times. I now invest you with the Jewel of your office, and I present you the Staff of Power. You will please be seated, and listen. It shall be the duty of the H. P. to preside at all meetings of the Tabernacle, call special meetings when the business of the Tabernacle requires it, decide all questions of order or of the rules, sign all money orders, preserve order, enforce the laws, instruct the candidates in the several degrees, and cause the members to learn well the Ritual. (Gives one sound, and all are seated.)

Meroe:—I now present to you Daughter —— —— ——, who was elected Vice-Priestess of —— Tabernacle, No. —.

INSTRUCTIONS TO THE VICE-PRIESTESS.

Inst. Off. :—Amisis, I now invest you with the Jewel of your office. You will please be seated. It is your duty to be present at all meetings of the Tabernacle, and assist the High Priestess in her several official duties; and, in the absence of the H. P., you are to preside in the meetings of the Tabernacle, and attend to the duties of the office.

Meroe:—I now present to you Daughter —— —— ——, who was elected Chief Recorder of —— Tabernacle, No. —.

INSTRUCTIONS TO THE CHIEF RECORDER.

Inst. Off.:—Sesotheni, I now invest you with the Jewel of your office. You will please be seated. It is your duty to keep the proceedings of each meeting, and the business, under proper heads. You shall have the minutes, the roll, and account books in your possession. You shall issue all notices, draw all warrants on the Treasurer, receive and record all moneys received into the Tabernacle, pay all moneys you receive into the treasury, make an annual report in full to the Grand Temple and Tabernacle, and report, every three months, the condition of the Tabernacle to the members and the Grand Chief. You shall notify the C. G. S., within five days, of the expulsion of a member, and why she was expelled, and fill out, sign and seal all certificates by order of the Tabernacle.

Meroe:—I now present to you Daughter —— —— ——, who was elected Vice-Recorder of —— Tabernacle, No. —.

INSTRUCTIONS TO THE VICE-RECORDER.

Inst. Off. :—I now invest you with the Jewel of your office. You will please be seated. It is your duty to assist the C. R. in her several duties, and attend to all the business of the office in the absence of the C. R. It is furthermore your duty to correspond with other Tabernacles, and to conduct the correspondence of the Tabernacle.

Meroe:—I now present to you Daughter —— —— ——, who was elected Chief Treasurer of —— Tabernacle, No. —.

Instructions to the Chief Treasurer.

Inst. Off.:—Seraphis, I now invest you with the Jewel of your office. You will please be seated. It is your duty to receive all funds coming into the Tabernacle from the C. R., keep an accurate account, and I pay all warrants. You shall report the condition of the treasury, every three months, to the Tabernacle, or at the regular quarterly meeting. Your further duties and instructions you will find in the Constitution.

Meroe:—I now present to you Daughter ——— ——— ———, who was elected Chief Priestess of ——— Tabernacle, No. —.

Instructions to the Chief Priestess.

Inst. Off.:—Hyerego, I now invest you with the Jewel of your office, and present to you the Shepherdess' Crook. You will please be seated. It is your duty to be present at every meeting, and open it with devotional exercises, give counsel to the sick or disabled members, and instruct candidates on the sacredness of their obligation. Your office is one of usefulness and benefit. Be true to duty.

Meroe:—I now present to you Daughter ——— ——— ——— and Daughter ——— ——— ———, who were elected Inner and Outer Sentinels respectively of ——— Tabernacle, No. —.

Instructions to the Inner and Outer Sentinels.

Inst. Off.:—Abassine and Lybenus, I now invest you with the Jewels of your office, and present to you the Rods of your authority. You will please be seated. It shall be your duty to guard the inner and outer entrances of the Tabernacle, and perform such other duties as are found in the Ritual. Your punctual and early attendance is absolutely required. Look well to your duty.

Meroe:—I now present to you Sir Knight —— —— ——, Sir Knight —— —— ——, and Sir Knight —— —— ——, who have been elected Tribunes of —— Tabernacle, No. —.

Instructions to the Chief Tribunes.

Inst. Off.:—Sir Meroes, I now invest you with the Jewels of your office, and present to you the Javelins of authority. You will please be seated. It shall be the duty of the Meroes to assist the H. P. in conferring the degrees, arrange the hall for meetings, conduct all public business, and attend every meeting. You will be members of the Tabernacle only during your term of office.

Meroe:—I now present to you Daughter —— —— ——, and Daughter —— —— ——, and Daughter —— —— ——, who were appointed the Board of Visitors of —— Tabernacle, No. —.

Instructions to the Board of Visitors.

Inst. Off.:—Hespers, I now invest you with the Jewels of your office. You will please be seated. It shall be your duty to visit the members in regular order, and report any who are sick, disabled, or need aid and attendance. It will also be your duty to attend, and report to the H. P. the condition of, the members. You shall cause orders to be drawn on the Treasury for all weekly benefits, and pay them to the members. You shall report your business to every regular meeting, in a written report, signed by all the members of the Board.

Meroe:—I now present to you Daughter ——
—— ——, and Daughter —— —— ——, and
Daughter —— —— ——, who were appointed a
Board of Examiners of —————— Tabernacle, No. —.

INSTRUCTIONS TO THE BOARD OF EXAMINERS.

Inst. Off. :—Cyrenes, I now present to you the
Jewels of your office. You will please be seated.
It shall be your duty to examine any matter or business of the Tabernacle that is referred to you.
You shall prepare candidates for the degrees, and
shall conduct visitors to their proper seats. You
shall make a written report to every regular meeting, signed by all the members of the Board.

The Installing Officer then gives three sounds,
and all stand, except the installed officers. He then
says:—By virtue of the authority in me vested, I
declare the officers of —————— Tabernacle, No. —,
installed and ready for duty for the ensuing Tabernacle year.

Response by the members:—*We declare! We
declare! !*

Meroe:—I now proclaim the officers of ——————
Tabernacle, No. —, duly installed in regular form.

The Sir Knights and Daughters give five claps,
and say: " *We declare!*" This is given three times.
The last time they say: " *We declare the officers of
—————— Tabernacle, No. —, regularly installed.*"

Inst. Off. gives one sound, and all are seated.

Music or singing; after which an oration may be
delivered, then they march three times around the
hall, and the Tabernacle closes in the usual form,
or, if in a public hall, the H. P. declares the Tabernacle at rest.

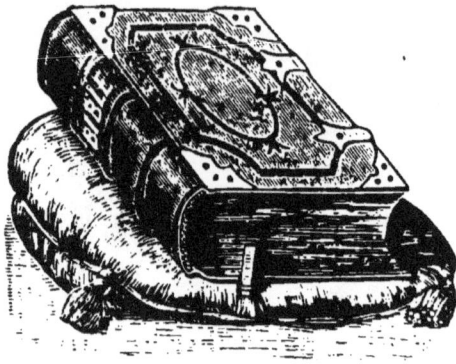

TABERNACLE FURNITURE.

(For Balance of Tabernacle Furniture, see page 358.)

TEMPLE FURNITURE.

(For Balance of Temple Furniture, see
pages 359 and 360.)

BURIAL SERVICE

OF THE

DAUGHTERS

OF THE

TABERNACLE.

FUNERAL CEREMONIES

OF THE

DAUGHTERS OF THE TABERNACLE.

———: o :———

The ceremonies which are observed at Tabernacle funerals, and for the interment of the dead, are very impressive and appropriate. They are performed as an imperative, yet a sorrowful duty, and as a token of affection and respect to the memory of a departed Daughter.

DIRECTIONS.

1.—No Daughter of the Tabernacle can be buried with the formalities of the Tabernacle, unless she is a Daughter Priestess in good standing; nor without the consent of her family.

2.—The Chief Priestess, having received notice of the death of a Daughter (the deceased being a Daughter Priestess in good standing), it shall be her duty to issue orders to the Tabernacle to make preparations to attend the funeral, and extend an invitation to the Temples and other Tabernacles. (Should the family of the deceased desire to arrange for the funeral, their wishes must be complied with, and it relieves the Tabernacle from all funeral expenses.)

170

3.—The whole arrangement for the burial of a Daughter by the Tabernacle must be made by the High Priestess and the Meroes. The ceremonies are conducted by the C. O. or C. M. of the nearest Temple, or any Grand Officer.

4.—Whenever other societies unite with the Tabernacle in the burial of a Daughter, the body of the deceased must be in charge of the Tabernacle having jurisdiction. Other societies are permitted to perform their ceremonies, but the services of the Tabernacle must not be omitted.

5.—If a sojourner, in good standing, dies within the jurisdiction of a Tabernacle, it shall be the duty of the Tabernacle to inter her with all the formalities of the Order, or attend to sending the body to its home. Where there are two or more Tabernacles, the oldest Tabernacle has precedence, unless otherwise arranged. The Tabernacle of which the deceased sojourner was a member shall pay all funeral expenses incurred to the Tabernacle which attended to this duty.

6.—The pall-bearers shall be Sir Knights of Tabor, selected by the High Priestess.

7.—No Tabernacle can unite with other societies in the burial of a person not a Daughter or a Knight of Tabor, without a dispensation from the Chief Grand Mentor, or the consent of the Grand Temple and Tabernacle having jurisdiction.

8.—The members of the Tabernacle shall attend the funeral of a deceased Daughter either on foot or in vehicles. The H. Ps. and P. H. Ps. carry their Staffs trimmed with crape. The I. S. and O. S. carry their Rods trimmed with crape.

9.—A Sir Knight attending the funeral of a Daughter shall wear a black suit, brown gloves, and the regulation undress. The Meroes shall carry their spears. The C. M.s and P. C. M.s carry their swords trimmed with black. Should a C. G. M. or P. C. G. M. attend, the C. G.s march in their rear with swords reversed, the C. C. B., with two assistants, in front of them.

10.—When two or more Tabernacles are in procession, the Tabernacle of which the deceased was a member shall march nearest to the corpse. If the deceased member was a member of other secret societies, such society or societies shall bear a part of the funeral expenses.

The Service.

11.—The Tabernacle shall assemble at their hall, or some place that is proper near the residence of the deceased. The H. Ps. shall declare the Tabernacle opened, and announce the business that has called them together. The C. R. reads the name and age of the deceased member, how long she has been a member, the day and date of her death, and gives the date when she was interred. It shall be enrolled in the record-book.

Order of March.

12.—After the procession is formed, they march to the residence of the deceased member, receive the corpse, and proceed in the following order to the church or place appointed for the services:

Two Meroes, with spears.
High Priestess.
Past High Priestesses, by twos.
Inner and Outer Sentinels.
Chief and Assistant Recorder.
Vice-Priestess.
Chief Treasurer and Hyerego.
Members, two by two.
Other Tabernacles, in the same order.
Chief Orator and Clergy.

Marshal.

* HEARSE. *
* *
* *

Family.
Knights, in their marching order.
Other Societies.
Carriages.

13.—A Tabernacle in procession is under the discipline of an open Tabernacle, and no one must leave the ranks without positive permission from the High Priestess, conveyed through one of the acting Meroes.

AT THE CHURCH.

14.—The Tabernacle and Sir Knights will open ranks, and the corpse and family will pass into the church. The Daughters and Knights will follow, and take their seats.

After the church ceremony and sermon by a minister or the Chief Orator, the Daughters and Sir Knights shall rise, whereupon the Chief Orator repeats the following invocation, and the Daughters and Knights respond:

Chief Orator:—Almighty Father, may we realize that Thine all-pervading presence is with us; may Thy spirit perfect us in truth and obedience to Thy will.

Response:—May the Lord's will be done!

C. O.:—May we meet our Sister Daughter in the fadeless light of God's kingdom.

Res.:—Into the Lord's hands we commit our souls!

C. O.:—Behold, O Lord, we are in sorrow. O Lord, let the light of Thy countenance shine upon us in our distress. Comfort us, and turn our mourning into joy.

Res.:—The Lord will hear and answer our prayer; only trust Him!

C. O.:—Blessed is the Lord. From the rising to the setting of the sun, praise the name of the Lord.

Res.:—Give thanks unto the Lord; his mercy endureth forever!

C. O.:—Hear us, O Lord, and comfort our mourning hearts.

Res.:—The Lord will meet us in our Tabernacles!

C. O.:—Our God dwelleth in the Heavenly Tabernacle; He hears the voice of our supplications.

Res.:—May He save us all with an everlasting salvation!

The Chief Orator (or the minister, if he is a member), then reads the following prayer, the Daughters and Knights holding up their joined hands during the same:

PRAYER.

O Merciful God, the Father of our Lord Jesus Christ, who is the resurrection and the life; in whom whosoever believeth shall live, though he die; and whomsoever liveth and believeth in Him, shall not die eternally; who also hath taught us, by His holy Apostle St. Paul, not to be sorry, as men without hope, for those who sleep in Him. We humbly beseech Thee, O Father, to raise us from the death of sin unto the life of righteousness; that when we shall depart this life, we may rest in Him, and that at the general resurrection on the last day, we may be found acceptable in Thy sight, and receive that blessing which Thy Well-Beloved Son shall then pronounce to all who love and fear Thee, saying: "Come, ye blessed children of my Father, receive the kingdom prepared for you from the beginning of the world." Grant this, we beseech Thee, O Merciful Father, through Jesus Christ, our Mediator and Redeemer. Amen!

Response.—In God alone is safety!

Whereupon the following hymn is sung:

I.

Dear as thou wert, and justly dear,
  We will not weep for thee;
One thought shall check the starting tear,—
  It is, that thou art free.

II.

And thus shall faith's consoling power
  The tears of love restrain;
Oh, who that saw thy parting hour
  Could wish thee back again!

176

III.

Triumphant in thy closing eye
The hope of glory shone;
Joy breathed in thine expiring sigh,
When thou wert taken home.

The following exhortation is delivered by the High Priestess:

EXHORTATION.

Daughters, this solemn scene tells us that our Tabernacle has been visited by that dread messenger—Death—against whose certain entrance sentinels and closed doors offer no stay or stop. The chain of our circle has been broken, and a link is gone, never more to return. We mourn the loss of a dear companion. The dead body of our beloved Sister, M—— N———, is now before us in its narrow house. This is the last of earthly Tabernacles for her whom we have met so often in our undisturbed retreat, away from the worldly-minded, to enjoy a brief season of happiness; and now we have assembled to bid our Sister a last, long farewell. She sleeps with the unnumbered dead. The storms and calms of life have passed over her pathway. She is at rest. Her toils on earth have ended. As it has pleased our Heavenly Father to call the soul of our departed Sister from its earthly Tabernacle, may she find joy and happiness in the Tabernacles of that peaceful land where the eternal light and love of the Eternal Father, Son and Holy Spirit will shed their rays forever, and, in the company of the angelic host and the redeemed of earth, may we meet our loved Sister, to part no more. Farewell, for a little while.

The Daughters and Knights stand, with arms folded across their breasts, during the reading of the exhortation. When the H. P. says *Farewell!* the Daughters and Knights drop their arms to their sides and fold them across their breasts—this is done three times—each time slowly repeating the word, *Farewell!*

The Knights and Daughter Priestesses, the family and friends, will march around and view the body, while the choir chants a funeral anthem, or a hymn is sung by the congregation. The Sir Knights and Priestesses then form in front of the church, and open ranks, when the casket is passed through to the hearse.

MARCH TO THE CEMETERY.

Chief Meroes.
Chief Orator and Clergy.

```
*   *
* HEARSE. *
*   *
```

Family Carriages.
Daughters in Vehicles.
Other Societies,
Sir Knights.
Other Vehicles.

AT THE GRAVE.

15.—The Daughters and Sir Knights form a circle around the grave (the casket being placed over the grave), with the family at the head, and the C. O. and ministers at the foot. The Daughters and Sir Knights join hands, and while the casket is being lowered, the following hymn is sung:

I.

Unveil thy bosom, faithful tomb;
    Take this new treasure to thy trust,
And give these sacred relics room
    To slumber in the silent dust.

II.

Nor pain, nor grief, nor anxious fear,
    Invade thy bounds; no mortal woes
Can reach the peaceful sleeper here,
    While angels watch the soft repose.

III.

So Jesus slept; God's dying Son   .
    Passed thro' the grave, and blest the bed:
Rest here, blest saint, till from His throne
    The morning break, and pierce the shade.

IV.

Break from His throne, illustrious morn!
    Attend, O earth! His sovereign word:
Restore thy trust; a glorious form
    Shall then ascend to meet the Lord!

The ceremonies may conclude with the church
order for the burial of the dead, or by the following, read by the C. O. :

PRAYER.

Forasmuch as it hath pleased Almighty God, in
His wise providence, to take out of this world the
soul of our deceased Sister, we, therefore, commit
her body to the ground—earth to earth, ashes to
ashes, dust to dust; looking for the general resurrection in the last day, and the life of the world to
come, through our Lord Jesus Christ; at whose
second coming in glorious majesty to judge the
world, the earth and the sea shall give up their
dead; and the corruptible bodies of those who sleep
in Him shall be changed, and made like unto His

own glorious body, according to the mighty working whereby He is able to subdue all things unto Himself. Amen!

The services close, and the procession returns to the place from whence it came; and after the necessary business is finished, the Tabernacle is closed.

PALATINE GUARDS' CHAPEAU.

Chapeau.

Button No. 1.

Button No. 2.

Helmet.

UNIFORM RANK HELMET.

PALATIUM

OF THE

Royal House of Media.

NINTH, TENTH AND ELEVENTH DEGREES

OF THE

Knights and Daughters of Tabor,

OF THE

International Order of Twelve.

PALATIUM

OF THE

ROYAL HOUSE OF MEDIA.

——:o:——

This is the highest department in the International Order of Twelve. It is the Royal Social House, where the Knights and Daughter Priestesses meet as equals. The business of this House is to exert a refining influence over the members of the order.

1.—It is proposed to be a part of the International Order of Twelve, with all the rights and privileges it confers.

2.—The Grand Temples and Tabernacles must make a Code of Laws or Constitution for the Government of Palatiums.

3.—Our order is so constituted, that the benefits for members are derived from Temples and Tabernacles; however, it is optional with Palatiums whether or not they will adopt the beneficial feature.

4.—Each Palatium may, if it desires to make By-Laws, have its members pay monthly dues and to give sick or distress benefits, and to aid the Temple or Tabernacle in paying funeral expenses.

182

5.—The Members of the Palatiums being a part of the Grand Temple and Tabernacle, they must pay grand dues, but not as much as is paid by the Temples and Tabernacles.

6.—A Palatium is divided into two departments: *First,* the Knightly Princes—that is, the Palatine Guards. These are to be ready to march and drill at any time. Special privileges are given to them to accumulate funds to prepare their outfits, and to get money into their treasury to pay travel-ing expenses when they are called to a distant point. They are permitted to have a Treasurer independent from the one of the Palatium, and shall be known as the Palatine Guards' Treasurer. They may give entertainments for the purpose of replenishing their Treasury. They must be ready when the C. G. M. orders them to meet the Grand Session for a Grand Parade.

Second, the Princesses of Media. These are the Ladies of the Palace. They shall have the same rights and privileges that the Knights have in the management of the Palatium. It is they who make the meetings of the Palatium pleasant and sociable. They shall aid the Palatine Guards in all their efforts. In a parade the Princesses shall turn out in carriages and in full dress.

7.—All Grand Officers should be members of the Palatium. This is necessary, because the Palatium is a department in the International as well as in the Grand Temple and Tabernacle, and Grand Officers cannot properly attend to all their duties, unless they become members of all the various departments of the Order.

8.—The Grand Temple and Tabernacle, in making a Code of Laws for the Palatium, shall define the duties of the officers.

9.—The C. G. M. may give a dispensation allowing the Vice-Princess to preside in case the Presiding Prince is required to act as Prince Marshal.

Officers of the Palatium.

1.—Presiding Prince,.................P. P.
2.—Vice-Princess,.....................V.-P.
3.—Recording Prince,.................R. P.
4.—Assistant Princess,................A. P.
5.—Prince Banker,....................P. B.
6.—Princess Nonna,...................P. N.
7.—Prince Clericus,...................P. C.
8.—Princess Revista,..................P. R.
9.—Prince Marshal,...................P. M.
10.—Prince Gonfalonier,...............P. G.
11.—Princess Sentina,................. S.
12.—Prince Wardship,.................P. W.

The officers are elected at the regular meeting in the month of March, and installed the fifth day of April, or within twenty days thereafter. The installation may be either public or private.

The installation ceremony may be performed by a Presiding Prince, Past Presiding Prince, Chief Grand Mentor, or International Deputy Grand Mentor.

PALATIUM OFFICER'S JEWEL.
Twelve Jewels, with Initials of Office on Each Jewel.

INSTALLING CEREMONY

OF THE

Officers of the Palatium,

OR

ROYAL HOUSE OF MEDIA.

INSTALLING CEREMONY

OF THE

OFFICERS OF THE PALATIUM.

————: o :————

The members of the Palatium shall assemble in their hall (or some place near to where the installation is to be held, if it is to be public). The Princes and Princesses shall appear in full dress. The P. P. declares the Palatium open for work. The Prince Marshal forms the procession. If a Grand or Past Grand Officer is present, proper respect must be shown him or her.

THE MARCH.

The procession marches around the hall four times. The ranks are opened and the officers are marched to the platform in the following order:

Tabernacle—Daughter Priestesses, in full dress.

Temple—Uniform Rank Knights, in full dress.

Grand and Past Grand Officers, in full dress.

Palatium—Princesses, in full dress.

Palatium—Palatine Guards, in full dress.

If the Maids and Pages take part in the ceremony, they shall march in front of the procession.

If there is room on the platform, the Grand and Past Grand Officers, and the C. M.s, C. P.s and Q. M.s are seated to the right and left of the officers about to be installed.

The Installing Officer shall be addressed as Sir Grand, the Presentor or Introducer as Prince Marshall.

CEREMONY.

The Prince Marshal places all the officers' Jewels on the altar.

Music; or, if there is no band, the following hymn is sung:

S. M.

I.

Through all the lofty sky,
  Through all the inferior ground,
The Almighty Maker shines confessed,
  And pours his blessings 'round.

II.

Each year the teeming earth,
  With flowers and fruits is crowned;
And grass, and herbs, and harvests, grow,
  And send their joys around.

III.

The world of waters yields
  A rich supply of food,
And distant lands their treasures send
  Upon the rolling flood.

IV.

To serve and bless our land
  The elements conspire;
And mercies mix themselves with earth,—
  With ocean, air, and fire.

V.

O that the sons of men
  To God their songs would raise,
And celebrate his power and love
  In never-ceasing praise!

Sir Grand gives four raps and all stand; he then says:—We have assembled at this hour to install the officers of Palatium, No. —, of the Royal House of Media. So important is the business which we are about to transact, that before we go any further, it is necessary to dedicate the work to God, our Ruler and Preserver, and ask his guidance and blessing upon the Palatium and its officers. Prince Clericus will favor us by addressing Him who sits on the throne of great grace. Palatine Guards and Knights, uncover!

Prayer by Prince Clericus.

Prince Clericus:—Holy and Divine Father, it is Thou that controls and rules in the world of mankind; Thou art the Supreme Dispenser of every good and perfect gift. We come, asking and pleading that Thou wouldst in mercy bless and protect the Royal House of Media. Grant unto us wisdom, that we may conduct the business of this Palatium in a manner that all its membership may be drawn to serve Thee and bless Thy holy name; breathe into our hearts Thy life-giving word, and save us with an everlasting salvation. Guide us in our counsels, shield us by Thy love. Thou Prince and Savior, bless·the nations, comfort the widows, care for the orphans, and receive us all into Thy favor. This is our prayer, and will be now, henceforth and forever. Amen!

Response by all the members:—May the Lord bless the Palatium!

Sir Grand:—Palatine Guards and Sir Knights, cover! (Gives one rap and all are seated.)

Music; or the following hymn is sung:

C. M.

I.

Eternal Sovereign of the sky,
  And Lord of all below,
We mortals to Thy majesty
  Our first obedience owe.

II.

Our souls adore Thy throne supreme,
  And bless Thy providence
For magistrates of meaner name,
  Our glory and defense.

III.

The acts of pious rulers shine
  With rays above the rest;
Where laws and liberties combine,
  The people are made blest.

Prince Marshal to Sir Grand:—I have the honor of presenting to you Prince —— —— ——, who has been elected Presiding Prince of —— Palatium, No. ——, and is now ready to be installed.

INSTRUCTIONS TO THE PRESIDING PRINCE.

Sir Grand:—Sir Prince, you have been elected by the members of your Palatium to preside over its important work. I place in your hands the charter—that makes —— Palatium, No. ——, a legal body. It must be present when the Palatium is open for business. You will carefully guard it as a sacred power. I present to you the Constitution of the Palatium, and the Laws of the International Grand Temple and Tabernacle, and of the Grand Temple and Tabernacle. It is your duty to have these Laws enforced in your Palatium. I present to you this sword, with the hilt in your hand. You are to teach the Royal Palatine Guards how to use it in the defense of their country when assailed by an enemy, and to protect the innocent. I now invest you with the Jewel of your office. Be an example to the Princes and Princesses. Sir Prince Marshal, please seat the Presiding Prince.

Prince Marshal:—Sir Grand, I have the honor of presenting to you Princess —— —— ——, who has been elected Vice-Princess of —— Palatium, No. —, and is now ready to be installed.

INSTRUCTIONS TO THE VICE-PRINCESS.

Sir Grand:—Princess, I take pleasure in saying to you that the members of the Palatium have expressed their confidence in your ability by electing you to the important office of Vice-Princess. Your duty is to assist the Presiding Prince by counsel and advice in his several duties. You shall preside during his absence from his seat. I now invest you with the Jewel of your office. May you attend to your duties punctually. Prince Marshal, you will please seat the Vice-Princess.

Prince Marshal:—Sir Grand, I now present to you Prince —— —— ——, who has been elected Recording Prince of —— Palatium, No. —. He is ready to be installed.

INSTRUCTIONS TO THE RECORDING PRINCE.

Sir Grand:—Sir Prince, you have been elected to the position of Recording Prince by the members of the Palatium. It is your duty to be present at every meeting of the Palatium, and record the business. You must keep a roll-book, and en-

roll the names of every member. You are to make
a quarterly report to the C. G. M. on the condition
of the Palatium, receive all moneys paid into the
Palatium, and draw all warrants for money on
Prince Banker, and see that they are properly signed
by the Presiding Officer, and countersigned by
yourself. Pay all moneys that you receive for the
Palatium to Prince Banker, and take his receipt
therefor. You are the corresponding officer of the
Palatium. I now invest you with the Jewel of
your office. Be careful in your business. Prince
Marshal, please seat the Recording Prince.

Prince Marshal:—Sir Grand, I take pleasure in
introducing Princess —— —— ——, who has been
elected Assistant Princess of —— Palatium, No.
—, and is now ready for installation.

INSTRUCTIONS TO THE ASSISTANT PRINCESS.

Sir Grand:—Princess, I congratulate you on the
honorable position which you have attained. It is
your duty to assist the Recording Prince in his several duties, and to attend to his business during his
absence. I now invest you with the Jewel of your
office. May you have good success. Prince Marshal, you will please seat the Assistant Princess.

Prince Marshal:—Sir Grand, I have the honor of
presenting to you Prince —— —— ——, who has
been elected Prince Banker of —— Palatium,
No. —. He is now ready to be installed.

INSTRUCTIONS TO PRINCE BANKER.

Sir Grand:—Sir Prince, by the suffrage of the
members of this Palatium, you are called to the
very important position of Prince Banker. It is

your duty to receive all moneys and valuables which are the property of the Palatium, and pay all warrants drawn on the Bank when they are signed by the P. P. and countersigned by the R. P. You must make a report to the Palatium of the condition of the Bank, when requested by the Presiding Officer. You must make a written statement to your successor of the condition of the Bank, and turn over to him all the moneys, valuables, books and other property belonging to the Palatium when he is installed. I now invest you with the Jewel of your office. Be true to your trust. Prince Marshal, please seat Prince Banker.

Prince Marshal:—Sir Grand, I have the pleasure of introducing to you Princess —— —— ——, who has been elected Princess Nonna of ——— Palatium, No. —, and is now ready for installation.

INSTRUCTIONS TO PRINCESS NONNA.

Sir Grand:—Princess, I congratulate you on the very responsible office that the Palatium members have entrusted to your care. The office requires that you should promptly attend all meetings, and be thoroughly versed in the Ritualistic work. I now present to you the Jewel of your office. Be active in your duties. Prince Marshall, please seat Princess Nonna.

Prince Marshal:—Sir Grand, I have the honor of presenting to you Prince —— —— ——, he having been elected Prince Clericus by ——— Palatium, No. —. He is now ready to be installed.

7—Dicksons' New Manual.)

INSTRUCTIONS TO PRINCE CLERICUS.

Sir Grand:—Sir Prince, you have been honored by the members of the Palatium by their electing you to the high office of Prince Clericus. It is your duty to conduct the devotional exercises of the Palatium, visit the sick or distressed Princes or Princesses, and to perform the funeral ceremonies of the Palatium. I now present to you the Jewel of your office. May you be well instructed in the Holy Scriptures. Prince Marshal, you will please seat Prince Clericus.

Prince Marshal:—Sir Grand, I have the pleasure of introducing to you Princess —— —— ——, who has been elected Princess Revista of —— Palatium, No—, and is now ready to be installed.

INSTRUCTIONS TO PRINCESS REVISTA.

Sir Grand:—Princess, the office to which you have been elected is one that requires your closest attention. Your duty is fully explained in the Ritual. I advise you to carefully study your part, so that you may be qualified in the business of your office. I now invest you with the Jewel of your office. May you honorably perform your duty. Prince Marshal, please seat Princess Revista.

Prince Marshal:—Sir Grand, I have the honor of presenting to you Prince —— —— ——, who has been elected Prince Marshal of —— Palatium, No. —. He is now ready to be installed.

INSTRUCTIONS TO PRINCE MARSHAL.

Sir Grand:—Sir Prince, it is with pleasure I hear that the members of the Palatium have elected you as Prince Marshal. It is your duty to instruct the Palatine Guards in the march, drill and the sword exercises, and conduct all public turn-outs of the Palatine Guards. Your station is to guard the inner door during the Session of the Palatium. I now present to you the Jewel of your office and this sword. You will find need for it in your duties. Be courageous. Prince Marshal, please seat the elected Prince Marshal.

Prince Marshal:—Sir Grand, I have the honor of presenting to you Prince —— —— ——, who has been elected Prince Gonfalonier of ——— Palatium, No.—. He is now ready to be installed.

INSTRUCTIONS TO PRINCE GONFALONIER.

Sir Grand:—Sir Prince, the members of the Palatium have conferred on you the honorable duty of unfurling and carrying the Royal Banner of the Royal House of Media. It is your duty to guard the Gonfalon, and defend it in time of danger. I now invest you with the Jewel of your office and place in your care the Gonfalon of the Palatium. Prince Marshal, please seat Prince Gonfalonier.

Prince Marshal:—Sir Grand, I take pleasure in introducing to you Princess —— —— ——, who has been elected as Princess Sentina, and is now ready to be installed.

INSTRUCTIONS TO PRINCESS SENTINA.

Sir Grand:—Princess, you have been honored by the members of the Palatium by their electing you to the very important office of Princess Sentina. It is your duty to guard the inner entrance of the Palatium during the hours of the Sessions. Your further duties you will find in the Ritual. I now invest you with the Jewel of your office, and the Poniard of defense. Be prompt to every duty. Prince Marshal, please seat Princess Sentina.

Prince Marshall:—Sir Grand, I have the pleasure of introducing to you Prince —— —— ——, who has been elected Prince Wardship. He is now ready to be installed.

INSTRUCTIONS TO PRINCE WARDSHIP.

Sir Grand:—Sir Prince, you have been elected Prince Wardship by the members of the Palatium. It is a responsible office, and in entrusting you with the position, the members have shown their confidence in your integrity and ability. Your station is at the outer post; you are to guard the entrance, and report all who desire admittance. I now invest you with the Jewel of your office, and present to you this sword; use it in defense of your position; may you perform your duties with honor. Prince Marshal, please seat Prince Wardship.

Sir Grand gives four raps, and all stand, except the newly installed officers. Prince Marshal forms a procession of the Palatine Guards, Princesses, Uniform Rank Knights and Priestesses (if there is room) who march four times around the hall, while the band is playing, or while some familiar hymn is sung.

At the conclusion of the fourth round, the Prince Marshal forms a circle around the installed officers—the Palatine Guards and the Princesses in the inner circle, and the Uniform Rank Knights and Priestesses on the outer circle.

Prince Marshal:—Palatine Guards and Uniform Rank Knights, Handle Swords! Draw Swords!! Present Swords!!! Princesses, Handle Poniards! Draw Poniards!! Present Poniards!!!

Sir Grand:—By virtue of the authority in me vested as Installing Officer, I now and here announce that the officers of———Palatium, No.—,' are duly installed and ready to perform the duties of their several offices for the ensuing Palatium year.

Prince Marshal:—Salute the installed officers. (The salute with swords and poniards is given four times.) Carry Swords! Return Swords and Poniards!!

The P. P. or V.-P. (while all the officers stand) says:—By virtue of the authority in me vested, I announce that ———Palatium, No.—, is at rest from work. Members of the Temples, Tabernacles and Palatiums, I thank you for your assistance. You are now disbanded.

Music or singing, after which addresses may be delivered, followed by a drill and march.

FUNERAL CEREMONY

—— : OF THE : ——

PALATINE GUARDS.

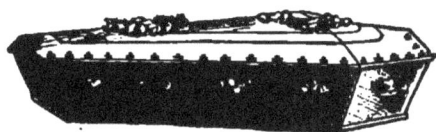

198

BURIAL CEREMONY

OF THE

PALATINE GUARDS.

————:o:————

INSTRUCTIONS.

1.—A Palatine Guard, to be enterred with the full honors, must be a member of the Uniform Rank, and in good standing in the Palatium.

2.—At the summons of the Presiding Prince, the Palatine Guards assemble to prepare for the interment.

3.—The Guards must attend in full uniform, with their sword hilts and banner draped in mourning,, the officers wearing their Jewels.

4.—On the day on which the remains are to be interred, the Guards shall assemble in their hall, and march to the residence, or wherever the remains are, in Palatine order. The sword and chapeau is borne in the rear of the P. P. On arriving at the place were the remains are, the lines are opened to the right and left, the pall-bearers pass through the lines, and place the sword and chapeau on the casket. The pall-bearers (Palatine Guards) take the casket, and, conducted by Prince Wardship pass through the lines and place it in the hearse.

5.—The procession is then formed by Prince Marshal and his Assistant Marshals, whereupon they march to the church or place where the services are to be held, in the following order:

Prince Wardship (on Foot or Horse).

Music.

Other Societies or Orders (Men).

Uniform Rank (Knights).

Palatine Guards.

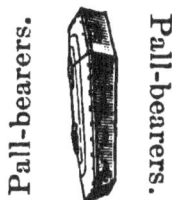

Pall-bearers. Pall-bearers.

Family (in Carriages).

Princesses (in Carriages).

Priestesses (in Carriages).

Grand and Past Grand Officers.

Citizens (in Carriages).

6.—After arriving at the church, the Palatine Guards and Knights shall enter in reversed order, preceding the casket, followed by the Princesses, Priestesses and Grand Officers.

7.—The P. P. shall preside during the ceremony, assisted by Prince Clericus. After the sermon, the Uniform Rank Knights open with their burial ceremony, which is followed by the Palatine Guards. The members of the order stand during prayer and the ceremonies.

8.—While the remains are lying in state, there shall be either two Uniform Rank Knights or two Palatine Guards on duty.

9.—The march to the cemetery shall be in the same order as the march to the church was. When the head of the procession arrives at the place of interment, the P. P., preceded by the P. M., pass through, followed by the Uniform Rank Knights and then by the other orders. On arriving at the grave or vault, they open. ranks, and the casket is conveyed through to the grave, and placed over the tomb. A circle is then formed around the casket, with the family at the foot and the P. P., P. C., C. M., C. O., and clergy at the head, the Uniform Rank Knights then form the inner circle and perform their part of the ceremony without lowering the casket. When they have finished, the Palatine Guards take the inner circle, and they finish the ceremony.

10.—The face of the deceased should be uncovered during the ceremony in the church, if thought proper.

11.—The funeral procession shall return from the cemetery to the place of disbandment in the same order in which it was originally formed. The P. P., on arriving at the place of disbandment, shall declare the Palatium at rest.

12.—Princesses and Priestesses shall wear their Badges of membership, and officers their Jewels of office, or full dress, if all the members decide to appear in full regalia.

CEREMONY IN THE CHURCH.

After the sermon and church services, and after
the Uniform Rank Knights have performed their
part of the church ceremony and are seated, the P.
P. commands, in a low voice:—Guards, Stand and
Uncover! *The Guards fold their arms, with
chapeaus resting on their left arms.

Presiding Prince:—Palatine Guards, we are sad
to-day; our ranks have been broken; a true and
trusted Guard has passed through the gates of
death; Prince ——— is no more of earth; he received the summons that must be obeyed; kind and
loving arms could not keep him here; our swords,
so ready to be wielded in defence of every Palatine
Guard, remain in their scabbards, our blades could
not shield him in that dreadful hour, nor defend him
in his struggle with death.   Prince ——— has
passed the portals, and we to-day mourn his demise.
The Royal House of Media will no more hear his
Princely voice.   He is silent; he is wrapped in lifeless mortality; he will never meet the Guards again
in the Palatine.   His hand will never wield his
sword.   His feet will never tread the earth again
in the royal march and drill; all that remains of
Brother Prince and Guard is his lifeless body
stilled in the embrace of death.   Palatine Guards,
Cover!   Let us reverently attend to the lessons of
the Sacred Scriptures.

Prince Clericus:—In my distress, I called upon
the Lord and cried unto my God.   He heard my
voice, and my cry came before Him.   I will rejoice
in Thy mercy!

Response:—Hear us, Lord, and in mercy save us.

P. C.:—The Lord will give strength unto His people; we trust in Thee, O Lord; shine upon Thy servants.

Res.:—Hear, O Lord, have mercy upon us.

P. C.:—God is our refuge and strength, an ever present help in trouble.

Res.:—Lord, remember us in love and mercy.

P. C.:—Help us, O God, of our salvation, for the glory of Thy name, and deliver us and purge away our sins, for Thy name's sake.

Res.:—Lord, let Thy tender mercies remain with us.

P. C.:—Teach us to number our days, that we may apply our hearts to wisdom.

Res.:—Bless the Lord, oh my soul.

P. C.:—Praise ye the Lord, O give thanks unto the Lord, for He is good; His mercy endureth forever.

Res.:—Save us, O Lord, we praise Thee, our Savior.

P. C.:—Teach us, O Lord, to do They will, for Thou art our God; lead us in the land of the upright.

Res.:—Deliver us, O Lord, and we will praise Thy holy name.

P. P.:—One by one we pass from earth. Shall we remember our Princely Brother?

Res.:—We will revere his name and his many virtues.

P. P.:—Shall his name be recorded in the Palatium?

Res.:—The record is made. It is written here, (hand on heart).

P. P.:—He was loved and respected; may he be enrolled in the heavenly land.

Res.:—May he rest in the never-fading light of glory.

The following is then sung:

C. M.

I.

Teach me the measure of my days.
  Thou maker of my frame:
I would survey life's narrow space,
  And learn how frail I am.

II.

A span is all that we can boast,
  An inch or two of time;
Man is but vanity and dust,
  In all his flower and prime.

III.

What shall I wish, or wait for then, .
  From creatures, earth and dust?
They make our expectations vain,
  And disappoint our trust.

IV.

Now I forbid my carnal hope,
  My fond desires recall;
I give my mortal interest up,
  And make my God my all.

Whereupon the following prayer is read by Prince Clericus:

PRAYER.

Our Heavenly Father, in the name of Jesus, our Redeemer, in our sorrow we come unto Thee. Thou art the heart's comforter, in mercy hear us. We thank Thee for Thy providential care over us during our past life. Oh let the light of Thy divine countenance shine within us at this hour. We know that Thou hearest our prayer. Death has entered our ranks. A Brother has passed through the dark valley. We mourn his departure. We humbly beseach Thee to give consolation to the bereaved friends and relatives, and teach us, who are assembled here, that we are but mortal, that we are frail, and that our days on earth are uncertain. O Lord, draw us unto Thee, that we may apply our hearts to holy wisdom, which will in the end bring us to a life of eternal joy and happiness, through the merits of Thy Only Son, Jesus Christ, our Redeemer. Amen! Amen!!

Response:—The Lord is merciful, and will hear our prayer!

P. P.:—Princes, Handle Swords! Draw Swords!! Present Swords!!! Sir Princes of the Palatine Guards, we are here to pay our last respects to a Prince Palatine. All that remains of Prince ——— lies before us, wrapped in the cold embrace of death. He will never meet us again in our pleasant Palatium; his seat is vacant; his voice, which mingled with ours in the Royal House of Media, is silent. When the command is given to *Fall in, Guards*, his absence will be felt; no more will he respond to his number at the call of the Prince Marshal; his sword, which he was ever ready to draw at the command, his hand will grasp it no more; the Guards that were ready at all times to defend him with their swords, and to protect him in the time of danger by a wall of steel, were impotent when the enemy—Death—claimed him; our

blades of steel could not shield our Princely Palatine; the guarded doors of our Palatium could not
prevent the entrance of the "grim slayer;" the loving hands of the Princesses of Media would have
held their Princely Brother to the earth, but smiles
and tears could not retain him, nor prevent the cold
touch of death to the silent rest we have brought
him; he sleeps with the unnumbered multitude;
camly he passed into the regions of the dead; may
he find that rest which is given to the believer in the
Presiding Prince of the Heavenly Land; may the
Son and Savior give him a place in the paradise
of bliss, and exchange his earthly armor for the
royal robes of eternal light; this sad and sorrowful circle tells how well we loved our Prince Palatine; with him we cannot again meet on earth; he
is gone, to return no more; we will remember his
many good qualities, and over his faults cast the
mantle of forgetfulness.   Princes and Princesses of
the Royal House of Media, one by one we must pass
from earth; our names will be dropped from the
roll-books of the Palatium; may we so live that
our names will be enrolled in the Lamb's Book of
Life; that when the chill of death clogs our blood,
and our hearts cease to respond to the call of life,
our unfettered souls will have clear passports into
the realms of eternal bliss and happiness.

After the usual custom of reviewing the body has
been observed by the congregation, Palatine Guards,
Uniform Rank Knights, Princesses and Priestesses,
the procession will then form and march to the
place of interment.   After the Uniform Rank
Knights have finished their ceremony, the Pala-

tine Guards form a perfect circle around the casket,
with the P. P. and P. C. at the head, and the family of the departed at the foot of the grave.

P. P.:—Palatine Guards, salute Prince Palatine
for the last time.   (Four salutes are given.)

If there is room, the Prince forms the Palatine
Guards in single file, and marches them around the
casket four times, each touching the head of the
casket with the point of his sword every time he
goes around, and says, *Farewell.*

Music; or the following hymn is sung:

C. M.

I.

Thy mighty arm!   O God, was nigh
  When we our foes assailed;
'Tis Thou hast raised our honors high,
  And o'er their host prevailed.

II.

The thund'ring horse, the martial band,
  Without Thine aid were vain;
And vict'ry flies at Thy command
  To crown the bright campaign.

III.

Their mounds, their camps, their lofty towers,
  Into our hands are given;
Not from desert or strength of ours,
  But through the grace of Heaven.

IV.

The faithful tablet of our heart
  These mercies shall record,
And never thence shall they depart,
  Nor we forget the Lord.

V.

To our young race will we proclaim
  The mercies God has shown;
That they may learn to bless His name,
  And choose Him for their own.

VI.

Thus, while we sleep in silent dust,
When threat'ning dangers come,
Their fathers' God shall be their trust,
Their refuge, and their home.

After the circle is formed, Prince Marshal gives the command to reverse swords and uncover. (The Guards stand with folded arms, their chapeaus resting on their right arms over the hilts of their swords.) The Prince Marshal removes the chapeau and sword from the casket, whereupon it is lowered into the grave.

The Prince Marshal points the deceased Prince's sword over the grave, and says:—Sir Princes, this is an emblem of defense and attack. Our deceased Palatine Brother was instructed that with the hilt in his hand he was to defend the innocent and protect the weak, and be true to every trust. The sword is a symbol of the Sword of the Spirit. He who possesses that symbolized sword has the pass into the holy presence of the Master Commander of Heaven and Earth. May the spiritual sword of love permit us to meet our Palatine Brother in the Heavenly Mansions.

Prince Marshal:—Palatine Guards, Cover! Return Swords!! Hear and Assist Prince Clericus!!!

P. C.:—I am the resurrection and the life. He that believeth in Me, though he were dead, yet shall he live. Whosoever liveth and believeth in Me, shall never die. To the earth we commit the mortal remains of our deceased Brother. May his soul rest in peace, Earth to earth, (*Cast earth*

on the casket.) Dust to dust. (*Cast again.*)
Ashes to ashes. (*Cast again.*) Until the morn
of the resurrection, when, like our risen Lord and
Savior, may he break every chain and bond of
death, and ascend to dwell forever in the sunshine
of heavenly beams.

Response:—*In Solo Deo Salus!*

The P. M. gives the command to uncover (the
Guards stand with folded arms and bowed heads.)

PRAYER.

Our Father which art in Heaven, hallowed be
Thy name. Thy kingdom come. Thy will be done
in earth as it is in heaven. Give us this day our
daily bread; and forgive us our trespasses as we
forgive those who trespass against us. Lead us
not into temptation, but deliver us from evil. For
Thine is the kingdom, and the power, and the
glory, forever. Amen!

Response:—Amen! Amen!! Amen!!!

P. M.:—Palatine Guards, Cover!

Prince Clericus, or a clergyman, gives the benediction. The lines are formed and they march
back to the hall, or the P. P. announces the Palatium at rest, and they disperse.

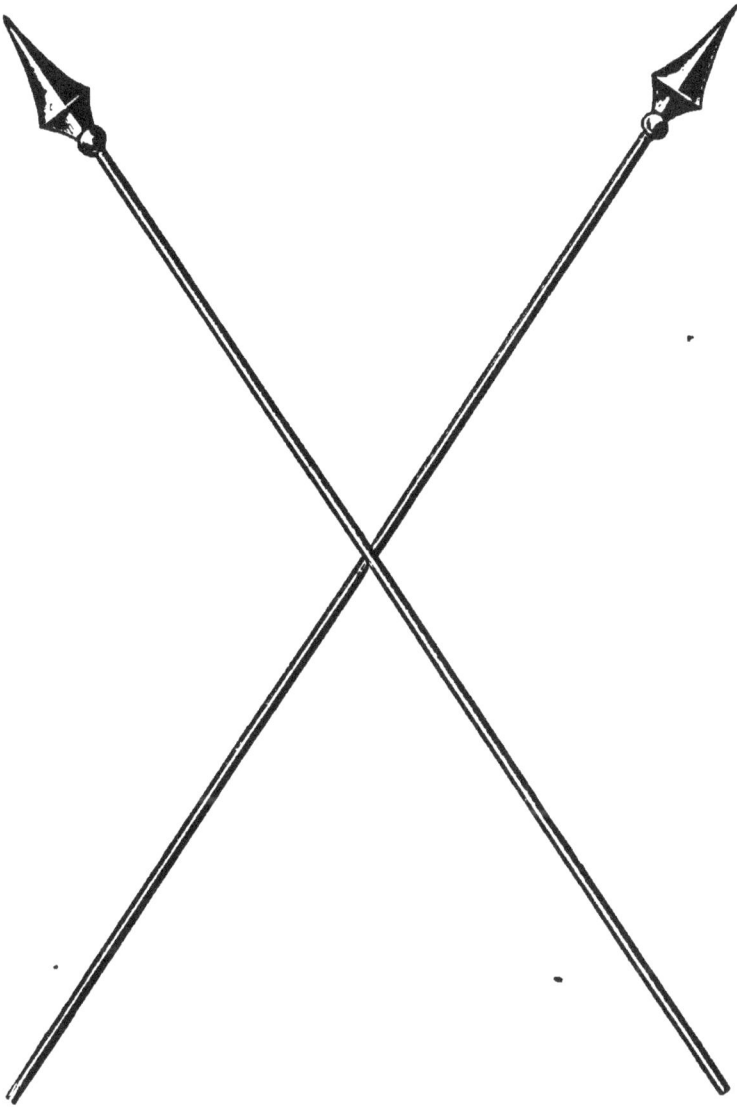

TABORIAN CADET JAVELINS.

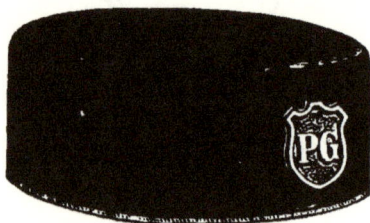

CAPS OF UNIFORM RANK KNIGHTS, PALATINE GUARDS AND TABORIAN CADETS.

General Laws

TENTS OF MAIDS

AND

PAGES OF HONOR.

212

GENERAL LAWS

GOVERNING

TENTS OF MAIDS AND PAGES OF HONOR.

————:o:————

INSTRUCTIONS.

1.—The membership of Tents shall consist of children ranging from the ages of six months to eighteen years.

2.—A Girl must join a Tabernacle when she arrives at the age of sixteen years. She cannot remain a member of the Tent after that age.

3.—A Boy must join a Temple when he becomes eighteen years of age. He cannot remain a member of the Tent after that age.

4.—The only adult members of a Tent shall be the Queen Mother, Vice-Queen Mother, and Father of the Tent; and they, to hold these offices, must be members in good standing in their respective Tabernacles or Temples.

5.—The Grand Temple and Tabernacle shall frame a Constitution for the government of Tents.

6.—The Boys of the Tent shall be known as Taborian Cadets.

7.—The Tent is one of the four departments in the International Order of Twelve. It is governed

213

by its own laws, and is subject to neither the Temple nor the Tabernacle Constitutions.

8.—The Queen Mother shall have full control or management of the Tent, and will be held accountable to the Grand Body, under which its charter is held, for the manner in which she administers the laws.

9.—The Queen Mother shall represent her Tent in the Grand Session, and make a full report of the work and business during the previous Tent year.

10.—Tents shall elect their own officers. After a Maid or Page moves to place a candidate in nomination—and being duly seconded—a standing vote is taken, and a majority of the votes given will elect. The Queen Mother, assisted by the Father of the Tent, shall conduct the election.

11.—The Tent has no secret degrees. The only secrets being the Password and Saluting Sign.

12.—When a Maid arrives at the age of sixteen years, she choses the Tabernacle which she desires to join. The Queen Mother gives her a transfer, recommending her to the Tabernacle which she desires to join, giving her age and stating how long she has been a member of the Tent, and shall certify as to her moral character, good deportment, and that she is in perfect health. A Tabernacle shall not receive a member from any Tent, unless acceptable as regards morality and good deportment, and is in perfect health.

13.—When a Taborian Cadet arrives at the age of eighteen years, he must choose the Temple which he desires to join. The Queen Mother gives him a transfer, stating how long he has been a member of the Tent, recommending him, giving his age, deportment, and general health. A Temple shall not receive a member from a Tent, unless his deportment is good, and he is in sound health.

14.—A Maid cannot remain a member of a Tent after she becomes sixteen years of age. A Taborian Cadet cannot remain a Page in the Tent after he arrives at the age of eighteen years.

15.—The Tabernacle to which the Maid is transferred, must confer all the degrees upon her, and enroll her name. (The Maid shall pay one dollar when her name is enrolled.)

16.—The Temple to which the Page is transferred, shall give him all the degrees. (He shall pay one dollar on being enrolled.)

———: o :———

GENERAL LAWS.

ARTICLE I.

REGALIA.

SECTION 1.—The regalia of the Maids shall consist of a white dress; white gloves; a pink sash, four inches wide, worn from either right or left shoulder; a wreath of leaves and flowers for head-wear, and a Tent badge.

SEC. 2.—The Taborian Cadets shall be neatly dressed in dark blue suits; knee pants and scarlet stockings; coat buttoned up in front; brown gloves; scarlet belt; Tent badge, to be worn on left breast; iron or tin-pointed javelin, five feet long, one inch and a half in thickness, of scarlet color; black cadet cap, with silver band, and letters T. C. thereon.

ARTICLE II.

SECTION 1.—The banner shall be two by three feet, one side deep scarlet, with the name of the city and State thereon. The other side light green, with the name and number of the Tent. The banner is trimmed with silver lace and fringe.

ARTICLE III.

SECTION 1.—The regalia of the Queen Mother shall be a white dress and a dark pink robe, en-train; a golden coronet, ornamented with white stones; pink gloves; emerald green belt, with silver clasps, and figures 333; a scepter, made to suit the taste. When she does not wear the robe, the regalia is an emerald green collar, trimmed with twelve silver stars and silver lace, and the letters Q. M. thereon.

SEC. 2.—The Vice-Queen Mother wears the same, excepting the robe and scepter.

SEC. 3.—The Father of the Tent shall wear the Uniform Rank dress and regalia.

ARTICLE IV.

SECTION 1.—The officers of the Tent may be installed by any Past Q. M., Grand Deputy, or G. Q. M.

SEC. 2.—The manner of installing is as follows: All the officers are seated in their proper stations. Their individual duties are read to them from the Constitution, commencing with the Queen Mother, and so on until all the officers are installed. When this is finished, the Installing Officer calls up all those present, except the officers who have just been installed; he then declares the officers installed, and all give the twelve claps—four times three.

SEC. 3.—At the conclusion of the installing ceremony, the Taborian Cadets may drill, or have other exercises, under the orders of the Queen Mother. Every Page over the age of six years is a Cadet. The Father of the Tent is required to give full instructions to the Tent Marshal in the drill and march.

ARTICLE V.

SECTION 1.—The Queen Mother must carefully instruct the children in deportment and politeness, and teach them to respect persons older than themselves, to love the members of the Tent, and to meet at the Sessions of the Tent punctually at the appointed hour.

SEC. 2.—The Queen Mother must not permit noisy and unruly children to remain members of the Tent. The Queen Mother has the authority to admit and enroll as many children in her Tent as she desires. She must have the Constitution and By-Laws read in open session at least once in every quarter.

SEC. 3.—The Queen Mother must report quarterly the condition of her Tent to the Grand Queen Mother, as also the number of members.

SEC. 4.—Every new member is introduced to the Tent, and received with twelve claps—four times three—and instructed in the Password and Saluting Sign, and impressed that they shall keep them secret from all who are not members of the Tent.

ARTICLE VI.

SECTION 1.—The Queen Mother shall be the Treasurer of the Tent. She shall receive all moneys and valuables belonging to the Tent, and shall report monthly, at a regular meeting of the Tent, the amount of money received and paid out during the month.

SEC. 2.—The Vice-Queen Mother shall receive all money paid into the Tent, and account for it in a book kept for that purpose. She shall also keep an account of all money drawn from the Treasurer.

SEC. 3.—Money can only be drawn from the Treasurer on a warrant signed by the V.-Q. M., and countersigned by the C. R. K.

FORM OF THE TENT.

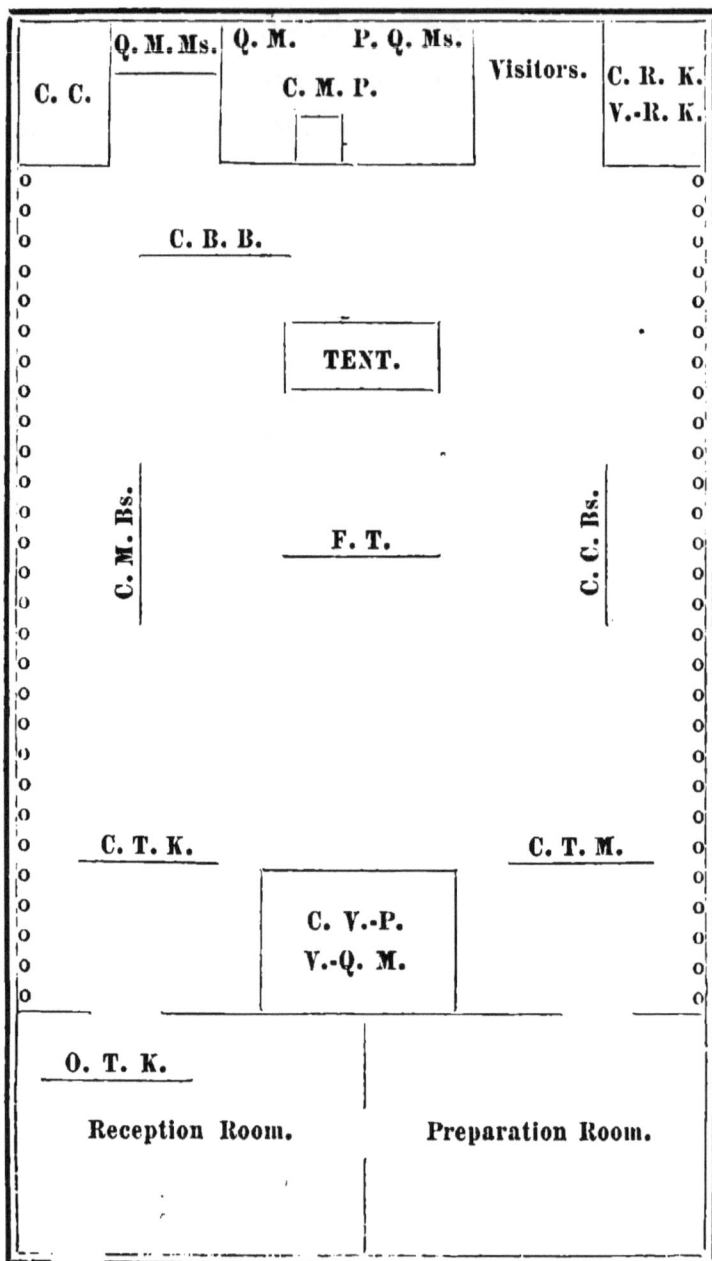

C. C.	**Q. M. Ms.**	**Q. M.**	**P. Q. Ms.**	**Visitors.**	**C. R. K.**
		C. M. P.			**V.-R. K.**

C. B. B.

TENT.

C. M. Bs.

F. T.

C. C. Bs.

C. T. K.

C. T. M.

C. V.-P.
V.-Q. M.

O. T. K.

Reception Room.

Preparation Room.

MAIDS AND PAGES

THE TENT BADGE.

220

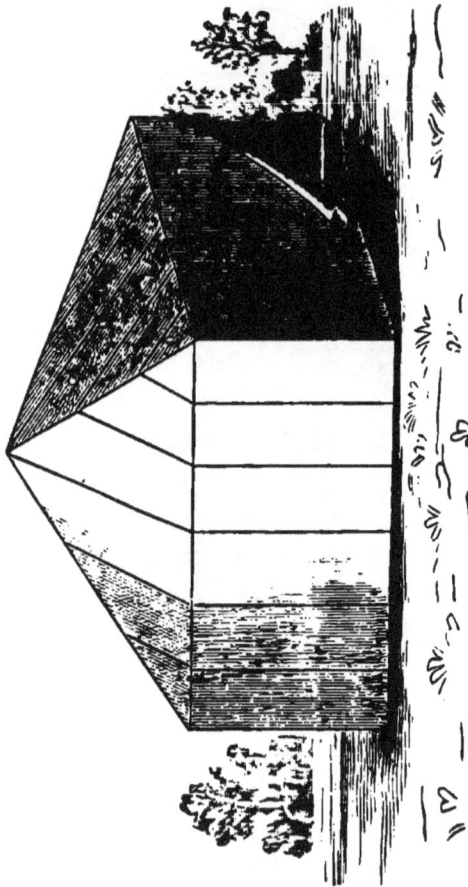

THE TENT HOUSE.

221

OFFICERS OF THE TENT.

1.—Queen Mother (Adult)............Q. M.
2.—Vice-Queen Mother (Adult)......V.-Q. M.
3.—Father of the Tent (Adult).......F. O. T.
4.—Chief Maid Presiding (Girl)......C. M. P.
5.—Chief Page Vice (Boy)..........C. P. V.
6.—Chief Record Keeper (Girl)......C. R. K.
7.—Vice-Record Keeper (Boy).......V.-R. K.
8.—Chief of the Chest (Girl)........C. O. C.
9.—Chief Tent Marshal (Boy).......C. T. M.
10.—Chief Banner Bearer (Boy)......C. B. B.
11.—Chief Cup Bearer (Girl).........C. C. B.
12.—Chief Cup Bearer (Girl).........C. C. B.
13.—Chief Cup Bearer (Girl).........C. C. B.
14.—Chief Mace Bearer (Boy)........C. M. B.
15.—Chief Mace Bearer (Boy).......C. M. B.
16.—Chief Mace Bearer (Boy)........C. M. B.
17.—Chief Tent Keeper (Girl)........C. T. K.
18.—Outer Tent Keeper (Boy)........O. T. K.
19.—Queen Mother's Messenger (Girl).Q. M. M.
20.—Queen Mother's Messenger (Boy).Q. M. M.

GENERAL REGULATIONS.

1.—The Queen Mother shall represent her Tent at the Grand Session of the Grand Temple and Tabernacle, and at the Triennial Grand Session.

2.—The Tent is a department in the International Order of Twelve, and the government of the Tent is under the control of the Queen Mother. She is responsible for any violation of the laws of the Order.

3.—The Taborian Cadets shall be commanded by the Chief Tent Marshal. He must instruct them in the drill and march. The Cadets must drill regularly.

4.—The Queen Mother shall instruct the Maids and Pages in mannerly behavior, the use of polite language, obedience* to parents, teachers and elderly persons, enforce cleanliness in dress and person, and inculcate a love for home and the Order.

5.—A Tent may make its own By-Laws, but they shall not conflict with the Constitution. The By-Laws may regulate the fees for membership, the monthly dues, the sick dues and burial benefits, and the day and hour of the regular meetings.

6.—Queen Mothers will be held responsible should they fail to enforce the general laws respecting Tents. All Tents must have precisely the same kind of dress, regalia and badges as the General Laws direct.

FUNERAL CEREMONY

OF

TENTS

OF

MAIDS AND PAGES OF HONOR.

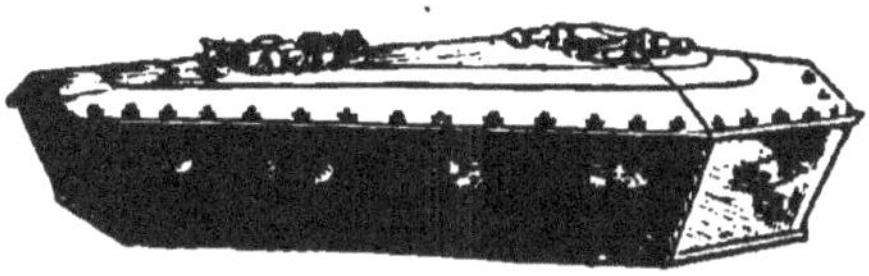

FUNERAL CEREMONIES

OF

TENTS OF MAIDS AND PAGES OF HONOR.

——: o :——

INSTRUCTIONS.

When the death of a member of the Tent is reported to the Queen Mother, it is her first duty to consult the parents or guardians of the child regarding the arrangements for the funeral. The Tent is not expected to pay the entire expense; it pays only the sum allowed by the By-Laws of the Tent. If the parents desire to have the child buried according to the ceremonies of the Tent, the Queen Mother proceeds to make all the needed preparation. The members of the Tent are called to meet, the children instructed, and other Tents are invited to attend.

THE FUNERAL DRESS.

The dress of the Maids shall be black, with a small white collar; on the left breast they shall wear the Badge of the Tent; on their heads a wreath of white flowers is placed, and white gloves are worn.

The Taborian Cadets shall wear the regulation dress, cap and white gloves; their javelins have a crape bow near the spear.

(8—Dickson's New Manual.)   225

The Queen Mother shall wear the Tabernacle funeral dress and her Jewel of office; her scepter is to be craped.

The Vice-Queen Mother shall wear the Tabernacle dress and her Jewel of office.

The Father of the Tent shall wear a black suit, white gloves, and his Jewel of office.

The Pall-bearers—either Maids or Cadets—shall wear, in addition to their other dress, white sashes.

The Banner of the Tent shall be trimmed with white and black crape.

THE MARCH.

The Maids and Pages shall assemble at a designated place near the residence of their deceased member, and form in line of march, as follows:

Tent Marshal

Father of Tent.
Queen Mother and Vice-Queen Mother.
Cadets, by twos.
Banner.
Maids, by twos.

Pall-bearers.   Pall-bearers.

Family, in Carriages.
Citizens, in Carriages.

The Knights and Daughters will show their respects by wearing their Jewels or Badges during the ceremony.

Ceremony at the Church.

If the remains are conveyed to a church, when the procession arrives there the lines are opened, and the casket is conducted by the Father of the Tent to the door of the church, where the minister meets it. They then enter in the following order:

Minister and Father of the Tent.

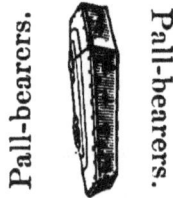

Pall-bearers.   Pall-bearers.

Family.

Queen Mother and Vice-Queen Mother.

Maids, by twos.

Cadets, by twos.

When the casket is rested, the C. M. P. sits at the head of casket, and the C. P. V. at the foot. The Q. M., V.-Q. M. and F. of T. in front of the altar, and the Maids and Pages in the rear of the family

The minister then opens the services, and preaches the sermon. After which the Queen Mother or Father reads the following (all stand):

Maids and Pages, we assemble at this hour, in obedience to a solemn duty which we owe to the memory of one who was a loving member of ——— Tent, No. —. We mourn the loss of a near and dear child. A golden link in the chain that formed around our Tent is broken, and a precious name is transferred from our roll-book to the roll-call in the Land of Eternal Bliss. Children of Tabor, we who are in life now are reminded that, though young in years, we may be called away at any hour. Let us trust and have faith in God, our Savior. To-day we bid farewell to (give the name), and pray that it may be our happy lot to meet her (or him) in the Paradise of Eternal Rest. Mothers, Fathers, Brothers and Sisters, remember that one by one we depart from earth. Let us pray to our Heavenly Father, that he may unite all the family in the Kingdom of Heaven, where there will be no more separation.

The following is then sung by the Maids and Pages:

"When blooming youth is snatched away."

I.

When blooming youth is snatched away
  By death's resistless hand,
Our hearts the mournful tribute pay
  Which pity must demand.

II.

While pity prompts the rising sigh,
  Oh, may this truth, impressed
With awful power, "I, too, must die,"
  Sink deep in every breast!

III.

Let this vain world engage no more:
  Behold the opening tomb!
It bids us seize the present hour;
  To-morrow, death may come.

IV.

Oh, let us fly—to Jesus fly!
  Whose powerful arm can save;
Then shall our hopes ascend on high,
  And triumph o'er the grave!

v.

Great God! Thy sovereign grace impart,
  With cleansing, healing power;
This only can prepare the heart
  For death's surprising hour.

The Queen Mother then gives one rap, and all are seated.

The Chief Record Keeper reads from the record of the Tent the name and age of the deceased, how long he (or she) was a member of the Tent, and the date of birth and death, parents' names, and date of burial. (This record must be carefully written in the record book, before the funeral takes place.)

The Queen Mother gives three raps, and all the Maids and Pages stand, with their arms folded across their breasts. The Queen Mother then leads the invocation, and the children respond.

INVOCATION.

Queen Mother:—Lord Jesus, Thou hast said:
Response:—Suffer little children
Q. M.:—To come unto me,
Res.:—And forbid them not,
Q. M.:—For of such is the Kingdom of Heaven.
Res.:—O Lord, teach our hearts to praise Thee.
Q. M.:—Thou art full of love and kindness.
Res.:—Lord Jesus, bless and save our parents.
Q. M.:—O Lord, bless the officers and children of the Tents.
Res.:—God, in mercy hear our prayers.
Q. M.:—Lord, save the world, and bless all mankind.
Res.:—Lord Jesus, bless Thy church and people.
Q. M.:—In God alone there is safety.

Res.:—Lord, hear our prayer, and bless and comfort all that mourn.

Q. M.:—Lord, dismiss us with Thy blessing.

CLOSING OF THE CHURCH SERVICE.

The Doxology is sung (the congregation standing). The minister then dismisses them, and requests the congregation to be seated until the Tent marches out.

While some familiar hymn is sung, the children of the Tents march around and view the remains, they then pass out and form in open ranks on the outside. The congregation is then permitted to view the remains, whereupon they pass out. The family bids a last farewell, and the casket is carried out in the following order: First, the minister; second, the Queen Mother and Vice-Queen Mother; third, the Father of the Tent; and fourth, the casket, with the family following. All pass through the lines to the hearse.

THE MARCH TO THE CEMETERY.

Q. M.   V.-Q. M.   F. of T., and Pastor.

Pall-bearers.   Pall-bearers.

Family.
The Children of the Tents.
The Friends of the Family.
(All of the above in carriages or vehicles.)

Ceremony at the Grave.

At the grave the children of the Tents open ranks, and the casket is conveyed through in the same manner in which it left the church, and is placed over the grave. The children form a circle around the casket, with the Q. M., V.-Q. M., F. of T. and the minister at the head, and the family at the foot.

The children join hands, and the following, or some other familiar hymn, is sung:

C. M.

"It is appointed unto men once to die."

I.

If I must die, Lord let me die
  With hope in Jesus' blood—
The blood that saves from sin and guilt,
  And reconciles to God.

II.

If I must die, then let me die
  In peace with all mankind,
And change these fleeting joys below
  For pleasures all refined.

III.

If I must die—and die I shall—
  Let some kind seraph come,
And bear me on his friendly wing
  To my celestial home.

IV.

Of Canaan's land, from Pisgah's top,
  May I but have a view,
Though Jordan should o'erflow its banks,
  I'll boldly venture through.

Prayer by the minister or the Father of the Tent. The casket is then lowered into the grave. The children forming the chain raise their hands until the casket arrives at the bottom of the grave, they then drop their hands and break the chain, they then fold their arms across their breasts until the ceremony is ended.

The minister or the Father of the Tent concludes the ceremony, as follows:

Forasmuch as it hath pleased Almighty God, in His wise providence, to take out of this world the soul of our deceased child, we therefore commit its body to the ground—earth to earth, ashes to ashes, dust to dust; looking for the general resurrection in the last day, and the life of the world to come, through our Lord Jesus Christ, at whose second coming in glorious majesty to judge the world, the earth and the sea shall give up their dead; and the corruptible bodies of those who sleep in Him shall be changed, and made like unto His own glorious body, according to the mighty workings whereby He is able to subdue all things unto Himself.

An appropriate hymn is sung, and the ceremony is closed by the Lord's Prayer: Our father who art in heaven, hallowed be Thy name; Thy kingdom come; Thy will be done on earth, as it is in Heaven; give us this day our daily bread; and forgive us our trespasses, as we forgive those who trespass against us; and lead us not into temptation, but deliver us from evil. *Amen!*

Benediction, and all return to their homes.

CEREMONY

LAYING CORNER-STONE.

233

CEREMONY

OF

LAYING CORNER-STONE.

——: o :——

The laying of corner-stones of churches, public buildings and bridges, is a part of the duty of the International Order of Twelve.

The ceremony of laying the corner-stone shall be under the control of the International Grand Temple and Tabernacle, or of the Grand Temple and Tabernacle.

Parties desiring the Order to lay their corner-stone, must make application to the Chief Mentor of the nearest Temple, stating the time and place at which they wish the ceremony to be performed. This petition must be signed by the committee that has charge of the building. A Chief Mentor, when he receives the petition, must lay the matter before the Chief Grand Mentor, with any recommendation that he and the other Chief Mentors (if there are other Temples in the city or town) have to make. The Chief Grand Mentor, when he receives the petition and the recommendation (if favorable), issues an official notice to the Chief Mentors to prepare for a procession, and to assist in laying the corner-stone.

On the day on which the ceremony is to be performed, the Uniform Rank Knights and Palatine Guards shall assemble in their hall in full dress regalia. The Chief Grand Mentor (if present) opens the Grand Temple and Tabernacle, and appoints Grand Officers *pro-tem.*, if the regular officers are not present. (If the C. G. M. cannot attend, he shall appoint a Deputy to represent him.)

If the Daughter Priestesses take part in the procession, they shall wear full dress regalia, or they may wear their Jewels and Badges.

The Vice-Grand Mentor carries the ewer with earth (sand).

The Chief Grand Scribe carries the ewer with corn.

The Chief Grand Treasurer carries the ewer with pure water.

The procession is under the command of the Grand Drill-Master and his aides.

FORM OF PROCESSION.
Chief Sentinel.
Music.
Taborian Cadets.
Uniform Rank.
Palatine Guards.
Past Chief Mentors.
Chief Mentor.
Banner.
C. G. St.
C. G. S.——C. G. T.
V.-G. M.
Grand Officers.

Past Grand Officers.
Past Chief Grand Mentors.
Chief Grand Mentor.

Guard,   Guard,
(with Drawn Sword.)   (with Drawn Sword.)

I. C. G. Sentinel.
I. G. Officers.
I. C. G. M.
Three Guards, with Drawn Swords.
Maids of Honor, in Vehicles.
Priestesses, in Carriages.

When the procession arrives at the place where the stone is to be laid, the ranks are opened, and the officer who is delegated to lay the stone, marches through, followed by those who were in the rear; they march around the stone four times, and then form a circle around it. The Daughter Priestesses form around the Knights; the following hymn is then sung:

L. M.

Laying the foundation.

I.

When to the exiled seer was given
A rapt'rous foregaze into Heaven,
All glorious though the visions were,
Yet he beheld no temple there.

II.

The new Jerusalem on high
Hath one pervading sanctity;
No sin to mourn, no grief to mar—
God and the Lamb its temple are.

III.

But we, frail sojourners below,
The pilgrim-heirs of guilt and woe,
Must seek a tabernacle, where
Our scattered souls may blend in prayer.

IV.

Oh Thou! who o'er the cherubim
Didst shine in glories veiled and dim,
With purer light our temple cheer.
And dwell in unveiled glory here.

The Grand Chief:—Sir Knights, Uncover! Let us bow our heads, while our Chief Grand Orator invokes the blessings of our Heavenly Father.

PRAYER.

Almighty and Everlasting Ruler of Heaven and Earth, Thou most Holy and Eternal Father, in the name of our Lord and Savior, hear our prayers and grant our petitions this day. In love and mercy let Thy presence be felt. Bless the multitude assembled here. Gracious Father, accept the work which the Knights and Daughers of Tabor have assembled to perform in Thy name. Grant us the power of quickening grace to prepare us, that we may receive Thy approval in laying this cornerstone. Bless the builder and workmen, protect them from danger, guide and direct them by Thy unerring counsel, so that this house may be completed to Thy glory, and be a benefit and blessing to all who may enter within its doors. Unto Thee, the Only Eternal God, and to Thine Only Begotten Son, Jesus Christ, our Lord and Redeemer, we will give honor, glory and praise now and forever. Amen!

C. G. M.:—Sir Knights, Cover!

A select piece of music, appropriate for the occasion, is rendered by the band.

C. G. M.:—Ladies and gentlemen, we have assembled to-day as members of the International Order of Twelve, to lay the foundation stone of a building to be occupied for a (give the purpose for which the house is to be built). One of the doctrines of our Order is to encourage all and any undertakings which have for their object the palliation of the sufferings of the human race. In obedience to the commands of our Order, we have assembled here to-day to take part in laying the corner-stone of this building. We feel honored at our being instrumental in laying the stone that is to firmly bind the building together. We apply the secret lock to the four corners and find them true, having passed upon every square. The large attendance here bespeaks the amount of interest which the friends and citizens share in the erection of this building. May it be an honor and benefit to this community, and may success crown every effort for good that has its origin in this house.

G. D.-M.:—Attention, Sir Knights. Handle Swords! Draw Swords!! Present Swords!!!

The C. G. M. places the box in the cavity, and the stone is lowered to its resting place and then fixed firmly by the architect (the band in the meantime rendering some appropriate music).

G. D.-M.:—Attention, Sir Knights. Carry, Comrades!

C. G. M. Let us now listen to the C. G. O., who will read from the Holy Scriptures:

Thus saith the Lord of Hosts: Consider your ways.

Go up to the mountain, and bring wood, and build the house; and I will take pleasure in it, and I will be glorified, saith the Lord.

Ye looked for much, and, lo, it came to little; and when ye brought it home, I did blow upon it. Why? saith the Lord of Hosts. Because of Mine house that is waste, and ye run every man unto his own house.

Therefore the heaven over you is stayed from dew, and the earth is stayed from her fruit.

And I called for a draught upon the land, and upon the mountains, and upon the corn, and upon the new wine, and upon the oil, and upon that which the ground bringeth forth, and upon men and upon cattle, and upon all the labor of the land.

Then Zerubbabel, the son of Shealtiel, and Joshua, the son of Josedech, the high priest, and all the remnant of the people, obeyed the voice of the Lord, their God, and the words of Haggai, the prophet, as the Lord, their God, had sent him, and the people did fear before the Lord.

Then spake Haggai, the Lord's messenger in the Lord's message, unto the people, saying, I am with you, saith the Lord.

And the Lord stirred up the spirit of Zerubbabel, the son of Shealtiel, governor of Judah, and the spirit of Joshua the son of Josedech, the high priest, and the spirit of all the remnant of the people; and they came and did work in the house of the Lord of Hosts, their God.

In the four and twentieth day of the sixth month, in the second year of Darius, the king.

In the seventh month, in the one and twentieth day of the month, came the word of the Lord by the prophet Haggai, saying:

Speak now to Zerubbabel, the son of Shealtiel, governor of Judah, and to Joshua, the son of Josedech, the high priest, and to the residue of the people, saying:

Yet now be strong, O Zerubbabel, saith the Lord; and be strong, O Joshua, son of Josedech, the high priest; and be strong, all ye people of the land, saith the Lord, and work: for I am with you, saith the Lord of Hosts:

According to the word that I covenanted with you when ye came out of Egypt, so My spirit remaineth with you: fear ye not.

For thus saith the Lord of Hosts: Yet once, it is a little while, and I will shake the heavens, and the earth, and the sea, and the dry land.

And I will shake all nations, and the desire of all nations shall come; and I will fill this house with glory, saith the Lord of Hosts.

The silver is Mine, and the gold is Mine, saith the Lord of Hosts.

The glory of this latter house shall be greater than of the former, saith the Lord of Hosts: and in this place will I give peace, saith the Lord of Hosts.

G. D.-M.:—Attention, Sir Knights. Carry Swords!

Music by the band.

C. G. M.:—Sir Chief Grand Orator, you will please mark the Taborian signs and the perfect figures on the top of the stone. ("777—333—12" is marked on the stone with green chalk.)

G. D.-M.:—Attention, Sir Knights. Present Swords!

C. G.-M.:—The emblematic figures "333" convey a deep significance, and prove the faith the Knights and Daughters of Tabor have in an overruling Providence. We believe in a triune God—the Father, Son and Holy Ghost. May He bless this building and the inhabitants of this city.

G. D.-M.:—Attention, Sir Knights. Salute! (They salute three times.)

C. G. M.:—The mystic "777" emblematizes the triple perfection of the International Order of Twelve, founded upon the solid principles of justice, equity, benevolence, prudence, loyalty, unity and impartiality. May these principles govern the business of this building.

G. D.-M.:—Attention, Sir Knights. Salute! (They salute four times.)

C. G.-M.:—We place the symbolized number "12" on this stone to express our unwavering confidence and trust in the motto of our Order: *In God alone is safety!*

G. D.-M.:—Attention, Sir Knights. Form a Wall of Steel!

C. G. M.:—Sir Vice-Grand Mentor, we will now consecrate this stone with earth. (The V.-G. M. scatters the earth over the stone. He stands by the side of the Chief.) May the building to be erected upon this stone be plentifully endowed with the riches of this earth.

C. G. M.:—Sir Chief Grand Scribe (the C. G. S. stands by the side of the Chief), we will now set apart this house that is to be erected on this stone (he states the purpose, and then the C. G. S. scatters the grains of wheat or corn over the stone.)

May there be gathered within these walls the golden harvest of success; may the seeds of eternal happiness be planted here and grow up to the glory of God and be garnered in the heavenly rest, to live forever.

C. G. M.:—Sir Chief Grand Treasurer (the C. G. T. stands by the side of Chief), with this pure water we consecrate the house to be erected upon this stone to Purity, Peace and Harmony. (The C. G. T. pours the water around the outside of the stone, touching the four sides.) Water is an emblem of purity. May all who enter this house live a pure life; may they inherit the waters of regeneration, and by a life in the service of the Lord be enabled to drink from the fountain of eternal life in the building not made with hands eternal in the Kingdom of Bliss and Glory.

C. G. M. strikes the stone four distinct times with his mallet, and says:—By virtue of the authority in me vested, I now and here announce that this foundation stone is truly laid and firmly laid and tried; may the Lord bless the work.

G. D.-M.:—Attention, Sir Knights. Present Swords! Return Swords!! (If there is a collection to be made, now is the time to announce it.)

Music by the band. The Knights and Daughters of Tabor form a procession and march by the stone slowly, and contribute what they may want to give on the stone. The strangers and citizens follow.

The return march to their hall is made in the same manner in which they marched out. On arriving in the hall the C. G. M. then declares the Grand Temple and Tabernacle at rest.

Mural Crown.

333

Belt Clasp—¼ Size.

SABA MEROE CORONETS AND BELT CLASP.

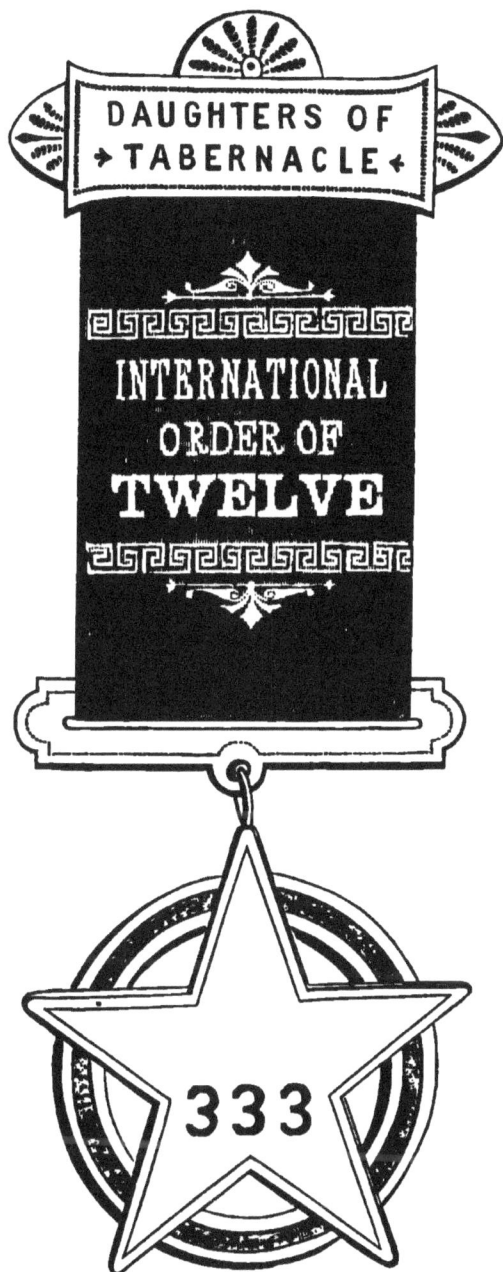

DAUGHTERS OF
+ TABERNACLE +

INTERNATIONAL
ORDER OF
TWELVE

333

BADGE OF DAUGHTER PRIESTESSES.

"In Solo Deo Salus!"

DEDICATING CEREMONY

OF

Knights and Daughters of Tabor

HALLS.

245

DEDICATION CEREMONY

OF

KNIGHTS AND DAUGHTERS OF TABOR HALLS.

——:o:——

The dedication ceremony of Temple and Tabernacle halls may be either public or private.

INSTRUCTIONS.

1. The hall, before it is dedicated, must be furnished with all the necessaries for the work and business of the Knights and Daughters of Tabor.

2. The ceremony must be performed by a C. G. M., P. C. G. M., or a D. G. M.

3. The Temple and Tabernacle Houses within the square, with their full furniture in sight, and candles burning.

4. The Daughters are marched into the hall, in full dress and regalia; the officers in their stations, and seated.

5. The Knights, in full dress and regalia, assemble in the ante-rooms, or some place near the hall, and march into and around the hall three times, and are seated; officers in their stations. Music; or the following hymn is sung:

I.

How lovely are Thy dwellings fair,
   Oh, Lord of Hosts! How dear
The pleasant Tabernacles are,
   Where Thou dost dwell so near.

II.

My soul doth long, and fainting, sigh
   Thy Temples, Lord, to see;
My heart and flesh aloud do cry,
   O, living God, for Thee!

III.

Happy, who in Thy house reside,
   Where Thee they ever praise;
Happy, whose strength in Thee doth bide,
   And in their hearts Thy ways.

IV.

They journey on from strength to strength,
   With joy and gladsome cheer,
Till all before our God, at length,
   In Zion do appear.

The C. M. of the Temple gives three raps, and all stand.　He then says:—We have assembled for the purpose of dedicating this hall to the work and business of the Knights and Daughters of Tabor. I now take pleasure in introducing Sir —— —— ——, the Dedicating Officer.

The C. M. then presents the gavel to the Dedicating Officer.

The Dedicating Officer gives one rap, and all are seated.　He then reads, as follows:—Sir Knights and Daughters, the solemn duties of the hour, and the importance of the business that has called us together, cannot be overestimated in an Order like ours, fulfilling a high and holy duty in this Christian age.　We are banded together for mutual aid and protection; to help each other in sickness; to comfort each other in distress; to support disabled members; to care for the lonely orphans of Knights or Daughters, and make glad the hearts of mourning widows. This is the misssion of our beloved Order. Then, how necessary it is that we should, in all our work and business, remember an overruling Providence, and ask that He may preside over our counsels, and give us wisdom to successfully conduct and guide the affairs of our Order, that it may continue a blessing for all time to come. Let us not only dedicate our hall to the Lord God, but give ourselves unto His keeping.

THE CEREMONY.

The Dedicating Officer gives three raps, and all stand. He then gives the following commands:—

1. Sir Knights, Form a Hollow Square! (The C. M., C. O. and C. P. in the center of the square, near the Temple House.)

2. Sir Knights, Handle Swords!

3. Sir Knights, Draw Swords!

4. Sir Knights, Present Swords!

5. Sir Knights, Deposit Swords! (The swords are laid down pointing to the Temple and Tabernacle Houses.)

6. Sir Knights, To the Right About Face! (Turn, face out.) Deposit Helmets!!

7. Sir Knights, To the Left About Face! (Turn, face in.)

8. Let us pray.

The Knights will kneel on their right knees, with their arms across their breasts, the Daughters standing.

The C. O., standing, will read the following prayer:—

PRAYER.

O, Eternal God, mighty in power, and majesty incomprehensible, whom the heaven of heavens cannot contain, much less the walls of Temples made with hands, and who yet hast been graciously pleased to promise Thy especial presence wherever two or three of Thy faithful servants shall assemble in Thy name to offer up their praises and supplications unto Thee; vouchsafe, O Lord, to be present with us, who are here gathered together, with all humility and readiness of heart, to consecrate this place to the honor of Thy great name. Accept, O Lord, this service at our hands, and bless it with such success as may tend most to Thy glory, and the furtherance of our happiness, both temporal and spiritual, through Jesus Christ, our blessed Lord and Savior. Amen!

All respond:—In God alone is safety!

The Dedicating Officer gives one rap, and all stand.

The Chief Mentor reads the following lesson:

LESSON.

Lord, what is man, that Thou takest knowledge of him! or the son of man, that Thou makest account of him!

Man is like to vanity; his days are like a shadow that passeth away.

Bow Thy heavens, O Lord, and come down; touch the mountains, and they shall smoke.

Cast forth lightning, and scatter them; shoot out Thine arrows, and destroy them.

Send Thine hand from above, rid me, and deliver me out of great waters, from the hand of strange children.

Whose mouth speaketh vanity, and their right hand is a right hand of falsehood.

I will sing a new song unto Thee, O God! upon a psaltery and an instrument of ten strings will I sing praises unto Thee.

It is He that giveth salvation unto kings; who delivereth David, His servant, from the hurtful sword.

Rid me, and deliver me from the hand of strange children, whose mouth speaketh vanity, and their right hand is a right hand of falsehood.

That our sons may be as plants grown up in their youth; that our daughters may be as corner-stones polished after the similitude of a palace.

That our garners may be full, affording all manner of store; that our sheep may bring forth thousands and ten thousands in our streets.

That our oxen may be strong to labor; that there be no breaking in, nor going out; that there be no complaining in our streets.

Happy is that people, that is, in such a case; yea, happy is that people, whose God is the Lord.

The Dedicating Officer, standing near the Temple House, says:—Attention, Sir Knights. Form the Living Chain! (The Knights clasp hands all around, so as to form a continuous chain. The command is then given to the Daughters to form a living chain around the Knights.)

The Chief Preceptress reads from Judges, chapter IV:

And the children of Israel again did evil in the sight of the Lord when Ehud was dead.

And the 'Lord sold them into the hand of Jabin, king of Canaan, that reigned in Hazor, the captain of whose host was Sisera, which dwelt in Harosheth, of the Gentiles.

And the children of Israel cried unto the Lord; for he had nine hundred chariots of iron; and twenty years he mightily oppressed the children of Israel.

And Deborah, a prophetess, the wife of Lapidoth, she judged Israel at that time.

And she dwelt under the palm tree of Deborah, between Ramah and Bethel, in Mount Ephraim; and the children of Israel came up to her for judgment.

And she sent and called Barak, the son of Abinoam, out of Kedesh-naphthali, and said unto him; Hath not the Lord God of Israel commanded, saying: Go, and draw toward Mount Tabor, and take with thee ten thousand men of the children of Naphthali, and of the children of Zebulon?

And I will draw unto thee, to the river Kishon, Sisera, the captain of Jabin's army, with his chariots and his multitude, and I will deliver him into thine hand.

And Barak said unto her, if thou wilt go with me, then I will go; but if thou wilt not go with me, then I will not go.

And she said, I will surely go with thee; notwithstanding the journey that thou takest shall not be for thine honor; for the Lord shall sell Sisera into the hand of a woman. And Deborah arose, and went with Barak to Kedesh.

252

And Barak called Zebulon and Naphthali to Kedesh; and he went up with ten thousand men at his feet; and Deborah went up with him.

Now Heber, the Kenite, which was of the children of Hobab, the father-in-law of Moses, had severed himself from the Kenites, and pitched his tent unto the plain of Zaanannim, which is by Kedesh.

And they shewed Sisera that Barak, the son of Abinoam, was gone up to Mount Tabor.

And Sisera gathered together all his chariots, even nine hundred chariots of iron, and all the people that were with him, from Harosheth, of the Gentiles, unto the river of Kishon.

And Deborah said unto Barak: Up, for this is the day in which the Lord hath delivered Sisera into thine hand; is not the Lord gone out before thee? So Barak went down from Mount Tabor, and ten thousand men after him.

And the Lord discomfited Sisera, and all his chariots, and all his host, with the edge of the sword before Barak; so that Sisera lighted down off his chariot, and fled away on his feet.

But Barak pursued after the chariots, and after the host, unto Harosheth of the Gentiles; and all the host of Sisera fell upon the edge of the sword; and there was not a man left.

All give three claps, and say, "Well Done! Well Done!! Well Done!!!

The C. M. says:—Attention, Sir Knights. To the Right About Face! Recover Helmets! To the Left About Face! Recover Swords! Present Swords! Return Swords! Form Procession! March Around the Hall, Daughters in front!

They march around the hall four times while the band renders some appropriate music; or, in lieu thereof, the following hymn may be sung:

I.

The spacious earth is all the Lord's,
  The Lord's her fulness is;
The world, and they that dwell therein,
  By sovereign right are His.

II.

He framed and fix'd it on the seas;
  And His almighty hand
Upon inconstant floods has made
  The stable fabric stand.

III.

But for Himself this Lord of all
  One chosen seat design'd;
Oh! who shall to that sacred hill
  Deserved admittance find?

IV.

The man whose hands and heart are pure,
  Whose thoughts from pride are free;
Who honest poverty prefers
  To gainful perjury.

V.

This, this is he, on whom the Lord
  Shall shower His blessings down;
Whom God, His Savior, shall vouchsafe
  With righteousness to crown.

The Dedicating Officer gives three raps, and says:—Sir Knights and Daughters, please form a living circle around the Temple and Tabernacle Houses. (The Dedicating Officer, C. M., and C. P. in the center.)

The Dedicating Officer gives two raps on the Temple and Tabernacle Houses, and says:—In the name of the Lord God of Heaven, Earth and the

Universe, in whom is all glory and power, I do solemnly dedicate this hall to the work of the Knights and Daughters of Tabor.

All give one clap, and pronounce: May He bless the work!

· The Dedicating Officer gives four raps on the Temple and Tabernacle Houses, and says:—In the name of Barak, the son of Abinoam, I do solemnly dedicate this hall to Charity and Friendship.

All give two claps, and pronounce: May we hear and obey!

The Dedicating Officer gives six raps on the Temple and Tabernacle Houses, and says:—In the name of Deborah, the prophetess, I do solemnly dedicate this hall to Honor and Virtue.

All give three claps, and say: May we remember! All join hands, and the C. O. offers the following invocation:

O, Most Glorious Lord, we acknowledge that we are not worthy to offer unto Thee anything belonging unto us; yet we beseech Thee, in Thy great goodness, graciously to accept the dedication of this place to Thy service, and to prosper this, our undertaking. Receive the prayers and intercessions of all those who shall call upon Thee in this house, and give them grace to prepare their hearts to serve Thee with reverence and godly fear; affect them with an awful apprehension of Thy divine majesty, and a deep sense of their own unworthiness; that, so approaching Thy sanctuary with lowliness and devotion, and coming before Thee with clean thoughts and pure hearts, with bodies undefiled, and minds sanctified, they may always perform a service acceptable to Thee, through Jesus Christ, our Lord. Amen! Amen!! Amen!!!

Dedicating Officer gives one rap, all are seated.

Any Chief Preceptress present may then read the following:

I.

Ye boundless realms of joy,
  Exalt your Maker's fame;
His praise your song employ
  Above the starry frame:
    Your voices raise,
    Ye Cherubim
    And Seraphim,
    To sing His praise.

II.

Thou moon, that rul'st the night,
  And sun that guid'st the day,
Ye glitt'ring stars of light,
  To Him your homage pay:
    His praise declare,
    Ye heavens above,
    And clouds that move
    In liquid air.

III.

Let them adore the Lord,
  And Praise His holy name,
By whose almighty word
  They all from nothing came;
    And all shall last,
    From changes free;
    His firm decree
    Stands ever fast.

IV.

Let earth her tribute pay:
  Praise Him, ye dreadful whales,
And fish that through the sea
  Glide swift with glitt'ring scales;
    Fire, hail, and snow,
    And misty air,
    And winds, that where
    He bids them blow.

The Dedicating Officer gives four raps, and all stand; he then says:—The dedicating of halls is legally set apart for the business and work of the Temples of Knights of Tabor, Tabernacles of Daughter Priestesses of Tabor, the Royal House of Media, and Tents of Maids and Pages of Honor. May success attend their efforts. (He gives one rap, and all are seated.)

If there is an oration to be delivered, or if the Uniform Rank Knights or Palatine Guards desire to drill, now is the time, after which the ceremony closes.

"In Solo Deo Salus!"

SWORD TACTICS AND DRILL

OF THE

Uniform Rank Knights,

AND

PALATINE GUARDS,

ALSO THE

JAVELIN DRILL OF TABORIAN CADETS.

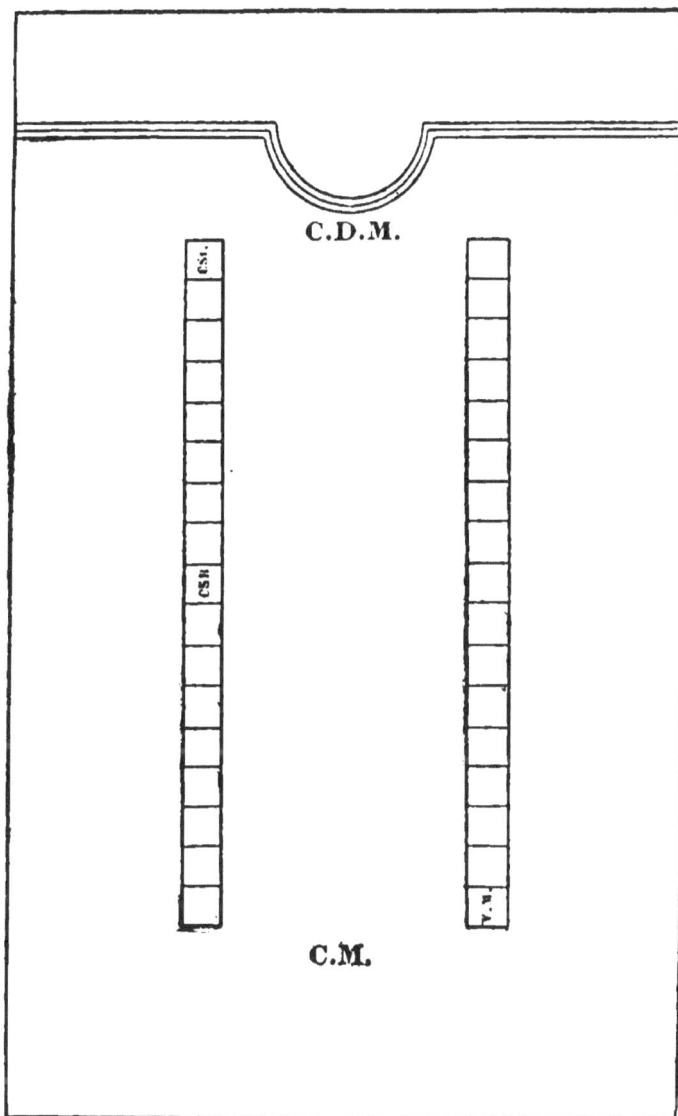

C.D.M.

C.M.

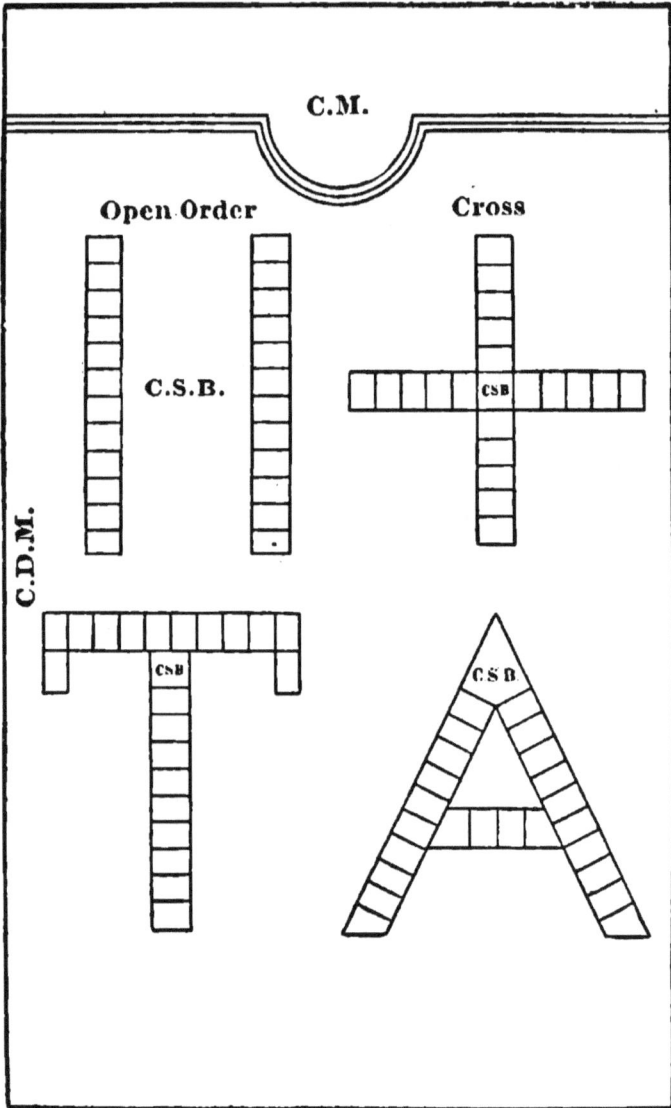

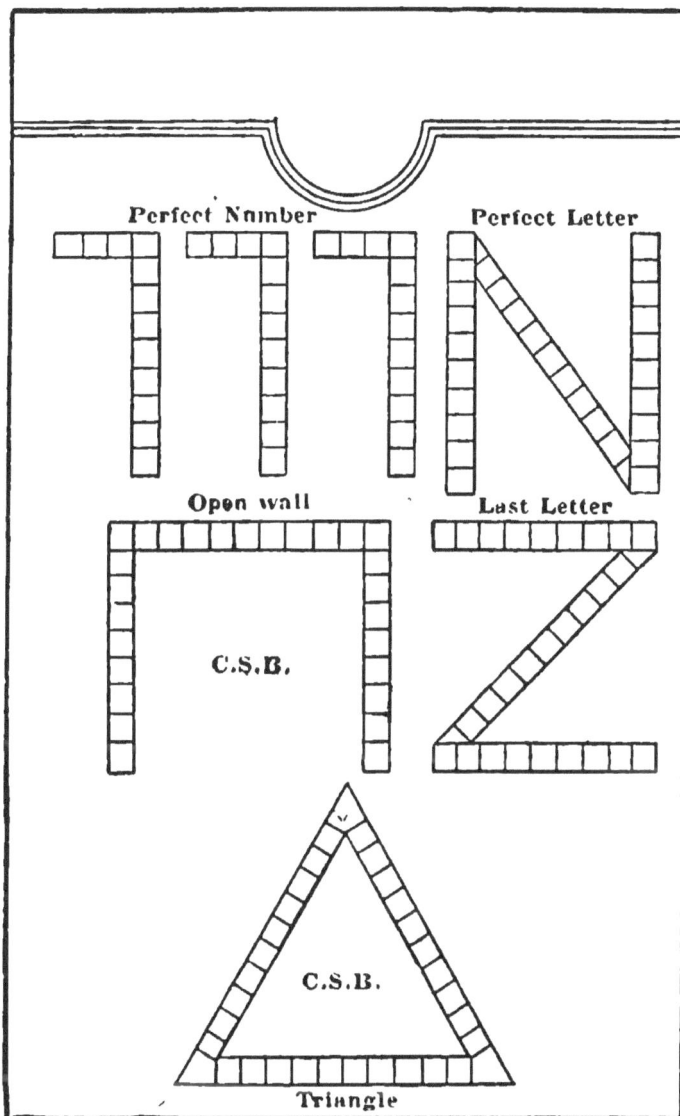

Perfect Number   Perfect Letter

Open wall   Last Letter

C.S.B.

C.S.B.

Triangle

SWORD TACTICS AND DRILL

OF THE

UNIFORM RANK KNIGHTS,

AND

PALATINE GUARDS.

——:o:——

COMMAND.

1. Cautionary, which is: Attention, Sir Knights!

2. The preparatory, which indicates the movement.

3. The command of execution, which causes the movement.

POSITION.

1. Heels on the same line, as near as possible.

2. The feet turned out equally; stand easy.

3. The knees straight.

4. The body erect, inclining a little forward.

5. Shoulders square, and falling naturally.

6. The arms hanging, with elbows near the body.

7. The head erect and to the front.

8. The chin drawn in.

9. The eyes fixed straight to the front.

10. The tallest man to the right of the line.

11. The smallest man to extreme left of the line.

12. Sir Knights will fall in, with swords in scabbard.

261

To Form the Lines.

To form the lines, the C. D.-M. will command:—

1. Attention, Sir Knights. Fall In!

(The Knights will form in one rank, face to the right.)

2. Front Face!

(Raise the right foot slightly and turn on the left heel half around, shoulders slightly touching.)

3. Right Dress!

(Each Knight will turn his head to the right and place himself on a line with the Sir Knight next to him on his right. The "left dress" is executed by the same movements reversed.)

4. Front!

(The head will resume the natural position.)

5. From the Right, Count Twos!

(At this command the Sir Knights will count from right to left in a distinct voice, "One, Two; One, Two;" until through the ranks.)

6. Form Divisions, Right Face!

(The Sir Knights will all face to the right; Division No. 2 will place itself on the right of Division No. 1, thus forming the Sir Knights into files of two abreast, No. 1 constituting the first Division and No. 2 the second.)

7. Officers in Ranks!

(At this command the V.-M. will take his place to the right of the Second Division, the C. S. to the right of the First Division, the C. S. B in the center.)

8. Form Lines, and Receive the C. M. (or P. P.)!

The V.-M. will command:—

9. Second Division, By File Left, March!

(At this command the Second Division will march promptly to the left.)

10. By File Left, March!

(Until they arrive opposite the First Division, the V.-M. will command. After placing his division exactly opposite the First Division by "right or left dress," he will resume his place to the right of his division. While this movement is being executed, the C. S. will command the First Division.)

11. (1) Mark Time! (2) Front!

12. First Division, Front! Right Dress! Front!

(The Sir Knights will thus be formed in two parallel lines, facing inward. The C. D.-M. advances to the C. M.'s station, salutes, and says: Sir Chief, the lines are now ready for inspection.)

The C. M. takes his place to the right between the two divisions, standing firm. The C. D.-M. then commands:—

13. Attention, Sir Knights! Handle Swords! Draw Swords! Carry Swords! Salute the C. M. (or P. P.)! Present Swords!

The C. M. passes down through the lines, then takes his place on the extreme left, and commands:—

14. Sir Knights, Carry Swords!
15. Sir Knights, Form Wall of Steel!
16. Sir Knights, Take Taborian Position!
17. Sir Knights, Carry Swords!
18. Sir Knights, Present Swords!
19. Sir Knights, Guard the Head!
20. Sir Knights, Guard the Body!
21. Sir Knights, Form Wall of Steel!

22. Sir Knights, Carry Swords!

23. Sir Knights, Present Swords!

24. Sir Knights, Carry Comrade!

25. Sir Knights, Give the Taborian Rest!

26. Sir Knights, Salute!

27. Sir Knights, Carry Swords!

The C. D.-M. commands:—

28. Sir Knights, Present Swords!

(The C. M. passes up through the lines and takes his seat.)

29. Sir Knights, Return Swords!

MARCHING DRILL.

The C. D.-M. commands:—

30. Second Division, Left Face!

31. First Division, Right Face!

32. Second Division, By File Right, March!

(They march until they reach the proper place at the right of the First Division.)

33. Second Division, Halt!

34. Sir Knights, Mark Time!

(In stepping off, always begin with the left foot.)

35. Sir Knights, By File Right, March!

(At each turn that is made, repeat command: By File Right!)

36. March Down the Center of the Hall!

37. First Division, File Right; Second Division, File Left, March!

(This movement separates the divisions—and unites them—in their march and counter-march around the hall.)

38. First Division, By File Left, March!

39. Second Division, By File Right, March!

(As they march around the hall and pass each other, they present swords.)

40. First Division, By File Right, March!

(This movement places the First Division by the side of the Second Division.)

41. Form Taborian Cross!

(This is formed by the odd numbers 15, 17, or 21. It will take some practice, and every man must know his place. When the command is given, ten Knights in the Second Division form across the hall, and eleven Knights of the First Division march in, thus forming the Cross. *See diagram.*)

42. Form Taborian T!

(The same twenty-one Knights form the T— the Second Division horizontal, and the First Division perpendicular. *See diagram.*)

43. Form Taborian A!

(Nine of the Second Division form the left line, and ten of the First Division form the right line, and one from each division form the center. They march with arms folded. *See diagram.*)

44. Divisions, Form in Open Order!

(*See diagram.*)

45. Sir Knights, Form in Single File!

(The Second Division marches around and falls in the rear of the First Division,—the First Division marking time.)

46. Sir Knights, Halt! Front Face! Right Dress!

To Form Three Divisions.

47. Sir Knights, Count by Threes!

(At this command, the Knights will count from

right to left: "One, Two, Three; One, Two, Three"—thus along the line.)

The C. D.-M. will now command:—

48. Sir Knights, Form Divisions! Right Face!

(The Sir Knights will face to the right, and No. 2 will take position to the right of No. 1, and No. 3 will take position to the right of No. 2. Mark time.)

49. Forward, March!

50. Open Order!

(At this command the Knights will take positions from three to seven feet apart, to the right and left.)

There are several fancy positions which may be taken by these divisions, but care must be had that each Knight knows his proper place. Do not attempt them in public, until you can go through them perfectly in the hall.

51. Form the Perfect Number—777!

(The Three Sevens cannot be formed with less than twenty-seven Knights. When the order is given, three Knights from each division, by one backward step, from the right or left, take position to the left. *See diagram.*)

52. Sir Knights, Resume your Place in Divisions!

53. Sir Knights, Form the Perfect Letter N!

(To form this letter properly, the divisions must be seven feet apart. The Second Division will rest their right upon the right of the First Division, and their left upon the left of the Third Division. *See diagram.*)

54. Sir Knights, Resume Places and Close Up Ranks!

There are several other beautiful positions that can be taken by these divisions:

The Triangle—△.

The Open Wall—⌐.

The Letter Z.

(*See diagram.*)

To Form Four Divisions.

55. Attention, Sir Knights.   Fall In!

(Always fall in with face to the right.)

The C. D.-M. commands:—

56. Front Face!

57. Right Dress!

58. From the Right, Count by Fours!

59. Form Divisions! Right Face!

(No. 2 will quickly take place to the right of No. 1; No. 3 to the right of No. 2; No. 4 to the right of No. 3.)

These divisions may be thrown into many fancy positions, and the C. D.-M. can exercise his skill in maneuvering the Sir Knights.   (1) Open Columns; (2) Two Divisions; (3) Three Divisions; (4) Four Divisions; (5) The Hollow Square; (6) The Double Square ⌐L; (7) The letter "M," and various other fancy positions.

Notice.

To become perfect in the Tactics and Drill, we must practice regularly, and all must attend if they would perform well.   One balk will throw the entire divisions into confusion.

Sword Exercise.

60. Draw Swords!

(First Motion.—At the word "draw," seize the scabbard with the left hand and grasp the sword with the right hand, and draw it out two inches.

Second Motion.—At the word "swords," draw the sword from the scabbard and extend the right hand to the front, and drop the sword in the hollow of the elbow.

Third Motion.—Bring the right hand to the thigh, the elbow a little bent, holding the sword between the thumb and two fingers, the blade perpendicular, being position of "Carry Swords.")

61. Present Swords!

(Raise the sword perpendicularly, the flat of the blade opposite the right eye, the guard at the height of the shoulder, and the elbow supported on the body.)

62. Carry swords!

(Extend the hand to the front, and replace the sword, as in the second and third motions of "Draw Swords.")

63. Taborian Position!

(First Motion.—Same as "Present Swords!"

Second Motion.—Drop the point of the sword by extending the arm, so that the right hand will rest on the right side of the thigh, the point of the sword resting on the floor or ground, about eighteen inches from the right foot; the Knight to your right takes position, his left foot touching the sword.)

64. Guard the Head!

(First Motion.—Same as "Present Swords."

Second Motion.—Hold the sword in a horizontal position above the head, about six inches in front of the forehead.)

65. Guard the Body!

(First Motion.—Same as "Present Swords," except in this case the blade is outward.

Second Motion.—Cut downward, and bring the sword to carry.)

66. Form a Wall of Steel!

(First Motion.—Same as "Present Swords."

Second Motion.—Bring your sword down horizontally, the right hand resting on the center of the breast, the point of your sword resting on the breast of the Knight to your left.)

67. Carry Comrade!

(First Motion.—Same as "Present Swords."

Second Motion.—Lay you sword across your shoulders and grasp the point with your left hand.)

68. Taborian Rest!

(First Motion.—Same as "Present Swords."

Second Motion.—Rest the sword in the hollow of the elbow joint, and grasp the blade near the guard with the left hand.)

69. Salute!

(First Motion.—Same as "Present Swords."

Second Motion.—Drop the point of the sword by extending the arm, so that the right hand may be brought to the side of the right thigh, the nails up, the elbow well back from the body.)

70. Return Swords!

(First Motion.—Bring the sword to the position of "Present," and seize the scabbard with the left hand near its mouth.

Second Motion.—Drop the point; turn the head to the left, and return the sword; bring your head to front, and drop the hands to their natural position by the side.)

71. Sir Knights, Disperse! Return to Quarters!

The Uniform Rank Knights and Palatine Guards may practice all the various sword exercises, maneuvers and drills.

When the Palatine Guards drill, instead of addressing them as Sir Knights, say Sir Guards. The Prince Marshal is styled Captain Marshal.

JAVELIN EXERCISES

AND

✤ DRILL ✤

OF THE

TABORIAN CADETS.

Javelin Exercises and Drill

OF THE

Taborian Cadets.

———:o:———

The javelins are made about five feet in length, steel-pointed, and one inch in diameter.

The ranks are formed in the same manner as designated in the Inspection Diagram.

Inspection.

The Chief Tent Marshal addresses the Chief Mentor:—Sir Chief, the Cadets are ready for inspection.

The Chief steps to the right front. The C. T. M. then commands:—

1. Attention, Taborian Cadets! Form Arch!

(First Motion.—Present javelins, holding them about one foot from the heel of the javelin.

Second Motion.—Carry the right foot about eighteen inches to the front; extend the javelin arm, and cross the head of the javelin, about three inches from the point, with that of the Cadet opposite.)

The C. T. M. passes down through the ranks slowly. On arriving at the extreme left, he turns and faces to the right, whereupon he commands:—

2. Cadets, Ground Javelins!

(First Motion.—Present javelins, and bring the feet together.

Second Motion.—Let the javelin slide down the right side until the heels rest on the ground (or floor), holding it between the thumb and two fingers; arm extended down, javelin resting against the right shoulder.)

3. Cadets, Repel Javelins!

(First Motion.—Grasp the javelin about the center, and present.

Second Motion.—Drop the javelin hand to the right hip, and let it firmly rest there, the point of the javelin to the front, and the heel to the rear— the point about one foot higher than the heel. Advance the left foot about eighteen inches.)

4. Carry Javelins!

(First Motion.—Present javelins, grasping the javelin about one foot above the heel.

Second Motion.—Drop the hand behind, so that it will rest on the right small of the back, nails out; arm over the javelin point, above the head; javelin near the right side of the face.)

5. Take Position, Right and Left!

(First Motion.—Grasp the javelin about the center, and present.

Second Motion.—Bring the hand to the breast, so that the javelin will extend horizontally across the breast. The First Division will side-step to the right, and the Second Division will side-step to the left, until the point and heel just touch the Cadets on either side.)

6. Poise Javelins!

(First Motion.—Present, grasping the center of the javelin.

Second Motion.—Rest the javelin in the hollow between the thumb and forefinger; raise the hand until it is on a level with the right eye, and point front.)

7. Ascend Mount Tabor!

(First Motion.—Bring the javelin into a position with the right hand about eighteen inches from its heel.

Second Motion.—Grasp the javelin with the left hand, near the center, and let the right hand rest on the hip; elevate the point about one foot. Keep time, or imitate walking.)

8. Division, Rest!

(First Motion.—Bring the javelin to a *present*.

Second Motion.—Rest the heel, and lean the point, on the right shoulder, and grasp the javelin with both hands.)

9. Present Javelins!

10. Right Face!

11. Mount Javelins!

(Throw the javelin across the shoulders, and grasp it with both hands.)

12. Present Javelins!

13. Front Face!

14. Right About Face!

15. Repel Javelins!

16. Present Javelins!

17. Left About Face!

18. Form Arch!

The C. T. M. may exercise in the various maneuvers, and marching or division drills. The Taborian Cadets shall appear in full regulation uniform on all public occasions. Due respect must be paid to the Queen Mother or Grand Officers, by opening ranks to receive them.

"IN SOLO DEO SALUS!"

GENERAL RULES

FOR THE

GOVERNMENT OF THE BUSINESS

OF THE

INTERNATIONAL

ORDER OF TWELVE.

RULES OF ORDER.

———:o:———

1. The Presiding Officer, at the proper hour, takes his (or her) seat, and gives one rap; the officers and members clothe themselves in proper regalia, and take their respective seats. The Temple, Tabernacle or Palatium is then opened in regular order.

2. The regular business of the Order shall be attended to without a motion, as prescribed in the "Rules of Business."

3. During the reading of the minutes, communications or other papers, silence shall be observed. After the minutes are read, if they are found correct, and if no objections are interposed as to their correctness, they shall stand approved; if, however, there is a question as to their correctness, the member who questions their correctness shall state what is not correct, and move that the correction be made.

4. Members and visitors must come to the hall cleanly dressed, wearing the working regalia, and white gloves.

5. A member, when addressing the Temple, Tabernacle or Palatium, shall stand and address the Presiding Officer (giving title of office).

6. During the time that the Temple, Tabernacle or Palatium is open and doing business, no refresh-

ments, smoking or chewing tobacco will be permitted.

7. When Grand Officers visit a Temple, Tabernacle or Palatium, they must be received standing.

8. All officers in open Session shall be addressed by the title of their office, all members as Daughter, or Sir Knight; these titles are to be used only in open Temples, Tabernacles or Palatiums, or when on duty or parade.

9. When it is necessary to get the sense of the Session on any question or resolution, it must be done by motion, duly seconded, stated by the Presiding Officer, and decided by the voting sign.

10. When an office is made vacant by death, resignation or for any other cause, the Presiding Officer shall appoint a member to discharge the duties until the next regular election.

11. The Presiding Officer shall control the business of the Session, and determine the time of closing without a motion.

12. The regular business of the Session shall be transacted according to the "Rules of Business." (See Constitution.)

13. The Presiding Officer shall be responsible to the Grand Temple and Tabernacle for the manner in which he administers the laws of the Order, and he shall decide all doubtful questions of Constitution, regulations and order; the decisions which he renders shall be final, until reversed by the C. G. M., or the Grand Temple and Tabernacle.

14. No member shall speak more than once on the same subject, until all who wish to speak have spoken; nor more than twice, nor longer than ten

minutes, without permission from the Presiding Officer.

15. A member speaking shall stand in front of either the Temple or Tabernacle House (as the case may be), and address the Presiding Officer, confine himself to the question at issue, and avoid personalities and irrelevant language.

16. A member shall not be interrupted while speaking, except to explain.

17. A motion shall not be in order until it is seconded, and stated by the Presiding Officer. A motion must be made in writing, when requested by the C. S., C. R. or R. P.

18. A motion to lie on the table shall be decided without debate.

19. A motion to postpone carries the question over to the next meeting.

20. When a question is laid on the table, it cannot be taken up until the next meeting, and then only by a majority vote.

21. A motion to reconsider can be acted upon only at the same Session; it must be made by a member who voted in the majority.

22. The first named on all special committees shall be the Chairman.

23. In all business meetings, they shall proceed according to the Order of Business.

24. A member wishing to retire from the Session during the evening, must come before the Temple (or Tabernacle) House, and make the request to the Presiding Officer. He announces the request, and if a majority are in favor of it, it is granted.

25. Members wishing to retire for a few minutes, shall rise from their seats and stand, and give the saluting sign; the Presiding Officer, on observing them, returns the sign, which signifies that permission is granted.

26. A member crossing the hall during the Session must give the saluting sign.

27. The strictest order and decorum must be observed during the hours of the Session.

28. Should an officer be absent from a meeting, the Presiding Officer shall fill the seat *pro-tem*.

29. A motion for indefinite postponement, if decided in the affirmative, quashes the proposition entirely, and is not debatable.

30. A motion, when regularly made and seconded, and proposed from the Chair, cannot be withdrawn without the consent of the Session.

31. Any member may rise to a point of order, whenever the speaker does not confine his (or her) remarks to the question, or is not quoting the law properly.

32. The previous motion cannot be entertained until two members have spoken for and against the subject at issue. The previous question is not debatable.

33. A new motion or resolution cannot be made until the one under consideration is disposed of, except a motion to lay on the table or previous question; these are not debatable.

34. A motion to postpone to a certain time, or a substitute, or an amendment, or to refer to a committee, is in order when a motion or resolution is pending.

35. A member, when speaking, must not use personalities or discourteous language. Should this occur, however, then the Presiding Officers shall call the speaker to order. If a member fails to come to order when requested, the Presiding Officer shall fine the speaker, and he must remain silent until the fine is paid, or remitted by the Session or Presiding Officer.

36. A motion to lay an amendment on the table, if it is carried, removes the whole question from the Session for the time, and if it is not taken from the table, it is indefinitely postponed; but it can be taken up for further consideration at any future time.

37. Privileged questions are in order at any time during the Session, such as: first, motion for the order of the day; second, a motion relating to individual members; third, questions of inquiry; fourth, questions of the rights and privileges of the Session; fifth, when a member desires to be correctly informed on any matter that is before the Session; and sixth, when a member desires to explain a matter wherein he has been misunderstood.

38. A motion to adjourn is always out of order, as the Session fixes the hour to open and the hour to rest. The Presiding Officer is goverened by these hours, unless a motion is carried to extend the time.

39. The Presiding Officer shall decide all points of order, without debate.

40. All motions or resolutions must be submitted in writing and laid on the Secretary's desk, and must be read when a member desires it.

41. When a motion or resolution is made, duly seconded, and stated by the Presiding Officer, it becomes the property of the Session, and cannot be withdrawn without the consent of the Presiding Officer, or a majority vote of the Session.

42. When a committee makes a report, if it is not satisfactory, it shall be referred back to the same for correction, with instructions.

43. If there is a majority and a minority report of a committee, the minority report must be acted upon first.

44. Members cannot vote, unless they are entitled to a vote, or are present in open Session.

45. All amendments to motions or resolutions must be disposed of before the main question can be acted upon. If the amendment is not adopted, the motion or resolution is put to a vote as amended; if the amendment is lost, the vote is taken on the previous question, without debate.

GRAND HONORS.

——:o:——

The grand honors shown to an International or Past International Grand Chief are given as follows: A suitable escort is sent to the reception room to conduct the visitor into the Session. As he enters, the Presiding Officer gives four raps, and all stand with their hands lifted up above their heads. When he arrives at the Altar, or Temple or Tabernacle House, he stops, and all give claps—four times three—and all then say: We Welcome! three times. He is then escorted to the Presiding Officer's station, and introduced by the Chief, whereupon one rap is given and all are seated. On invitation of the Chief, he may deliver an address.

An International Chief Grand Preceptress or Past International Chief Grand Preceptress is received in the same manner.

A Chief Grand Mentor, or Past Chief Grand Mentor, is conducted into the Session by an suitable escort. When he enters, the Presiding Officer gives four raps, and all stand, with folded arms, until he arrives at the Altar, or Temple or Tabernacle House, then all give seven claps, and say: We Welcome! three times. He is then conducted to the Presiding Officer's station, and introduced by the Chief, whereupom one rap is given and all

282

are seated. On invitation, he may address the members.

A Chief Grand Preceptress or Past Chief Grand Preceptress is received in the same manner.

All other Grand Officers and Past Grand Officers are received into Subordinate Temples, Tabernacles, Palatiums and Tents with the standing honors. When they arrive at the Altar, Temple or Tabernacle House, they are introduced by the Chief, and seated.

The grand honors shall only be conferred upon International or Past International Grand Chiefs and International and Past International Grand Preceptresses, Chief Grand Mentors and Past Chief Grand Mentors, and Chief Grand Preceptresses and Past Chief Grand Preceptresses, when received into a Triennial Grand Session or a Grand Session. The same grand honors are given to the above Officers and Past Officers when they visit a Temple, Tabernacle, Palatium or Tent.

RULES OF BUSINESS

GOVERNING THE

TRIENNIAL GRAND SESSIONS.

——:o:——

1.—On the day and hour fixed by the Constitution the members assemble. The I. C. G. M. takes his seat and gives three distinct sounds with the Taborian bell—this calls the Session to order.

2.—After being satisfied that all present are members, he orders the I. C. G. St. and I. I. G. St. to their posts (with instructions).

3.—The I. C. G. S. calls the roll of Grand Temples and Tabernacles. If the Representatives of five of them are present, he shall proceed to open the Triennial Session in the Saba Meroe Degree.

4.—The I. C. G. S. calls the roll of Grand Officers, and they are seated in their stations. If an Officer is absent, the I. C. G. M. shall fill the vacancy *pro-tem.*

5.—If the hall has not been dedicated to the Taborian work, it is now attended to.

6.—The Committee on Credentials is appointed by the I. C. G. M.

7.—Report of Committee on Credentials.

8.—The I. C. G. M. appoints all the committees, as prescribed by the Constitution.

9.—The I. C. G. M. reads his message, and it is referred to the proper committee. The I. C. G. P. reads her report, and it is referred. The I. G. Q. M. reads her report, and it is refered.

10.—The Grand Temples and Tabernacles make their reports through the C. G. M.s or C. G. P.s

11.—The International Districts make their reports through their D. G. M.s

12.—At the opening of the Sessions, the I. C. G. R. reads the proceedings of the previous Session, unless otherwise ordered.

13 —Immediately after the proceedings are read and disposed of, the I. C. G. M. calls for the reports of the various committees, in their regular order.

14.—Motions, resolutions, and new business.

15.—Election of International Grand Officers.

16.—Installation of Grand Officers.

17.—The I. C. G. M. declares the International Grand Temple and Tabernacle at rest.

Grand Temples and Tabernacles shall make their own Rules of Business, as well as those governing the business of their Temples, Tabernacles, Palatiums and Tents.

FORM OF REPORT

GRAND TEMPLES AND TABERNACLES

TO THE

TRIENNIAL GRAND SESSION.

————:o:————

1.—Number of Temples, - - - - ......
2.—Increase of Temples since last Triennial
    Grand Session, - - - - ......
3.—Number of Tabernacles, - - - ......
4.—Increase of Tabernacles since last Triennial
    Grand Session, - - - - ......
5.—Number of Palatiums, - - - - ......
6.—Increase since last Triennial Grand Session,......
7.—Number of Tents, - - - - ......
8.—Increase since last Triennial Grand Session,......
9.—Number of Knights of Tabor, - - - ......
10.—Increase since last Triennial Grand Session,......
11.—Number of Daughters of Tabor, - - ......
12.—Increase since last Triennial Grand Session,......
13.—Number of members in the Palatiums, - ......
14.—Number of Palatine Guards and how many
    Companies, - - - - - ......
15.—Number of Maids and Pages, - - - ......
16.—Increase since last Triennial Grand Session,......
17.—Names of the members of the International
    Grand Temple and Tabernacle that have
    died since last Triennial Grand Session,......
18.—Number of Knights and Daughters in the
    State and Jurisdiction, - - - ......
19.—Amount of International Grand Dues:
    First year, - - - - - $......
    Second year, - - - - - ......
    Third year, - - - - . ...

              Total Grand Dues, $ .....

20.—Palatium Grand Dues, at one dollar per
year for each Palatium:

First year, - - - - - $......
Second year, - - - - - ......
Third year, - - - - - ......

Total Grand Dues, $......

21.—Tent Grand Dues, at one dollar per year for
each Tent:

First year, - - - - - - $......
Second year, - - - - - ......
Third year, - - • - - - ......

Total Grand Dues, - $......

22.—Grand Total, - - - - - - $......

I hereby certify that this is a true and correct report
for the three years ending the .... day of ...., A.
D. 18.., A. O. T..., for the Grand Temple and Tabernacle for the State of .... and its Jurisdiction.

....................C. G. M.

I hereby attest this report to be correct and confirm
the same. Witness my hand and seal.

[SEAL.] ....C. G. S.

The I. C. G. S. is hereby authorized to collect the International Grand Dues from the Grand Sessions of each
Grand Temple and Tabernacle annually, and give his receipt for the amount.

REPORT

FROM

INTERNATIONAL DISTRICTS

TO THE

TRIENNIAL GRAND SESSION.

———: o :———

1.—Number of Temples, - - - - ......
2.—Number of members, - - - - .. ...
3.—Number of Tabernacles, - - - - ......
4.—Number of members, - - - . ...
5.—Number of Palatiums, - - - - ......
6.—Number of members, - - - - ......
7.—Number of Tents, - - - - - ......
8.—Number of members, - - - - ......
9.—The amount of Grand Dues paid:

First year, · - - - - $......
Second year, - - - - - ......
Third year, - - - - - ......

Total Grand Dues, $......

10.—The amount of expenses:

First year, - - - - - - $......
Second year, - - - - - ......
Third year, - - - - - ......

Total Grand Dues, $......

11.—Clear balance, - - - - - $......

I hereby certify that this is a true report of International District, No. ....

................D. G. M.

The I. C. G. S. is hereby authorized to collect the Grand Dues from the Districts annually, and give his receipts to the D. G. M. for the amount received.

"In Solo Deo Salus!"

SYNOPSIS

OF

OFFICIAL FORMS,

USED BY THE

INTERNATIONAL

ORDER OF TWELVE

TABORIAN FORMS.

———: o :———

777—INTERNATIONAL ORDER OF TWELVE.—333.

PETITION.

To the Members of................*Temple, No*......
Your petitioner has formed a good opinion of the International Order of Twelve, and desires to be made a member of your Temple.   If admitted, I promise to obey the Laws and Regulations of the Order.

Age...., Residence......, Recommended by.........
Signed this the......day of......, A. D. 18...
Enclosed Fee, $......   ....

———

333—INTERNATIONAL ORDER OF TWELVE.—333.

PETITION.

To the Members of.............*Tabernacle, No*......
Your petitioner has formed a favorable opinion of the International Order of Twelve.   I desire to be made a member of your Tabernacle.   If I am admitted a member, I promise to obey the Laws and Regulations of the Order.

Age...., Residence......, Recommended by........
Signed this the......day of......, A. D. 18...
Enclosed Fee, $......   ....

———

INTERNATIONAL ORDER OF TWELVE.

PETITION.

To the Members of................*Palatium, No*......
Your petitioner has been a member of the International Order of Twelve for............   I am now in good standing in..........Temple, (or Tabernacle.) No....

I desire to be enrolled a member of the Royal House of Media, if found worthy.

Residence........., Recommended by.............

Signed this the......day of......, A. D. 18...

Enclosed Fee, $......   ....

777—INTERNATIONAL ORDER OF TWELVE.—333.

GRAND TEMPLE AND TABERNACLE TRANSFER.

To All Whom These May Concern, Greeting:

After careful examination, I am satisfied that the bearer.............is a member of the International Order of Twelve, and is worthy. By virtue of the authority he (or she) is hereby transferred to any Temple of the Knights of Tabor (or Tabernacle) that elects him (or her) a member, upon payment of one dollar.

Signed and sealed this the......day of......, A. D. 18..., A. O. T......

   [SEAL.]   ....C. G. M.

For.................and Jurisdiction.

777—INTERNATIONAL ORDER OF TWELVE.—999.

TRANSFER.

This is to certify, that the bearer, Sir..............,
was a member in good standing when the transfer was granted, in.............Temple, No... He is hereby transferred to any Temple working under the International Order of Twelve; *provided*, he is elected by a majority vote of the members present at any Regular Session, and upon payment of one dollar. This transfer is good for sixty days from date only.

Witness our hands and seals this the........day of........, A. D. 18..., A. O. T......

              ....C. M.

   [SEAL.]   ....C. S.

The Temple granting this transfer is authorized to charge one dollar for it. No transfer can be granted, unless all dues and fines are paid.

INTERNATIONAL ORDER OF TWELVE.

R. M.—TRANSFER.—P. M.

This is to certify, that Prince (or Princess) was a member in good standing at the time this transfer was granted, of............Palatium, No... He (or she) is hereby transferred to any Palatium that is working under the International Order of Twelve; *provided*, he (or she) is elected by a majority of the members present, and upon payment of one dollar.

Witness our hands and seals this the.........day of........., A. D. 18..., A. O. T......

[SEAL.]   ....P. P.
.............................R. P.

The members who receive a transfer shall pay one dollar for it.

333—INTERNATIONAL ORDER OF TWELVE.—333.

TRANSFER.

This is to certify, that the bearer, Daughter Priestess ....,was a member in good standing when this transfer was granted, of.............Tabernacle, No... She is hereby transferred to any Tabernacle working under the International Order of Twelve; *provided*, she is elected by a majority vote of the members present at a Regular Session, and upon payment of one dollar. This transfer is good for sixty days from date only.

Witness our hands and seals this the.........day of........., A. D. 18..., A. O. T.....

[SEAL.]   ....C. P.
.............................C. R.

The Tabernacle granting this transfer is authorized to charge one dollar for it.

INTERNATIONAL ORDER OF TWELVE.

TRANSFER.

This is to certify, that the bearer was a member in good standing of.............Tent, No..., at the time this transfer was granted. He (or she) is hereby transferred to any Tent of Maids and Pages working under the International Order of Twelve.

Signed this the........day of........, A. D. 18.....

[SEAL.] ....Q. M.

..........................C. R. K.

777—INTERNATIONAL ORDER OF TWELVE.—333.

TRAVELING CERTIFICATE.

To All Whom These May Come, Greeting:

This is to certify, that the bearer is a member in good standing in...........Temple, No..., situated in the City of........., State of.........

This certificate is granted to Sir.............for the term of.........months. His monthly card will show that he is clear with the Chief Scribe's books, and he will give the Quarterly Pass that was used at the date of this certificate. Chief Mentors are requested to give and impart to him the Quarterly Pass whenever it is changed.

Members of the International Order of Twelve, everywhere, are requested to receive Sir............as a true and loyal member of the Knights and Daughters of Tabor, of the Uniform Rank.

Signed this the........day of........, A. D. 18...,
A. O. T.......

..........................C. M.

Attested by the seal of the Temple, and sig-

[SEAL.] nature of the Chief Scribe.

..........................C. S.

This certificate is good only for the time for which it is granted.

777—INTERNATIONAL ORDER OF TWELVE.—333.

TRAVELING CERTIFICATE.

To All Whom These Come, Greeting:

This is to certify, that the bearer is a member in good standing in..........Tabernacle, No..., situated in the City of.........., State of..........

This certificate is granted to Daughter Priestess...... ......, for the term of..........months. Her monthly card will show that she is clear with the Chief Recorder's books, and she will give the Quarterly Pass which was used at the date of this certificate. The High Priestesses are requested to give and impart to her the Quarterly Pass whenever it is changed.

Members of the International Order of Twelve, everywhere, are requested to receive Daughter Priestess..... ....as a true and loyal member of the Knights and Daughters of Tabor, and Priestess of Saba Meroe.

Signed this the........day of.........., A. D. 18..., A. O. T.......

..............................C. P.

Attested by the seal of the Tabernacle and [SEAL.]   signature of the Chief Recorder.

..............................C. R.

This certificate is good only for the time for which it is granted.

QUARTERLY REPORT.—FORM 1.

1.—Number of members, - - - - ......

2.—Number suspended for dues, - - - .....

3.—Number expelled, - - - - .....

4.—Amount of sick dues paid this quarter, - ......

5.—Died this quarter, - - - - ......

6.—The amount of dues received this quarter, ...

7.—Number of new members received this quarter, - - - - - - - ......

8.—The amount received for fees, - - ......

9.—Total amount received from all sources, - ......

10.—Amount paid out for regular expenses, - ......

11.—Amount paid out for funeral expenses this
quarter - - - - - - ......

12.—Amount given to distressed Knights or
Daughters, - - - - - ......

13.—Amount paid for C. G. P. or C. G. M. visits,......

14.—Total amount paid out during the quarter, ...

15.—Balance in the treasury and bank, - - ......

16.—Do you own a hall? - - - - ......

17.—Do you hold your regular sessions? - - ......

18.—Are your sessions pleasant and instructive?......

I hereby certify this to be a correct report of
[SEAL.]   the condition of.................Temple,
No.... (or Tabernacle, No....)
.........................C. M. (or C. P.)
Attested and sealed this the........day of........,
A. D. 18..., A. O. T.......
.........................C. S. (or C. R.)

All Temples and Tabernacles must report to the Chief Grand Mentor the first week in March, June, September and December. A Temple or Tabernacle that fails to report quarterly, will be considered in bad condition.

The address of the C. M. or C. P. is.........Street, City of...........State of............

QUARTERLY REPORT.—FORM 2.

1.—Number of members, - . - - - ......
2.—How many boys? - - - - - ......
3.—How many girls? - - - - ......
4.—How many boys transferred to the Temple? ......
5.—How many girls transferred to the Tabernacle? - - - - - - ......
6.—What is the amount of dues received this quarter? - - - - - - ......
7.—What amount of fees received this quarter?......
8.—Total amount received from all sources, - ......
9.—How much paid out for regular expenses? ......
10.—The amount paid to sick members, - ......
11.—The amount paid on funerals this quarter, ...
12.—The amount paid on other expenses, - ......
13.—Balance in treasury _ - - - ......
14.—Do you hold your sessions regularly? - ......

I certify the above to be a true report of...........
Tent, No....

..........................Q. M.

(ATTESTED.)..........................C. R. K.

All Tents must make a report to the Grand Queen Mother the first week in March, June, September and December.

The address of the Queen Mother is................
Street, City of............., State of................

THE QUARTERLY PASS.

The Quarterly Pass is issued to all Temples and Tabernacles every three months. When it is received by the C. M. or C. P. they impart it to their members at the first Regular Session after it is received. If members are not at the Session, they cannot receive it until the next Session, as it is not to be given outside of a Session, and then only by the Presiding Officer. C. M. and C. P. are not permitted to give it to any but their members, except to one having a traveling certificate from some other Temple or Tabernacle. The Quarterly Pass is a safe-guard against imposition. C. M.s and C. P.s must carefully follow these rules, and instruct their members not to give it to any one, not even to a member of their own Temple or Tabernacle, who have not received it.

———:o:———

REGULAR SESSION.

Temples and Tabernacles must hold at least one Session in each month, if they fail to meet, they forfeit their charter or warrant. If for reasons which make it impossible for the Temple or Tabernacle to have their Regular Session, the C. M. or C. P. must write immediately to the C. G. M. and give him the reason, and get his dispensation. Unless this is done the charter or warrant will be forfeited just as soon as the C. G. M. is notified.

International Order of Twelve

OF

Knights and Daughters of Tabor.

ITS MOTTO:

"In Solo Deo Salus!"

————:o:————

WORK AND BUSINESS OF MEMBERS.

This Order was organized for the benefit of its members, and the people among whom Temples, Tabernacles, Palatiums and Tents are organized. It is the duty of the Order,

First, to take care of its sick and distressed members, to relieve its poor and helpless members, and to sustain the widows and orphans.

Second, to advance the standard of virtue and morality, encourage and aid in multiplying schools and institutions of learning, and to impress upon its members the necessity of investing in real estate, and acquiring homesteads.

Third, to impress upon its members that they shall be loyal to the Government in which they live, and to be temperate, law abiding and trustworthy.

Fourth, our Order is non-sectarian and non-political, therefore no denominational or political discussions shall be permitted in our Temples, Tabernacles or Palatiums.

Fifth, when a member in good standing dies, it is the duty of the Temple or Tabernacle and Palatium to have the member respectably interred.

Rights of Chief Mentors.

A Chief Mentor is responsible to the Grand Temple and Tabernacle for the manner in which he conducts the business of his Temple. It is his business to enforce the Laws of the Order, and the Edicts of the C. G. M. He must have a thorough knowledge of all the Laws and Rules of the Order. He must not permit any one to assume control of his Temple. His decisions are final, until reversed by the C. G. M.

Rights of High Priestess. (C. P.)

A High Priestess is responsible to the Grand Temple and Tabernacle for the manner in which she conducts the business of her Tabernacle. She must enforce the Laws of the Order, and the Edicts of the C. G. M. She must have a thorough knowledge of the Laws and Rules of the Order. She must not permit any one to assume control of her Tabernacle. Her decisions are final, until reversed by the Chief Grand Mentor or Chief Grand Preceptress.

Rights of Members.

Members of the International Order of Twelve are obligated to obey all the Laws, Rules and Edicts. It is the right of members in good standing to receive the weekly benefit when sick or disabled, and to receive aid when in distress. It is their right to demand and receive a traveling certificate upon their compliance with the Laws. It is their right to receive a transfer, when they have paid all their dues and taxes. There is no power that can suspend or expel a member without a trial, by due process of the Laws of the Order. The right of appeal, in accordance with the laws of appeals, must not be denied to a member. A Knight of Tabor, in good standing, has the right to visit any Temple or Tabernacle, by producing proof that he is in good standing in the Temple that he is a member of. A Daughter of Tabor has the right to visit any Tabernacle, by producing proof that she is in good standing in the Tabernacle that she is a member of. It is the right of members, who die in good standing, to receive a respectable burial, in accordance with the Laws of the Order.

RIGHTS OF QUEEN MOTHERS.

A Queen Mother has full control of her Tent, and must administer the Laws governing the Tents, and the Edicts of the C. G. M. She is to open and close her Tent without a motion, in accordance with the By-Laws of her Tent. She must have a thorough knowledge of the Laws of the Order. Her decisions are final, until they are reversed by the Grand Queen Mother.

RIGHTS OF PRESIDING PRINCES.

A Presiding Prince has full control of his Palatium, and must administer the Laws that govern Palatiums, and the Edicts of the C. G. M. He is to open and close the Palatium without a motion, in accordance with the By-Laws. He must have a thorough knowledge of the Laws of the Order. His decisions are final, until they are reversed by the C. G. M.

A Recommendation.

It is recommended that the Daughters' Tabernacles hold their Sessions during the hours of the day. If this is done, they will avoid being out late at night, and will save themselves great inconvenience, and for many other reasons not necessary to mention. It will surely be for the best interests of our Daughters to meet during the day.

The Degrees.

The degrees of the International Order of Twelve must be given according to the form as laid down in the Rituals, and care must be taken to give the candidate full and perfect instructions. No part of the ceremony must be omitted. One or two degrees should only be conferred at any one Session; in fact, it is best to confer but one degree on the candidate at each Session. This will give the candidate a better idea of the different degrees. This law applies only to chartered and warranted organizations, and not to the setting up of Clubs.

International Districts.

The I. C. G. M. may organize Districts in any State, Territory or country, where there is no Grand Temple and Tabernacle. These Districts are to remain under the Government of the International Grand Temple and Tabernacle, until they are organized into Grand Temples and Tabernacles. The I. C. G. M. shall appoint a District Mentor and District Preceptress. A District must hold an Annual Session, to be presided over by the I. C. G. M. or District Mentor. The District must be composed of all the Temples, Tabernacles, Palatiums and Tents, in one, two or more States or Territories.

DUTIES OF THE DISTRICT MENTOR.

It shall be the duty of the District Mentor to make organizations in all parts of the District he shall visit, and instruct Temples, Tabernacles, Palatiums and Tents, when they request his presence. - When he visits, his traveling expenses and *per diem* must be paid by the Temple, Tabernacle, Palatium or Tent which invites him. He must, when ordered by the I. C. G. M., visit any part of the District on special business for the Order. His expenses must be paid out of the International Grand Treasury. He is to represent his District in the Triennial Grand Session, and the Temples, Tabernacles, Palatiums and Tents in the District will be assessed *pro rata* to pay his traveling expenses and *per diem*. He is to keep a list of all organizations, and report to the I. C. G. M. their condition from time to time. C. M.s and C. P.s will make their quarterly reports to him, and he will furnish them with the Quarterly Pass. His office expenses will be paid out of the funds of the District Session, that is, for his stationery and postage stamps.

DUTIES OF THE DISTRICT PRECEPTRESS.

It shall be the duty of the District Preceptress to visit all Tabernacles and Tents, when invited by the C. P. or Q. M. Her expenses are to be paid by the Tabernacle or Tent that she visits. She is authorized to organize Tabernacles, Palatiums and Tents in all parts of her District. She is the Representative of the District in the Triennial Grand

Session, and the organizations in the District will be assessed *pro rata* to pay her expenses.

GRAND DUES.

The amount which each Temple, Tabernacle, Palatium and Tent shall pay for each member, will be named from year to year, and collected at the District Session. Any Temple, Tabernacle, Palatium and Tent, which fails to pay Grand Dues every year, shall pay the penalty awarded by the District Session.

DISTRICT SESSIONS.

The C. M. must represent his Temple either in person or by his Vice.

The C. P. must represent her Tabernacle either in person or by her Vice.

The P. P. or V.-P. must represent the Palatium.

The Queen Mother must represent her Tent in person or by her Vice.

Each of the above organizations must pay the traveling expenses and *per diem* of their Representatives.

TIME.

The time and month for holding the District Sessions, shall be fixed by the International Chief Grand Mentor.

REGALIA.

The full dress of the Uniform Knights of Tabor shall be as follows:

A black coat, single-breasted, buttoned up to the neck in military style, yellow metal buttons, with letters "U. K. T.;" black pants; helmet, trimmed with gold lace; a shield, with the letters "U. K.

T.," ornamented with a scarlet feather; a baldric, four inches wide, colors black in the center and scarlet on each side, trimmed with half inch gold lace; on left breast the letters "U. K. T.," made of yellow metal; a twelve-pointed star on the shoulder, with the figures "777" in the center; guantlets of same colors as the baldric, made to reach half way to the elbow, ornamented with letters "U. K. T.;" gloves buck-skin or lisle-thread, color light yellow; regulation sword, silver scabbard with shield letters "U. K. T.;" silver chains, scarlet belt, with hooks for cap and cup, on sword blade the words Uniform Rank of Tabor; black navy cap, trimmed with silver lace, letters "U. K. T."

UNDRESS UNIFORM.

When giving the degrees or on fatigue duty the uniform is the cap, sword, belt, gloves and badge. The badge is a ten-pointed star, made of white metal, with "777" in the center, scarlet ribbon, with letters International Order of Twelve printed thereon. The badge is attached to the left breast by bar and pin.

C. M.s AND P. C. M.s

Colors are emerald green, and gold; baldric, green and black; helmet, green feather; sword, yellow metal scabbard and chains; cap, gold lace; badge or jewel, yellow metal.

SABA MEROES REGALIA.

FULL DRESS.

The High Priestess, Tharbis, white dress, a royal purple robe entrail, spangled with small gold stars fastened at the shoulders with "333" golden pins. The jewel of office is pinned to left breast. The staff in her right hand. An emerald green belt, gold clasp "333," gloves long, pink silk or lisle-thread. A golden coronet, ornamented with different colored stones. A Maid and Page accompany her on all public occasions.

THE DRESS OF OTHER OFFICERS.

Amisis, Scsotheni, Seraphis, Hyerego, Abassine, Lybenus, three Hespers, three Cyrenes, white dress, sky blue robe entrail, spangled with small silver stars; sky blue belt; silver clasp "333;" pink silk or lisle-thread gloves; a golden coronet, ornamented with white stones.

DRESS REGALIA.

The C. P.s and P. C. P.s will wear the following: A collar, emerald green, ornamented with twelve golden stars; pink gloves; staff; coronet; emerald green sash or belt; jewel of office; yellow metal star, resting on a ring; lettered in center, C. P. or P. C. P. and emerald green ribbon on which is printed, "International Order of Twelve" (with bar and pin).

OTHER OFFICERS.

V.-P., C. R., C. T., C. Ps., I. St., O. St., B. Vs. and B. Es., emerald green collar, trimmed with twelve silver stars, pink gloves, emerald green sash or belt (333), coronet, jewel of office, white metal star resting on a ring, with initials office in the center; sky-blue ribbon on which is printed "International Order of Twelve" (with bar and pin).

OTHER MEMBERS.

Emerald green collar, ornamented with twelve silver stars, buff colored gloves, emerald green sash or belt ("333"), a silver coronet or wreath of flowers. The Badge—a white metal star resting on a ring ("333") in the center. Sky-blue ribbon on which is printed, "International Order of Twelve" (with bar and pin).

All regalia may be ornamented with either gold or silver lace or fringe to match the color of the stars worn by the member.

UNDRESS OF DAUGHTERS.

The undress of the Daughters is the Jewel or Badge, which must be worn at all Sessions when the full regalia is not required, as also gloves. The Jewel or Badge can be worn at any time to designate that you are a member of the Order on any public occasion, when the full regalia is not needed.

MOURNING BADGE.

The Mourning Badge is a small rosette made of crape, with an emerald green center. This must be worn for the time set by the Temple or Tabernacle after the death of a member, not less than thirty nor more than sixty days.

STAFFS AND RODS.

The C. P.'s staff is about three feet long, one inch in diameter, surmounted with a golden ball; color of staff, emerald green.

Inner and Outer Sentinels' rods are seven feet long, one inch in diameter; color, emerald green, surmounted with spear and golden ball.

The C. Ps.' rod is seven feet long, one inch in

diameter; color, emerald green, surmounted with a golden crook.

FORM OF TABERNACLE HOUSE.

The House shall be three stories high. First story, fifteen inches square, twelve inches high; second story, ten inches square, twelve inches high; third story, open on four columns, fifteen inches high. Color: First story, pink; second story, pea-green; third story, white.

Rings for carrying; two pink poles.

The moulding of the Tabernacle may be gilded and ornamented to suit the taste.

Lettering on first story, first side, the name and number; second side, the date of warrant; third side, "Daughters of the Tabernacle;" fourth side, the name of city and State.

Second story, first side, 333; second side, the Bible; third side, the cups; fourth side, the golden shoes.

FORM OF TEMPLE HOUSE.

The Temple House shall be three stories high. First story, eighteen inches square and one foot deep; second story, fifteen inches square and one foot deep; third story, ten inches square and one foot deep, made to open in each story. Color: First story, light scarlet; second story, pea-green; third story, white; moulding gilded. Lettering: First story—On one side, the name of the Temple and number; next side, the date of its organization; third side, the city and State; fourth side, "Knights of Tabor." Second story—First, 777; second, 999; third, 444; fourth, 333. Third story—First, the eye; second, the clasped hands; third, the ear; fourth, the emblematic star; rings and pole for carrying.

TEMPLE FURNITURE.

The Holy Bible, two cups, gavel, three pitchers, sword, girdle, star, shield, key, Manual, three candle-sticks, and staff.

TABERNACLE FURNITURE.

Holy Bible, two golden shoes, roll of flax, two cups, ball of wool, curious girdle, five candle-sticks, coronet, robes, bells, door, chariot and chair, and faces.

ALTAR.

The altar is two feet six inches in height, one foot six inches wide, and one foot deep, painted emerald green on one side, on one side scarlet, on one side blue, and on one side black, with figures "777," "333," "444," "999" (one set of figures on each side), the top white.

GOVERNING DEPARTMENTS

1.—Temples of the Knights of Tabor.
2.— Tabernacles of Daughter Priestesses of Tabor.
3.—Palatiums of the Royal House of Media.
4.—Tents of Maids and Pages of Honor.
5.—Grand Temples and Tabernacles.
6.—International Grand Temple and Tabernacle.

SICKNESS.

One of the fundamental principles, as well as most important, of the International Order of Twelve, is the care of its sick, disabled or distressed members. An order or society which does not make provision for its sick, has no right to exist.

The Temple or Tabernacle that does not amply provide for its sick, disabled or distressed members, ought to and should close up, for they are a disgrace to the Order. Each Temple and Tabernacle must pay a weekly benefit, and if the sick members need more, arrangements may be made to meet the expenses; make your monthly dues on each member sufficient to keep money in your treasury to meet expenses. Members, who know that they will be cared for when sick, will not object to paying the monthly dues.

District Grand Mentors.

Under the authority of Grand Temples and Tabernacles, the appointing of D. G. M.s and arranging their Districts, is entirely the business of the Chief Grand Mentors. He alone has the authority to appoint. He is a Special Deputy of the C. G. M., and the limits of his District are fixed by the C. G. M.'s commission. The duties of the D. G. M. must be named in his commission. If he is ordered to visit a Temple, Tabernacle, Palatium or Tent by the C. G. M., he must be paid out of the Grand Treasury for his time, traveling expenses and *per diem*. He cannot be received into an open Temple, Tabernacle, Palatium or Tent on official business, without showing his authority from the Chief Grand Mentor. The D. G. M. is not permitted to control the business of Temples, Tabernacles Palatiums or Tents, nor can he preside in the election of officers in any of the departments.

SUPPLIES.

The supplies which must be furnished, with the charter, to new Temples, are as follows:—

6 Constitutions, 2 Complete Rituals, 6 Blank Transfers, 6 Blank Traveling Certificates, 25 Monthly Cards, 12 Blank Petitions, 4 Blank Quarterly Reports, the Quarterly Pass and Key.

New Tabernacles, with the warrant:—6 Constitutions, 2 Third Degree Rituals, and 2 Fourth Degree Rituals, 25 Monthly Cards, 6 Blank Transfers, 6 Blank Traveling Certificates, 12 Blank Petitions, 4 Blank Quarterly Reports, the Quarterly Pass and Key.

New Palatiums, with the charter, 12 Rituals and 1 Manual. Palatiums make their own Constitution and By-Laws, but they shall not conflict with the General Laws and Constitution of Grand Temples and Tabernacles.

New Tents, with charter, 25 Monthly Cards and 12 Constitutions.

Every Temple, Tabernacle, Palatium and Tent must have and own a Manual within three months after having been organized and set up.

INCORPORATION.

Grand Temples and Tabernacles are a part of the International Order of Twelve, yet they are set apart as a Governing Power under the General Laws in their States, Territories or Provinces. For the purpose of legalizing these organizations and their departments, they must be incorporated. The Board of Grand Curators shall be the incorporators.

Real Estate.

Grand Temples and Tabernacles should secure Real Estate, by having it deeded to the Board of Grand Curators and their successors in office, the ownership to be vested in the Grand Temple and Tabernacle of Knights and Daughters of Tabor, for the State of ——.

A Temple or Tabernacle which is making preparations to build a hall, or is about to buy a lot or building, may secure the same as follows:

First, call a meeting and elect Trustees. A deed can be made to these Trustees and their successors in office, the ownership to be vested in —— Temple, No. —, of Knights of Tabor. (If a Tabernacle, in —— Tabernacle, No. —, of Daughters of Tabor), name town or city, county and State.

When a Temple and Tabernacle unite to purchase, they call a joint meeting and elect Trustees. The property is deeded to these Trustees and their successors. The ownership is vested in —— Temple, No. —, and —— Tabernacle, No. —, of Knights and Daughters of Tabor. Name town or city, county and State.

In cities where there are a number of Temples and Tabernacles, a joint meeting is called of all the numbers, and Trustees are elected. A deed is made to these Trustees and their successors in office. The ownership is vested in (the name and number of each Temple and Tabernacle is given in the deed to the Knights and Daughters of Tabor, also name of city, county and State.)

The Number of Trustees.

There may be three, five, seven or nine Trustees. In some States they must all be males, in others a woman may be a Trustee. Whatever the law is, comply with it.

Election.

The Trustees are elected annually, at a meeting called for that purpose. Thirty days' notice must be given, or the day and date fixed in the By-Laws.

Stocks and Shares.

When one Temple or Tabernacle buys real estate, it is not necessary to form a joint-stock company, but when two or more join together, the amount of stock should be fixed and that divided into shares. Temples and Tabernacles may take shares, or it can be made so that the individual members can be shareholders. None but members of the International Order of Twelve, however, shall be shareholders.

Incorporation.

Real estate, upon which halls are built, or to be built, must be incorporated in accordance with the form of the law of the State in which the real estate is situated.

Palatium Regalia.

The Regalia of a Palatine Guard shall be as follows:

Baldric, made of leather, four inches wide, length to suit the height of the person. The center emerald green, on each side of the green scarlet, trimmed with gold lace. A yellow metal star, with seven points, on the shoulder; letters on the breast "P. C.;" epaulet on left shoulder, ornamented with green and gold. Regular Palatium Badge. A black chapeau; a yellow metal star with seven points, lettered "P. C." in the center. Green and white feathers; chapeau ornamented with gold lace. Guantlets or gloves of brown leather; guantlets ornamented with "777" on yellow metal. Dress black military suit, with double row of yellow metal buttons, lettered "P. C."

Undress Uniform.

Black skull-cap, with gold lace band, lettered "P. C.;" sword and belt; brown lisle-thread gloves; and regulation badge, of yellow metal.

Regalia of a Princess of Media.

Light buff dress, sash six inches wide, colors emerald green and dark pink, three inches of each color. The sash to hang from the left shoulder. A seven-pointed star of yellow metal, lettered "P. M." The star on the shoulder. The sash is made to suit the height of the person. The belt dark pink, with a five-pointed star made of yellow metal, used as a clasp, and lettered "P. M." Gauntlets and gloves dark pink, letters on guantlets "P. M.;" a poniard suspended by a gilded chain near the left side; a silver cup attached to the belt, and a mural crown, ornamented with a variety of colored stones.

The regalia may be ornamented with gold lace and fringe, to suit the taste.

Undress Regalia of Princess of Media.

Any colored dress may be worn; the regulation badge, color emerald green and dark pink; Palatium Badge, attached to left breast by a bar and pin; also dark pink gloves.

The flag of the United States—the "Star Spangled Banner"—with flags of other nations (if thought proper), shall be displayed by the Uniform Rank Knights and Palatine Guards at all public parades.

Temple—Plateau.

Knights of Tabor may call their place of meeting or hall either a Temple or Plateau.

Chief Preceptress—High Priestess.

The Presiding Officer of a Tabernacle may be called either C. P. or H. P.

REGALIA BADGES.

"In Solo Deo Salus!"

COMPLETE LEXICON

OF

ABBREVIATIONS AND TERMS

USED IN THE

INTERNATIONAL

ORDER OF TWELVE.

TABORIAN LEXICON.

——:o:——

Abbreviations—The abbreviations which are used in the Order are fully explained for the benefit of the members, as follows:

A. D.—*Anno Domini*—in the year of the Lord, dating from the birth of Christ up to the present time.

A. M.—*Anno Mundi*—the year of the world, the age of the world.

A. O. T.—Age of Taborians.

I. S. D. S.—"*In Solo Deo Salus*"—"In God Alone is Safety"—The motto of the Order.

K. O. T.—Knights of Tabor.

U. R. T.—Uniform Rank of Tabor.

D. T.—Daughter of Tabor.

D. P.—Daughter Priestess.

Q. M.—Queen Mother.

M. A. P.—Maids and Pages.

T. C.—Taborian Cadets.

P. P.—Presiding Prince of the Palatium.

V.-Ps.—Vice-Princess of the Palatium.

P. R. M.—Prince of the Royal House of Media.

P. O. M.—Princess of Media.

P. P. P.—Past Presiding Prince.

P. V.-Ps.—Past Vice-Princess.

C. M.—Chief Mentor—the Presiding Officer of the Temple.

P. C. M.—Past Chief Mentor.

C. P.—Chief Preceptress—The Presiding Officer of the Tabernacle.

P. C. P.—Past Chief Preceptress.

H. P.—High Priestess—Presiding Officer in the Ancient Tabernacle.

C. S.—Chief Scribe of Temple.

C. T.—Chief Treasurer of Temple.

C. O.—Chief Orator of Temple.

C. C. B.—Chief Color Bearer of Temple.

C. D.-M.—Chief Drill-Master of Temple.

C. G.—Chief Guard of Temple.

C. St.—Chief Sentinel of Temple.

V.-P.—Vice-Preceptress or Vice-Priestess of Tabernacle.

C. R.—Chief Recorder of Tabernacle.

C. Tr.—Chief Treasurer of Tabernacle.

C. Ps.—Chief Priestess of Tabernacle.

C. T.—Chief Tribune of Tabernacle.

I. St.—Inner Sentinel of Tabernacle.

TITLES.

Temple—C. M. or Sir Chief.

Tabernacle, in the Fourth Degree, H. P. or Tharbis.

Palatium—P. P. or Sir Prince.

Tents—C. M. P. or Chief Maid.

Grand Temple and Tabernacle.—C. G. M. or Grand Chief.

International Grand Temple and Tabernacle.—I. C. G. M. or International Grand Chief.

I. O. T.—International Order of Twelve.

C. M. P.—Chief Maid—the Presiding Officer of the Tent.

C. G. M.—Chief Grand Mentor—the Presiding Grand Officer of a Grand Temple and Tabernacle.

P. C. G. M.—Past Chief Grand Mentor.

C. G. P.—Chief Grand Preceptress.

P. C. G. P.—Past Chief Grand Preceptress.

G. Q. M.—Grand Queen Mother.

P. G. Q. M.—Past Grand Queen Mother.

D. G. M.—Deputy Grand Mentor, or District Grand Mentor.

D. G. P.—Deputy Grand Preceptress.

G. T. T.—Grand Temple and Tabernacle.

I. C. G. M.—International Chief Grand Mentor —the Presiding Officer of the International Grand Temple and Tabernacle.

P. I. C. G. M.—Past International Chief Grand Mentor.

I. C. G. P.—International Chief Grand Preceptress.

P. I. C. G. P.—Past International Chief Grand Preceptress.

I. G. Q. M.—International Grand Queen Mother.

P. I. G. Q. M.—Past International Grand Queen Mother.

I. D. G. M.—International Deputy Grand Mentor.

I. G. D.—International Grand Deputy (a Daughter).

I. G. T. T.—International Grand Temple and Tabernacle.

A.

Agla—One of the twelve cabalistic names which the ancient Magies of Persia and other mystic workers used to express the incommunicable name of the Deity—the names given are as follows:

Ehi, Azazel, Eloho, El-Gibbor, Eloah, Sabaoth, Tseboath, Shaddai, Adonai, Makom and Agla. The followers of Mithra, in practicing their mystic rites, worshipped God under the name of Agla.

Amath—A noted Prince of the Tribe of Benjamin. He was a giant in strength, and one of Israel's mightiest warriors, a cotemporary with Barak and Deborah; and history tells us that he was one of the leaders, with ten thousand warriors, who conquered Sisera and his army in a battle near Mount Tabor, B. C. 1336.

Adonia—The Jews did not believe it right to pronounce the true name of God. Josephus, the Jewish historian, said it was not lawful to pronounce His holy name. In reading, whenever the word Jehovah occurred, they abstained from pronouncing it, and used the word Adonia instead. The definition of this word is Lord or Master. It is one of the twelve cabalistic names of God. The number "12" is a perfect number, and a symbol of purity.

Aya—In the mysteries of Ethiopia we find the name Aya used to express the Goddess of Thunder, the wife of the River Nile. She was supposed by the ancient Ethiopians to have full command of the rise and fall of the Nile. When it thundered, it was Aya speaking. She was supposed to be seated at the entrance of the ancient Tabernacle of

Saba Meroc, guarded by a great serpent. The precepts of her thunder-bolts were light from Heaven.

Arcanum—A mystery, a hidden secret. In Latin, Arcanus, a closed secret, a chest or box, or a secret repository. The Past Arcanum is the Twelfth Degree in the International Order of Twelve, and is the Presiding and Past Presiding Officers' Degree. The members are regularly organized, and have monthly sessions. They represent their Temples, Tabernacles, Palatiums and Tents.

Adoption—The title of the First Degree in the Tabernacle. When a Daughter takes this degree, she is adopted a Daughter of Tabor, and her name is enrolled on the C. R.'s roll-book.

Advance—The title of the Second Degree in the Tabernacle. When the adopted Daughter has served her full time, she is prepared to advance to the more serious and trustworthy dignity of a Daughter of Tabor.

Altar—Just after the dawn and sun-rise of creation, very early in the history of the world, Altars were erected, and sacrificial offerings were made upon them in honor of and thank-givings to God. The first Altar that history gives an account of was built by Cain and Abel, sons of Adam and Eve. Through the pages of history, for four thousand years, we read of Altars having been erected for sacrificial offerings and praises to God.

In the Uniform Rank, or Fourth Degree of the Knights of Tabor, the Altar takes a very prominent part. In the Saba Meroc, or Fourth Degree of the

(11—Dickson's New Manual.)

Daughters of Tabor, the burning Altar is a very interesting part of the ceremonies. The Presiding Officer of the Temple and of the Tabernacle is seated South of the Altar, the Vice in the North, the C. R. in the East and the Chief Treasurer in the West.

Ammon—(See Jupiter Ammon).

Amen—An expression used at the closing of prayer, and signifies "So be it." When it is used in a declaration, it means "Truly, faithfuly fulfilled."

Abassine—The name of the Inner Sentinel of the Ancient Tabernacle of Saba Moroe. Abyssinia, a country in Africa, situated South of Nubia and West of the Red Sea, once was a powerful ancient government, but with the fall of Ethiopia, Abyssinia gradually lost its civilization and internal wars debased the people to barbarism. The Abyssinians embraced Christianity under the reign of Constantine the Great, and for a time these people lived a peaceful life, and the prospects were that they would return to their ancient greatness, but internal strife again reduced this favored country to its savage practices. The population at this date is about 3,000,-000, divided into many distinct tribes, most of whom are in a barbarous condition. Abassine, the guardian of the inner entrance of the ancient Tabernacle was a native of that country.

Amisis—The name of the Priestess of the Temple which was situated in ancient Nubia, in the famous city of Beyt-El-Welee. A drawing taken from ancient sculpture found in Nubia, represents Amisis seated in the northern part of the ancient Taber-

nacle, on a throne representing the Moon. She is
receiving a delegation of rank which has come to
consult Isis, by order of Ramesis the II, about the
conducting and management of victory. The name
Amisis is purely Ethiopian, and means that the
bearer is a representative of the universal power
of the Supreme Ruler of the World, or one able to
fortell future events.

B.

Bible—The Book of Books, the Sacred Word of
God, in which are contained the revelations of
the Supreme Being. The Old and New Testament.
The rules and principles of Christian faith and
practice. It is humanity's sacred treasure. The
revealed will of God to mankind. No person can
become a member of the International Order of
Twelve, unless a firm believer in the teachings of
the Holy Volume.

Barak—About the year 1336, B. C., the children
of Isreal were held captives by the Canaanites.
They prayed unto God to deliver them. He heard
their petition, and sent Deborah, a prophetess, who
was Judge of Israel at that time, to call Barak, a
son of Abinoam, of Kedesh-Naphthali, to go to
Mount Tabor, and take with him ten thousand men
of the tribes of Naphthali and Zebulon, Barak and
Deborah gathered ten thousand men, fully armed and
equipped, on the Plateau of Mount Tabor, and gave
battle to the immense hosts of Canaanites, who were
under the command of Sisera, and by the help of
God secured a great victory, and freed the captive
Isaraelites. Knights of Tabor will not forget the
inner history which secured to Barak this extraordinary victory.

Book of Laws—Law is that which is set and fixed by statute, an edict, a rule of government, an expressed degree, a command, an enactment. No government could exist for any length of time without a code of laws founded upon the principles of justice and right. All who are enrolled members of the International Order of Twelve are presented with a book of laws—the Manual and the Constitutions. The unwritten law is impressed upon their memory in such a manner that it cannot be forgotten.

Ballot—It is the lawful duty of the members of a Temple and Tabernacle to ballot on every candidate. The balls are white and black. All members present at the Session must vote. If a candidate is reported on favorably by the Committee, the ballot box is prepared by one of the Chief Guards or Chief Tribunes, who puts all the balls into one apartment of the box and then places it on the altar. The C. S. or C. R. calls the roll. As each member's name is called, the vote is cast; when the roll is finished, the Guard or Tribune takes the box to the V.-M. or V.-P. who examines the balls, but does not announce. The box is then placed before the C. M. or C. P., and is examined, and the result announced. If four black balls are found, the candidate is rejected. If the C. M. or C. P. thinks a mistake has been made by some member voting a black ball, another ballot is ordered.

Blue—One of the appropriate colors found in the Second Degree in the Tabernacle. It is an emblem of universal love, and of that charity which is as broad as creation. It is emblematic of true friendship and constant benevolence.

Banner—In the International Order of Twelve four different banners are used. The Temple Banner is made of heavy silk; colors, one side, emerald green; on the other side scarlet. The trimming is gold; the lettering on the green side is "*In Solo Deo Salus*," a twelve-pointed star in the center, with figures "777," "999," and at the bottom "U. R. of K. of T;" on the scarlet side the name and number of the Temple is given, a seven-pointed star, and the name of the city and State or country.

The Tabernacle Banner is made of heavy silk, one side emerald green, the other side light pink. Lettering on the green side is "Saba Meroe." A shield with the following colors: gold, blue, purple, scarlet and white, with "333" in the center of the shield.

The Banner of the International Order of Twelve is trimmed with gold lace and fringe; on the pink side the name and number of the Tabernacle and the name of the city and State and country.

The Palatium Banner is made of heavy silk or satin, trimmed with gold. The four colors are green, scarlet, purple and white, arranged to suit the taste. The lettering on one side is "Royal House of Media," and a blazing star with twelve points. "International Order of Twelve" on the other side. The name and number of the Palatium, a globe, the name of city and State and country.

The Tent Banner is made of silk or linen, trimmed with silver lace and fringe. The colors are pink and scarlet; on one side a bee-hive: "The Children of Mount Tabor;" on the other side the name and number of the Tent, and city and State and country. The Taborian Cadets carry a United States flag also.

The flag of the United States of North America must be carried in all public processions, and also the flag of other nations wherein the Order is established.

Badges—A badge is a mark of distinction; it is worn by Orders and Societies to designate to which Order or Society the wearer belongs. They that wear a badge, ought to be prepared to prove their right to display it. The various badges worn by the members of the International Order of Twelve are hereby fully explained.

The Badge of a Knight of Tabor is a ten-pointed star, made of silver or white metal, with figures "777" in the center; a scarlet ribbon, with the words "International Order of Twelve" printed thereon. The fastening is a bar and pin, worn on left breast. The Badge of a Chief Mentor and Past C. M. is gold or yellow metal, with an emerald green ribbon.

The Badge of the Daughter of the Tabernacle is a five-pointed star on a ring of silver or white metal, with figures "333" in the center; a sky-blue ribbon, with the words "International Order of Twelve" printed thereon. The fastening is a bar and pin, worn on the left breast. This is the Saba Meroe Badge. The Badge of a C. P. or H. P. is either gold or yellow metal; the ribbon is emerald green. The Past C. P. or Past H. P. wear the same.

The Badge of the Royal House of Media is a ten pointed star within a ring, made of gold or yellow metal, lettered "R. M." in the center of the star, with fastening bar and pin.

The Badge of Maids and Pages is a white metal or silver star, on the face of which are crossed javelins, with letters "T. T.," and fastening bar and pin.

C.

Candace—History informs us that for two or three centuries the reigning Queens of Ethiopia were called Candace. Ethiopia, at the time that our Savior was on earth, was not the brilliant government that it was when Queen Nicaulo visited Solomon, yet it was one of the recognized nations, under its own monarchs. Candace, Queen of Ethiopia, was enrolled among the sovereigns of the earth. One of her cabinet officers visited Jerusalem about the time that Jesus was crucified, and on his way home he had the Scriptures expounded to him by Phillip, an apostle; he believed and was baptized. This Eunuch was a man of authority under Queen Candace, and no doubt taught the Christian doctrine in Ethiopia. The name of Candace, Queen of Ethiopia, will be perpetuated in the Saba Meroe.

Cabalistic—The ancient traditions or a mysterious science, used by the ancients to interpret unpublished history of events. The Jewish doctors used a combination of words, letters and numbers in interpreting the Scriptures, and the cabalistic doctors pretended to foretell future events by the study of this science.

The Egyptian and Ethiopian priesthood used this secret science and mystery in their mystic work. It was by this means they taught the greatness of Jehovah; by this system they illustrated the great truths of the resurrection and immortality of body and soul. The Knights of Tabor, in their Third and Fourth Degrees, have clearly unfolded the mystical modes of the Cabala, in explaining sacred things.

Calanthe—A very interesting history is attached to this word. The great mysteries of Mithras were instituted by Zeradusht, a learned sage of ancient Persia. The mysteries of Mithras were divided into seven degrees. No one was accepted to membership until he had passed through the most severe tests, to prove that he was worthy to be admitted to that mystic and binding friendship which could not be severed. The aspirant for membership was first purified by water in seven baths, each bath of seven hours' duration. He was made to pass through what he supposed was flames of fire. If he had courage and determination he went through unhurt. The next was a fast of seven days to test his endurance. After these preparations he was permitted to enter a cavern, representing the world; on its walls were inscribed the celestial signs. Mithras was represented as seated in the sun, denoting that his followers paid adoration to the sun's light, heat and fire; to the right of Mithras were Dalmon and Phyletus, two men, with their right hands clasped together, around them was a bright rain-bow. They represented true friendship, and were votaries of the mysteries of Mithras. They had been tested, and proved their ability to keep an obligation.

Dalmon had been arrested for killing a man, and was tried before Dionysius, the Governor, holding office under the authority of Astyages, King of Media. (Persia at that time, 575 years, B. C., was a province governed by Media.) Dalmon was condemned and sentenced to be thrown into a den of tigers within five days. Phyletus felt it his duty to save Dalmon or die for him. He appealed to Dionysius, and stated to him that Dalmon had a wife and children who depended on their husband and father for sustenance, and that if Dalmon could not be pardoned, he would take Dalmon's place and die in his stead. He said: "I have no wife nor children depending on me, like Dalmon."

The Governor declared that he would not issue a pardon, nor would he accept the proposition which Phyletus made to him. Phyletus, finding that Dionysius would not hear him, decided to make a personal appeal to King Astyages. The king resided in a distant city. Phyletus, with two other friends, mounted on fast horses, made the journey, and appeared before the king the next day after they had started.

Phyletus gave a history of the case, the friendship that existed between him and Dalmon, and his desire, if Dalmon could not be pardoned, to be permitted to die in his stead. The king questioned Phyletus, so as to find out the workings of the mystic brotherhood, and the mysteries of Mithras. The answers were so interesting and extraordinary that the king was surprised to hear that such an order existed in Persia, a province that had been lately added to his kingdom. Calanthe, the only

daughter of the king, stood near her father when
Phyletus made his appeal, and was so pleased with
what she had heard, that she requested the king to
visit the Province of Persia and investigate the
statements that had been made. The king con-
sented, and preparations were at once made for the
journey. The king, with a large escort, arrived in
the morning of the very day on which Dalmon was
to suffer the penalty at sun-down.

After a short rest, the king summoned Dionysius,
Dalmon and Phyletus to appear before him. The
governor explained to the king all that transpired
on the trial, and that the laws of Persia demanded
life for life; and he further stated, that on the trial
it was proven that Hieatus had made the attack on
Dalmon; but the law was positive, and Dalmon
must die, unless the king decreed otherwise.
Phyletus again appealed to the king, and said that
he did not wish the king to abrogate the law, nor
would he ask a pardon, but that if a life must be
given for a life, he should permit him to die in
Dalmon's stead. On hearing this, Dalmon (though
his wife and children were present) protested that
he alone was guilty, and he never would consent to
let his friend Phyletus die for him. Phyletus reminded Dalmon of his family, and that the Mystis
would approve of his action, and the bonds of friendship required the sacrifice; but to all his entreaties
Dalmon refused to listen. Calanthe pled with her
father, the king, to pardon Dalmon. She contended
that he was the most noble man she ever heard
speak, and that the friendship between Phyletus
and Dalmon was wonderful beyond expression, and

that such greatness of courage and fidelity should merit the king's approval.

Astyages conferred apart with Dionysius. When he returned, he stated that the laws of the Meads and Persians could not be abrogated or annulled, and Dalmon must be cast into the tigers' den, and that he would not permit Phyletus to take his place. The sentence was that Dalmon must be cast into the tigers' den. Calanthe and Phyletus attempted to speak, but the king would not listen to them. The king, with his escort, accompanied the guards with Dalmon to the den. Just as the sun was setting, they lifted Dalmon to cast him into the den, amid the cries of his wife and children. Phyletus made one more effort to take his place, but was held back by the guards. Dalmon asked to speak, and the king gave him permission, he said, "Phyletus I leave my wife and children in your care; now, O king, I die contented." The king gave the signal, and the guards lifted Dalmon and let him down into the den. (The manner in which Dalmon was saved appeared wonderful to those who were not let into the secret. Under the orders of the king, secretly given to Dionysius, he instructed the keepers of the tigers to fasten them up in the second room of the den. Dalmon was let down into the empty room. The keepers were instructed to open the middle door as soon as Dalmon was drawn out. Those who looked into the opening could see the tigers as they walked around. All this was kept a secret from the people by the keepers.)

At length the king said, Calanthe, go to the opening and call Dalmon. The guards removed the cover, and Calanthe called Dalmon; he answered, O, Calanthe, Agla has preserved my life. The king, on hearing his voice, ordered the guards to let down a rope and lift Dalmon out of the den. The law and the sentence has been complied with, and he is free. When Dalmon was drawn out, the people gave a great shout of joy. They said it was a wonderful deliverance. Calanthe was represented in the cavern, seated in the moon, an emblem of her care over the members of the mystic order of Mithras, during the night of danger and distress.

Candidate—One who seeks and aspires to an office, elective or appointive. A petitioner to any Order or Society is a candidate for membership.

Chief Mentor—The title of the Presiding Officer in a Temple of The Knights of Tabor.

Chief Preceptress—The title of the Presiding Officer in a Tabernacle of the Daughter Priestesses of Tabor.

Cush—The name of Ham's eldest son. He was the founder of the Kingdom of Ethiopia. The descendants of Cush, or Cushites as they were called, were the most ancient civilized nation on earth. Saba Meroe, the capital of Ethiopia, was, according to ancient writers, one of the most beautiful cities in the world. It was the residence of the proud kings and queens of Ethiopia for over two thousand years. In that city was situated the ancient Tabernacle. The title of Priestess, in the Daughters of Tabor, is derived from that Tabernacle.

The musty pages of ancient history give but an item here and there of the grandeur of this magnificent empire. A great part of its history is so mixed with that of Egypt, that unless the searcher for the truths of history carefully separates the historical facts pertaining to these two noted countries, there will be a tendency to award to Egypt what belongs to Ethiopia. The opening to civilization of Central Africa by Cush is traced back to 2,000 years before Christ. The writings of Herodotus, Diodorus, Siculus and Josephus, and the testimony given in the Bible, and the admirable work of Major Martin R. Delaney, on the "Origin of Races and Colors," clearly proves that the Ethiopians were the first enlightened and civilized people on earth. Major Delaney gave this subject years of careful research and study, and to the unprejudiced mind establishes the truth of Ethiopia's ancient civilization. The definition of the word Cush, or Kush, is black, or dark brown.

Cushites—The descendants of Cush.

Cabri—The mysteries of Cabri originated among the Syrians. It was the name of the Phenician God. The worship of Cabri was first established by the children of Sydyk, and they were taught how to build ships by Cabri. The mysteries were practiced by the Samothracians, Thebians and the Lemnos. The object of the mysteries was to make men just and virtuous.

Chus—(See Abassine.)

Cyrene—A noted city in Africa. It was one of the cities cotemporary with ancient Saba, and was celebrated for the learning and refinement of its citizens. The Ethiopic mysteries were taught by the priesthood. They were represented in the ancient Tabernacle. The part performed by the Priestesses of Cyrene was to attend the Altar and keep a perpetual fire burning on it. They did this for hundreds of years. A school of philosophy was sustained. Aristippus and many others of note were the instructors. Josephus speaks of Cyrene as one among the powers in African civilization.

D.

Dalmon—The mysteries of Mithras were founded upon the influence of true friendship. The members were bound together by the mystic rite of initiation, which emblematized the union of soul and body. Death could only part them. The followers of Mithras were always prepared to defend a member or sacrifice their lives to save him, and to die for him if necessary. Dalmon and Phyletus proved by their courage and fidelity to each other that the cords of Mithrian true friendship could not be broken. (See Calanthe.) It was from this part of the history of the mysteries of Mithras that the legend of Damon and Pythias was written. The name Dalmon signifies true and unalterable friendship.

Deborah—The fourth chapter of Judges (Bible) informs us that Deborah was a prophetess and a judge in Israel. This distinguished woman lived between Ramah and Bethel, on Mount Ephraim, and was a judge and prophetess of the Israelites 1,296 years before Christ. This part of the Scriptures is a pleasing study. It proves that God entrusts his work and the accomplishment of great events to the brain and hands of women as well as men, and establishes one of the teachings of the International Order of Twelve, which is that a woman is man's equal.

E.

Egypt—This famous country is situated in the northeastern part of Africa, between Nubia and the Mediterranean See. Egypt was settled by Mizraim, the second son of Ham. Owing to the close proximity to Ethiopia and the close relationship of the founders, the Egyptians soon adopted the Ethiopian civilization. For many years these two nationalities were united under one government. Ham, the father of Cush and Mizraim, lived, after settling in Africa, about three hundred years. He resided for a number of years in Egypt, and was a co-ruler with Mizraim, until his death. Modern writers make the mistake of awarding to Egypt the title of the first civilized government on earth. This is the fault of not taking the proper means to explain the two forms of government, and in giving of each the true historical facts. When the truth is told, without prejudice, Ethiopia stands at the head of civilization. It is a proud title, and the descendants of this noble ancient people must not permit this honor to be taken from them; in fact, it cannot be lost—historical facts must and will stand. The hieroglyphical records on the sculptured stones, found in various parts of Ethiopia, are evidence of African greatness. The symbolized columns of the Temples in Nubia, which have been covered by the dust of ages, have recently been excavated, and the student of history can read on them the history of a great people.

Ethiopia—(See Cush, and Egypt.) It would take too much space to give a history of this country in detail.

Elohim—This is one of the names of God. It is a sacred and mystic name. The name symbolizes the Holy Trinity, a mysterious union in the Godhead. The ancient Jews had a deep reverence for this name of the Deity, and never pronounced it, but substituted the word Adonia, or Father.

East—In the Saba Meroe, the Priestess of Memnon is seated in the East, symbolizing the rising of the sun, and the beginning of another day.

Elion—The candidates in the Ethiopic mysteries had to pass through a purification, divided into three parts. The first, *air;* the second, *fire;* the third, *water*. A subterranean chamber was so arranged that a fierce wind sweept through it. If the candidate succeeded in passing through the chamber, he was informed that he had been favored by Elion. The chamber of fire was presided over by Eloi. The chamber of water was presided over by Noil. In passing these three chambers, the candidate proved his courage and will-power. Elion means mortality; Eloi, immortality; Noil, true happiness. These words have a prominent place in The Key Knights' history.

F.

Four—In searching among the mysteries of Mithras, we find the figure four (4) one of the mystic numbers. God was worshiped under the name of Agla. When they desired their members to assemble in case of a sudden emergency, the trumpet was sounded distinctly three times four. It made no difference what a member was doing at the time, everything was dropped to obey that call.

G.

God—The word God is of strictly Anglo-Saxon origin, and means Good Being, from the attribute of Goodness, Jehovah, a Supreme Being, All-powerful, Divine. The only one for mankind to worship, The Creator, Eternal and Sovereign Ruler of the Universe. In our investigations of the ancient mysteries, we find that in many of them the pure worship of God is veiled in symbols and metaphors, and yet, when we sift the language, and find its allegorical meaning, it is the highest and most exalted worship of the true God.

H.

Hyerego—In the ancient Tabernacle of Saba Meroe, there was a Priestess, whose duty it was to offer incense on the burning altar. She was the Oracle, was gifted with knowledge, could solve problems, and foretell future events. She symbolically represented the power of faithful prayer. "Whatsoever ye ask in faith, believing it shall be given," is the words of our Savior.

Hesper—The ancient Tabernacle was so situated, that the approach to it was very difficult for those who were strangers. The Priestesses of Hesper were detailed for the special duty of guiding strangers through the winding and intricate passages to the entrance. Their name implies that they were from the western part of Ethiopia. The symbol worn by them consisted of three stars, as a sign that they belonged to the Hesperine Priesthood, and had direct communication with the Garden of Hesperides.

Hesperides—An Ethiopic legend, handed down from the remotest period, speaks of the Garden of Hesperides. It was said to have been situated in Central Africa, and was a most beautiful and brilliant garden—a Paradise to live in. The ancient Ethiopians believed that it was the abode of those who originally taught their forefathers and founders the great lessons of social civilization—morals, literature, religion, and all the sciences. The emblems and precepts taught by them are of the highest order. The Phenix—Motto: We regenerate ourselves. The Ram—Motto: Peace, patience, friendship. The Thunderbolt—Motto: Light from heaven. The Great Serpent, whose body surrounded the entire garden—The precepts: Fear not God's works, they are good. The Pyramid—Motto: The Lord has been merciful to us.

The philosophy of the Hesperides is replete with beautiful legendary instructions. It shows the ideal consummation of social and religious civilization. The Garden of Hesperides was a symbol representing ancient Ethiopia in the lead of the civilized world.

I.

Indian—In some parts of the ritualistic work of the International Order of Twelve, reference is made to the Indian mysteries. Nearly all the ancient mysteries had their origin in Ethiopia or Egypt. After a thorough search for a derivation of the mysteries of India, we find that they originated in the East. The Gymnosophists were celebrated for their learning. They inculcated a belief in the triad of Gods, under the names of Brama, Vishnu, and Siva, and these were represented as the supreme, eternal, and uncreated God. They taught the immortality of the soul. The mysteries were divided into four degrees. The initiation was very severe, and required courage and endurance. The ceremonies were interspersed with prayer, fasting and ablutions. The candidate was required to serve in a preparatory state for several months, by prayer, fasting, and cleansing and purifying by water. The First Degree represented our first parents in Paradise—in happiness. The Second Degree represented them expelled from the garden, and their sufferings. The Third Degree represented the life in the world, with its cares and toils. The candidate was impressed with what he saw and heard, and that a pure life in this world and a firm belief in Brama, Vishnu, and Siva, would insure an eternal life of happiness. The Fourth Degree represented the soul entering Paradise. He was entrusted with the sacred word, "Aum," which signifies: created, preserved and saved.

The object of the Indian mysteries was to teach the unity of God, and the necessity of living a pure life.

J.

Jabin—One thousand three hundred years before the advent of Christ, the Lord, the children of Israel were held in bondage by Jabin, King of Canaan. Deborah, a prophetess, being inspired by the Lord God, caused Barak to gather from the tribes of Naphthali and Zebulon ten thousand men on Mount Tabor, to do battle against the large army of Jabin. Deborah said that God had promised them the victory, and Israel would be freed. History tells us that a desperate battle was fought— God fighting for Israel—Jabin's hosts were conquered and Israel's bondage was broken. The definition of the word Jabin is: he will cause pain.

Jewels—The accepted definition of the word Jewel, is personal ornaments of gold, silver and precious stones. In the International Order of Twelve the official badges worn by the officers are called Jewels. The following is a description of the various official Jewels worn in the different departments. .

The Temples have twelve Jewels. Ten-pointed stars, made of silver or white metal; ribbon, light scarlet, with the words "International Order of Twelve" printed thereon, fastened by a bar and pin; in the center of the star the initial letters of the different officers are placed. The C. M.'s Jewel has green ribbon and yellow metal star.

The Tabernacle has eighteen Jewels. Five-pointed star, resting on a ring made of silver or white metal, in the center of star the initials of the different officers are placed; ribbon, sky-blue, with

"International Order of Twelve" printed thereon, fastened by a bar and pin. The C. P.'s ribbon is green, and yellow metal star.

The Palatium has twelve Jewels. Seven-pointed star, made of gold or yellow metal, the star enclosed in a ring. The initials of the various officers are placed in the center of the star; ribbon, green and scarlet, and lettered "I. O. of 12," fastened by a bar and pin.

Grand Temples and Tabernacles have twenty-seven Jewels. Ten-pointed star, made of gold or yellow metal, enclosed in a ring, ornamented with a wreath; in the center of the star the initial letters of the various officers are placed; green ribbon, on which "Grand Temple and Tabernacle" is printed, fastened by a bar and pin.

The International Grand Temple and Tabernacle has thirty-three Jewels. A twelve-pointed star, made of gold or yellow metal, with six long and six short points, enclosed in a ring, ornamented with green, red and white stones. In the center of the star the initial letters of the various officers are placed; green ribbon, on which is printed "International Order of Twelve," fastened by a bar and pin.

K.

King—The word king occurs several times in various parts of the ritualistic work of the Knights and Daughters of Tabor. In the primary, ancient sense, the word king means the head or chief of a family or race; the common term means a monarch, sovereign or chief ruler, over a nation or countries, and they usully have hereditary succession.

Knight—The institution of the Knighthood was first conferred by kings and emperors as a mark of honor upon some distinguished soldier or statesman. The ceremonies of the Knighthood were very impressive. Organized Knighthood commenced about the year 302 B. C. by St. Helena, the mother of Constantine the Great. The Order of Knights of the Holy Sepulchre was instituted by her. These Knights were eminent for their courage and fidelity to the Christian religion. There are at this day a large number of organized Knights among the various Secret Orders.

Kush—(or Cush)—The eldest son of Ham.

Kushites—(or Cushites)—The descendants of Kush (or Cush).

L.

Law-Book—A book containing or treating of the laws.

Lybenus—In the mystic work of Ethiopia Lybenus was a very prominent figure, and was entrusted with especial duties. The Priestess of Lybia, or we will say the several Priestesses of that country, under the name of Lybenus, were always on duty as guards of the entrance to the ancient Tabernacle, at the mystic door. All who approached must give the Niolotic word and sign. In the Taborian formula Lybenus is symbolized in a true representative manner.

M.

Media—This remarkable country was a civilized government nearly one thousand years before Christ. They traced their origin to the ancient

Zend Tribes. The Sacred Book of Zendavesta un-
folds a system of ceremonial religion which is traced
back to the Ethiopic mysteries. The history of the
Medes is well worthy of careful study.

Meroe—The city of Meroe, situated in Central
Africa, was built on the banks of the river Nile.
It was the most ancient city in the world. Its
African name was Saba. The sacerdotal and
palatial city of Ethiopia, the residence of the kings
and queens. Within its walls was the ancient
Tabernacle, which was instituted to preserve the
name and worship of the true God. Two thousand
years before Christ this city was the seat of learning and refinement. It is said to have been the
most beautiful city that was ever built. Strangers
and foreigners, who visited this city, call it the
Celestial City. During the time that Solomon, King
of Israel, was in the height of his glory, this city
sent one of its most learned women, Queen Nicaule
of Ethiopia, called Queen of Sheba in the Scriptures,
to test his wisdom. After a contest of many days, the
queen declared that Solomon was the wisest man
whom she had ever met, and Solomon said she was
the most learned woman in the world. These two
distinguished monarchs, who stood at the head of
their respective governments, were the wonder and
admiration of all the other nations. Meroe, with
its marble palaces and impregnable walls, which the
large Egyptian army, under the command of that
able general, Moses, the Hebrew, after months of
battering, could not make an impression upon, this
city, which from its strength seemed to be enabled
to stand for all time to come, has passed away,

buried under the dust of ages. No vestige now remains of this once powerful city, and the people of Ethiopia are scattered. The wheel of time which rolled Ethiopia to the bottom of the hill, that same wheel—mark what I say—will some day roll it to the top of the hill again. God is just.

N.

Nicaule—History speaks of several queens of Ethiopia. In this Lexicon we will only refer to two of them. Nicaule was crowned Queen of Ethiopia and Egypt about the year 980 before Christ. These two powerful kingdoms had for a number of years been united under one government. This queen excelled in learning and diplomacy. It was this queen who visited King Solomon when he was in the zenith of his glory, 992 years before Christ. Josephus speaks of this visit, and says she was admired for her many accomplishments and learning. Chapter 10, 1st Kings (Bible) tells us that she visited Solomon to test his wisdom by propounding very difficult questions. This chapter refers to her as Queen of Sheba. The word Sheba means conversion. It is certain that this queen was converted to the Jewish faith during her visit to Solomon. Some modern writers have endeavored to prove that this queen was not the reigning monarch of Ethiopia and Egypt, by asserting that she was a Sabean, from South Arabia; but Josephus, with full access to the records of Jewish history, could not make a mistake, and he was an unprejudiced writer. The truth will prevail, and that is that she was an Ethiopian, and the most learned woman of the age in which she lived.

O.

Odin—The founder of the Odonic mysteries was born in the city of On, in Lower Egypt, about the beginning of the Christian era. He traveled among the Asiatic tribes, and assisted by Segge, the Chief of the Asers, initiated them into the mysteries of Odin. The precepts were peculiar, some of which we here give, as follows: "Let not your right hand know what your left hand doeth," and "a secret is not a secret, when it becomes the property of those who have no right to it."

Odo—The sacred Ethiopic name of the Wife of Thunder. When the thunder rolled, the wife shed tears, and the river Nile overflowed its banks, and Egypt was blessed with a plentiful harvest. This mystic legend is a beautiful one.

Om—This peculiar word, in the Ethiopic language, signifies the central power. When joined with two other words, it means all-powerful.

Ophir—(See Seraphis).

Order—Rank, class, division of men or women; as the Order of Twelve, etc.

Osiris—(See Rameses).

P.

Power—The physical ability to act, strength, endurance, force, energy, activity; the mental or moral faculty of thinking, reasoning and judging; the exercise of any kind of control, influence, command, sway, governing, dominion; there are various other powers, however, such as in mechanics, in optics, in law, in arithmetic, in Scripture, etc.

Palatium—A Latin word, meaning a palace. One of the seven hills of Rome, on which Augustus Cæsar had his residence, was called a Palatium. The Ninth, Tenth and Eleventh Degrees in the International Order of Twelve compose the third department or Royal House of Media. The place of meeting is called the Palatium.

Palatine Guards—The Guards of the Palace. This is the name of the drill department of the Palatium.

Preceptress—A teacher or instructor. It is the proper title of the Presiding Officer in the Daughter's Tabernacle, a department in the International Order of Twelve.

Q.

Queen—The wife of a king, a woman who is the sovereign ruler of a kingdom. Queen Mother is the title of the executive officer in a Tent of Maids and Pages, the fourth department in the International Order of Twelve.

R.

Revista—A noted Princess of the Median empire during the reign of Zendacer, 600 years before Christ. His daughter, Revista, was his principal advisor, and her influence was very great throughout the kingdom, so much so, that the king consulted her on all State matters.

Rameses—To obtain a partial history of ancient Ethiopia, careful search must be made. Upon investigation it is found that Ethiopia and Egypt, for the first four hundred years of their existence, were so closely and intimately connected that they seemingly had but one government, and yet the careful searcher can trace the line that divides the two kingdoms. The founding and settling of Ethiopia and Egypt is clearly written. Ham, a son of Noah, had four sons; Cush, Mizraim, Phut and Canaan. Biblical history is plain in its details of what parts of the world were settled by the families of these sons. Noah lived three hundred and fifty years after the flood. Since then the number of people increased considerably, and at the building of the Tower of Babel, when their languages were confounded, the Lord scattered them abroad to people all the earth. The families of the different sons of Noah must have been very large. The various boundaries of their individual countries were fixed. Canaan, the youngest son, settled in the land of Judea, then known as the land of Canaan. Nimrod remained in the land of Shinar, and became the founder of the two mighty empires of antiquity, Assyria and Babylon. Ham and his three sons, Cush, Mizraim and Phut, took up their line of march for Africa. They remained for a short time in the land of Media. They finally crossed the Isthmus of Suez and from thence crossed over into Africa. Ham, Mizraim and Phut settled on the Delta (Egypt), and Cush with his families pushed into the interior of Africa. That part of the country from the borders of Egypt to the interior of Africa was called Ethiopia. Cush laid the foundation of Saba, the capital city, on the banks of the river Nile. This beautiful city was called Meroe by the Greeks. Under the wise administration of Cush, Ethiopia soon became a flourishing kingdom, with all

the attributes of a polished, enlighted people.
Egypt, from the close relationship of the people, soon
adopted the Ethiopian manners and customs. These
two countries were for years conjointly under the
governorship of Ham, Cush and Mizraim. Ham,
during his lifetime, was the chief ruler, bearing the
title of Rameses I; after his death Cush was the
chief, bearing the title of Rameses II; after his
death Mizraim governed, under the name of Rameses III. Ham died at an advanced age, being much
loved by the people. He was deified under the
name of Jupiter Ammon, and was worshiped as a
God. He is represented as having the head of a
ram, with a man's body.

Cush, when he died, was deified under the name
of Sesostris. He was represented as having a dog's
face, with a human body.

Mizraim, when he passed from earth, was deified
under the name of Osiris. He was represented as
having a bull's face, with a man's body.

A work, "The Antiquities of Africa," which was
published in London, England, in 1703, informs
us that ancient Ethiopia was divided into forty-five
kingdoms. Diodorus, Siculus, and other ancient
historians tell us that the laws, manners and customs of Egypt were nearly the same as those of
Ethiopia.

There is no doubt but that Cush and Mizraim,
after the death of Ham, governed conjointly for
the benefit of both countries. The pyramids were
undoubtedly built by them. The principal ones
are the monuments of Rameses I, Rameses II, and
Rameses III. The catacombs and the numerous

temples of Ethiopia and Egypt are evidence of the kindred styles in architecture. Their statuary and heiroglyphic characters were the same. The Ethiopians invented the first alphabet. Job Ludolphus, the learned Israelite in Ethiopic literature, gives the form of 16 letters which were used by the royal family and the priesthood. I might proceed and speak of the twenty-five dynasties under the Rameses, and the splendor of Ethiopic civilization for ages, but must desist for want of space.

S.

Sesotheni—The Priestess in the ancient Tabernacle of Memnon—sometimes called the Temple of the Sun. When the sun arose and cast its rays on the roof of this beautiful Temple of Memnon, sweet music continued to play until the sun was at its meridian. Sesotheni was seated at the east side of the ancient Tabernacle. Her duty was to record the beginning of another day, and announce the coming of the Day-God.

Sesostris—(See Rameses)—Sesostris was the first to settle in Egypt with his family.

Seraphis—An ancient Priestess, who represented the value of gold and silver. Her place in the ancient Tabernacle was at the west side. It was her duty to teach the votaries of the Saba Meroe the value of time, and that a minute, hour or day lost was irretrievable.

Sisera—The name of the general who commanded the Canaanite Army, which was defeated by Barak with his ten thousand in the memorable battle on and around Mount Tabor, one thousand three hundred years before Christ.

Shamgar—The name of one of Israel's mightiest men. Shamgar was a son of Anath. 1336 years before Christ the Israelites and Philistines were almost continuously at war. In one of the battles Shamgar slew six hundred Philistines with an ox-goad.

T.

Tabernacle—The definition of Tabernacle is a flimsily built temporary habitation, a tent or portable structure, moveable at the will of those who owned it. A sacred Tabernacle was a moveable tent-like house, for the worship of God. The most ancient Tabernacle known was erected within the walls of the ancient city of Saba, in Ethiopia. It represented the temporary existence of human beings on this earth. The Tabernacle erected by Moses in the Wilderness of Sin, 1491 years before Christ, for the worship of God, while the children of Israel were journeying from the Red Sea to the Promised Land, was the most costly one ever built. In our Order, the place of meeting for the Daughters of Tabor is called a Tabernacle.

Temple—An edifice erected to worship the Deity. Temples, for the worship of idols, were numerous in ancient times, even now there are numerous Temples erected for the worship of idols. The Jewish Temple, built by Solomon, and dedicated to the worship of the true God, is acknowledged to have been the most artistic structure ever built by man. Any Christian church, or any place used for divine worship, is termed God's Temple. The place where the Knights of Tabor meet is called a Temple.

Tabor—A lute, or a kind of drum-guitar. Mount Tabor, a conical mountain in Galilee, is about eighteen hundred French feet high, on the top of which is a beautiful plateau, about one mile in circumference. It is a historical mountain, and a land-mark where events transpired which made it memorable. About the year 1396 B. C. Deborah, a judge and prophetess of Israel, summoned Barak to gather ten thousand men of the tribes of Zebulon and Naphthali on the top of Mount Tabor and to give battle to the mighty hosts of Sisera. The scene in that battle was grand—God fought for Israel that day. The stars of Heaven (angels) fought against Jabin's army. The lightning and thunder of Jehovah's power was hurled against the Canaanites, and Israel was victorious.

The second scene was under the new dispensation—the transfiguration of Jesus, the Son of God—this glorious sight was witnessed by three Apostles: Peter, James and John.

Tetra—This word is from the Greek, and means four. Among the ancients the figure four (4) had a mystic significance. The inexpressible name of the Deity was expressed in four letters, the most prominent of the mysteries which originated in Ethiopia and Egypt and which were transmitted to the surrounding nations. We find that the figure four (4) represented the Great Ruler of Mankind. A. G. L. A. and E. L. J. E. were the cabalistic letters representing the ineffable name of God. The figure four (4) represents the four necessary elements to perpetuate the existence of mankind, namely : earth, fire, air and water. It represents the four principal departments in the International Order of Twelve, viz: Temples, Tabernacles, Palatiums and Tents; also the four Presiding Officers: Chief Mentor, Chief Preceptress, Presiding Prince, and Queen Mother.

Three—Among the ancient mysteries the figure three (3) occupied a prominent place. It is a perfect number. It designates the triune God—the Father, the Son, and the Holy Ghost—the Holy Trinity. Among the pagan nations, the figure three was prominent as a mystic number. Cerberus, the Dog-God, had three heads. The scepter of Neptune was a trident. A triple cord was used in the Ethiopic mysteries. Three colors: red, black and white, were worn as a charm to protect the wearer in time of danger. The three-fold cord was not easely broken. Three times three are strong numbers in the ritualistic work of the Order of Twelve. The three principal colors of the International Order of Twelve are: red, black and green. Red is emblematic of the blood of Jesus, which saves all who come unto Him in faith. Black is an emblem of death, and reminds us of the fact that all mortals must pass through the narrow passage-way before becoming immortal. Green is emblematic of eternity, and admonishes us that if we would enjoy eternal rest and happiness we must live the life of true Christians on earth. Knights and Daughters of Tabor, when you wear the regalia, remember its instructions.

Tent—A movable or portable lodge. It was the
first covering or shelter which our ancestors used.
The fourth department in the International Order
of Twelve is called the Children's Tent. The
members of it are known as Maids and Pages. But
three adults are permitted to be members. Tents
were organized to gather in the children, to give
them moral instruction, to teach them the difference
between right and wrong, to guide their young
minds in the ways that will ultimately make them
good men and women, and to discipline them in
the obeying of the laws and rules. As they grow
up, the impression of right and justice will be impressed upon them, and they will be moral and
good citizens and faithful members of the Order.
The Tent is governed by the Constitution and By-
Laws; it has no rituals nor degrees. Provision is
made, when the boys become 18 years of age and
the girls 16 years of age, so that they can become
members of either a Temple or a Tabernacle. If
they have been properly instructed in the Tent,
they will understand the nature of a sacred obligation. The Queen Mother must carefully train the
girls in ladylike manners and deportment, and the
boys in good manners and manliness. The Father
of Tents must teach the Taborian Cadets the march
and drill. It is not necessary that the girls shall be
drilled in public. Teach them how to be modest,
virtuous, and retiring. The Tent is the Order's
school-house.

Twelve—Three times four, or four times three,
a symbol representing twelve units, as 12 or XII.

(12—Dickson's New Manual.)

Twelve is a perfect number. A study of the twelve Apostles in the Holy Scriptures is pleasing and instructive to the biblical student. In many of the ancient mysteries the figure twelve (12) had a prominent part. In the mystic ancient Tabernacle of Saba Meroe there were twelve divisions of officers and members—the most notable were the Priestesses of Twelve. In the Key Knights of Tabor the figure twelve (12) represents a perfect Temple of the Uniform Rank. There must be twelve officers present to constitute a Taborian Temple. There must be twelve officers to all perfect Palatiums, of the Royal House of Media. The Past Arcanum must have twelve officers. The twelve requisites demanded of every Knight and Daughter of Tabor, if they are true and worthy, are: 1st, Justice; 2d, Temperance; 3d, Prudence; 4th, Constancy; 5th, Morality; 6th, Industry; 7th, Benevolence; 8th, Love; 9th, Truth; 10th, Perseverance; 11th Courage; 12th, Mercy. Knights and Daughters are requested to define these twelve requisites, and make proper application in their lectures.

U.

Unite—To combine, to join together, to form a whole, to become one, cemented, consolidated, acting in concert, a united compact body. The International Order of Twelve of Knights and Daughters of Tabor is a unit, bound together by the twelve secret degrees.

Unity—Means oneness, indivisibility, uniformity, a circle. The obligations of the Knights and

Daughters of Tabor bind together the members in one body. The entire circle is a unity.

Union—The act of uniting, combining, joining, consolidating an agreement on the part of persons to form a unit, under the general laws and rules. The International Order of Twelve forms a union of Grand Temples and Tabernacles, by its General Laws.

Uniform—The dress regalia of a Knight of Tabor. It is designated by the number of Degrees he has received, if he has received the full four, he is classed as a Uniform Rank Knight of Tabor.

V.

Vote—To signify will or preference either by ballot, signs or *viva voce*. It is the duty of every member of the Order to vote, just as conscience dictates, and for the protection of the good name of the Order. When a vote decides a question or the business under consideration, the minority must rest satisfied. There are three forms of voting in the International Order of Twelve: 1st, the secret ballot, in the degrees; 2d, the written ballots, on electing officers; 3d, the vote by signs. The taking of a vote in public can be expressed either standing or by yeas or nays.

Votaries—Those who are devoted, or consecrated by a vow or promise. The Priestesses of Saba Meroe were votaries of the ancient Tabernacle, and devoted to its service and worship.

W.

West—The ancient Tabernacle of Saba Meroe, faced north and south. When the Fourth Degree is opened for work or business, the official position of the four prominent officers is as follows: Tharbis, the High Priestess, is seated in the South; Amisis, the Vice-Priestess, is seated in the North; Sesotheni, the Priestess of Memnon, is seated in the East; Seraphis, the Priestess of Ophir, is seated in the West. When a Temple of the Knights of Tabor is opened in any of the degrees, the C. M. is seated in the South; the V.-M. in the North; the C. S. in the East, and the C. T. in the West.

X. ·

Xanthian—When ancient Ethiopia was in its height of power and culture, a sect of Ethiopians formed a settlement east of Central Africa, and built a city called Xanthus. They were a peaceful people, and excelled in sculpture. The Xanthians were noted for their extreme temperate habits. After the downfall of Ethiopia, it is supposed that a remnant emigrated into Asia, and settled in Italy, and were known as Xerophagists or dry livers. They worshiped God under the name of Jupiter Ammon. During their residence in Xanthus they were represented in the ancient Tabernacle of Saba Meroe by the Meroes.

Y.

Yarubas—The Ethiopic definitions of the symbols, mottoes and precepts, found in the Garden of Hesperides. The Yaruban language is supposed to be the ancient Ethiopic, and is spoken to this day by the tribes south of the Desert of Sahara.

Z.

Zendavesta—Nearly one thousand years before Christ the Medes were a civilized people. They drew their origin from the ancient Zend races. These people possessed a mystic religion, which they learned from the Cushites. The sacred book, or Zendavesta, unfolded a mysterious system of ceremonial religion, which is traced back to the mysteries of Ethiopia. The members of the Royal House of Media should refer to the history of Media for further instructions.

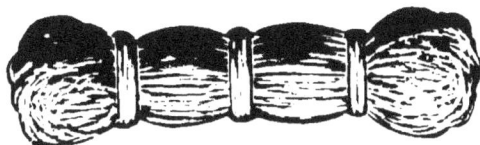

Flax.

Girdle.

Wool.

TABERNACLE FURNITURE.

(For Other Tabernacle Furniture, see page 167.)

TEMPLE FURNITURE.

(For Other Temple Furniture, see page 168.)

TEMPLE FURNITURE.

(For Other Temple Furniture, see pages 168 and 359.)

PALATIUM BADGE.

GENERAL INDEX.

——:o:——

362

PAGE.

LIST OF ILLUSTRATIONS.

PALATINE GUARD, WITHOUT BALDRICK.

www.ingramcontent.com/pod-product-compliance
Lightning Source LLC
Chambersburg PA
CBHW030914270326
41929CB00008B/695